SOVIET PERCEPTIONS
OF THE UNITED STATES

SOVIET PERCEPTIONS OF THE UNITED STATES

Morton Schwartz

University of California Press

BERKELEY   LOS ANGELES   LONDON

University of California Press
Berkeley and Los Angeles, California
University of California Press, Ltd.
London, England
Copyright © 1978 by
The Regents of the University of California

First Paperback Printing 1980
ISBN 0-520-04094-5
Library of Congress Catalog Card Number: 76-7767
Printed in the United States of America
Designed by Dave Comstock

1 2 3 4 5 6 7 8 9

FOR RUNA, DAVID,
AND JONATHAN

CONTENTS

INTRODUCTION

Among the problems confronting American policy makers, few are more vexing than that of assessing the images others, especially adversaries, have of the United States. While there clearly are limits to American power and influence, much of what transpires in the world arena hinges on the actual and anticipated behavior of the United States. This is especially true in the case of the world's other superpower, the USSR. A great deal of what the Kremlin rulers attempt to do, or not to do, rests on their estimation of how we will behave. While their choices are undoubtedly influenced by other factors—external circumstances, dangers, opportunities, internal pressures—the Soviet "image of America" has an important, often critical, bearing on the formulation of policy.

The relationship between Soviet perceptions and behavior is in principle well understood. The facts, however, have been a source of puzzlement. How, indeed, do the makers of Soviet policy view the United States? This issue is vastly complicated by the central role played by Marxism-Leninism in the Soviet scheme of things. Given their adherence to these doctrines as the official ideology of the Soviet Communist Party, the leaders of the USSR are obliged to see the United States in a particular light. After all, as the most powerful nation, economically and militarily, in the non-Communist world, this country is regarded as the "citadel" of world capitalism, its "mightiest bulwark." As such it is by definition presumed to be dominated by a "bourgeois" socio-economic and political system, i.e., one which is

1

basically exploitative, oppressive, decadent, and crisis-ridden, and to pursue an "imperialist"—hence aggressive, predatory, anti-socialist and anti-Soviet—foreign policy.

And, indeed, the United States has been described precisely in such terms for much of recent Soviet history. The political leadership during Stalin's last years in the late 1940s and early 1950s gave voice to a particularly crude version of the Marxist-Leninist formulation. The United States, according to their expressed views, was ruled by a small clique of Wall Street finance capitalists dedicated to the pursuit and protection of their immediate class interests. All else in American life—the political process, the press, domestic social and economic arrangements, culture, foreign policy—was said to be ruthlessly subordinated to the defense of these interests. In the strange realm of Stalinist political mythology, as Frederick Barghoorn wrote more than twenty-five years ago,

> America resembles more closely the horrid fantasy of Orwell's *Nineteen Eighty-Four* than the country we know. The America in Soviet propaganda is ruled by force and fraud. Its handful of rulers pull the strings to which their subjects dance like puppets. Its domestic policy is one of exploitation and oppression and its foreign policy is characterized by deception and aggression.[1]

As an integral part of his cold war campaign—waged with equal vigor both at home and abroad—Stalin insisted that all materials pertaining to the United States had to be presented in these sinister terms. The official Party attitude which then prevailed was reflected in the *Pravda* (2 September 1950) statement: "Every Marxist work on the economics of capitalist countries must be a bill of indictment."

In the two decades or so since Stalin's death in 1953, the situation has significantly changed. Seeking to break with the obscurantist practices of the Stalin period, top Party leaders in the mid-1950s instructed Soviet scholars to abandon the "dogmatic and oversimplifying" attitudes of the past. They were urged, in particular, to provide a more objective assessment of the outside world. And, as numerous writers have indicated, Soviet writings started taking on an increasingly less dogmatic tone in the Khrushchev years and slowly but steadily improved.[2] However, it was only after the creation of the

Institut Soyedinennykh Shtatov Ameriki i Kanada (Institute of the United States of America and Canada) or *Institut SShA* (USA Institute) in 1967 and the major research efforts of its director, Georgi A. Arbatov, and his fellow Americanists, that, relatively speaking, more realistic accounts of America began to appear.* Although they are clearly not free from the normal requirements of Soviet scholarship and must hew closely to the political leadership's ideological and policy line, the analyses of Moscow's Americanists, especially in the past few years, have been significantly better informed and more sophisticated than any previously published in the USSR.

While there is general agreement on these basic facts, there is little consensus on their implications. Some have argued that greater familiarity with the United States, resulting from their research activities and frequent visits to this country, has led to a considerably greater objectivity. Issues of American politics, writes Hannes Adomeit, tend to be discussed "on their merits." Thus, it is suggested, the weight of doctrinal preconceptions has been reduced, a development which, at least potentially, could lead to a more pragmatic and realistic approach to political reality and to the making of Soviet policy.[3]

Others take an even more optimistic view. As a result of their greater competence and sophistication, it is suggested, Soviet experts today tend to regard American foreign policy as more benign and less threatening than did the more dogmatic political analysts of the past. This evolution in Soviet thinking has been especially important and helps explain recent achievements in Soviet-American relations. After all, the willingness of the Kremlin leaders to negotiate agreements with the United States on, say, strategic arms limitation, rests on their belief that Washington is pursuing a policy course which poses no immediate threat to basic Soviet security interests.[4]

* Originally established in November 1967, it was known as the *Institut SShA* (USA Institute)—the only Soviet institute initially designed to concentrate its research on one country. Its coverage was later expanded, however, to include Canada, and in late 1974 it was renamed accordingly. As the heart of its interests remains the United States, we shall continue to refer to it by its original (and more accurate) title, the USA Institute. For a brief summary of the background and organization of the institute and biographic sketches of its leading staff members, see *Biographic Report: USSR Institute of the United States of America and Canada* published by the Central Intelligence Agency (CR 76–10864), April 1976.

There are still some who view Soviet research as primitive and devoid of understanding. Robert Byrnes, for example, argues that Soviet analysts lack any feel for "what makes us tick."

> The work they do is not only propagandistic but also shows an inability to understand our culture. Some of the writing is not even malicious—it simply displays a total lack of comprehension. . . . [E]ven those Russians who have spent a year in America work on a mental frequency that will just not pick up American signals.

The level of Soviet scholarship, in Byrnes' view, "is incredibly low."[5]

More respectful but much more pessimistic is the position of Uri Ra'anan, who suggests that the current Soviet effort to gain a better understanding of America may have a disturbing, perhaps even destablizing influence on Soviet-American relations. What troubles Ra'anan is the fact that the Kremlin is pursuing this effort precisely at a time in our history when we are faced with increasingly serious internal difficulties. Domestic problems—unemployment, inflation, racial tension, urban violence—appear intractable, and political processes are working uncertainly: two presidents have been forced to retire, the Congress, the press and the American public are increasingly mistrustful of the executive branch. All these facts are carefully studied and duly noted in Moscow. The Soviet leaders, it is feared, are thus being led to the conclusion that the United States is gradually being turned into a "paper tiger."[6]

This clash of views, it should be noted, is no mere academic squabble. As is true for divergences among Soviet views themselves, these various assessments of Soviet beliefs about the United States have important—and very different—policy implications. Putting it somewhat crudely, to the extent that Soviet scholarship is seen to reflect relatively moderate views (and that important elements in the Soviet political leadership are judged to share similar beliefs), the makers of American policy might want to consider adopting a "strategy of reassurance." That is to say, the American government should strive to avoid actions which will discredit this view; it should, where feasible, actively seek to encourage the belief that American purposes vis-à-vis the USSR are friendly, that its interests are indeed being taken into account by Washington and that the United States and the USSR share numerous interests in common. To the extent that dogmatic

4

anti-American views have in fact declined in Moscow, this "strategy of reassurance" should help reinforce this development, help build mutual trust and, it may be hoped, stimulate further improvement in Soviet-American relations.

If, on the other hand, one assumes that the Soviet rulers see the United States as beset by serious social, economic and political crises, the adoption of a much more forceful policy may be in order. To help discourage the USSR from assuming that because of chronic domestic turmoil American power on the world scene is becoming increasingly irrelevant, Ra'anan suggests the American government pursue a policy of "intentional unpredictability." Only by occasional and somewhat unpredictable demonstrations of U.S. determination and strength, he argues, will the Soviet leadership be dissuaded from pursuing a more assertive and more dangerous foreign policy course.[7]

The present study addresses itself to the questions raised above, viz., it seeks to examine the Soviet conception of the "internal springs" of American foreign policy. Its main purpose is to explore current Soviet perceptions of the United States, the extent and character of such changes in Soviet beliefs as seem to have occurred in recent years, and the significance of these views for Soviet-American relations. More specifically, the study will analyze Soviet perceptions regarding four main areas: (1) the American socio-economic system, its strengths and weaknesses, and its influence on the goals and conduct of U.S. policy; (2) the political system of the United States, the presidency, the executive agencies formally responsible for foreign policy, the Congress, interest groups, the media and public opinion; (3) the characteristics and behavior of American policy makers; and (4) expectations regarding future American behavior. These findings will be examined in the context of domestic Soviet political arrangements. Their policy implications for the United States will also be explored.

A word about methodology. The analysis which follows is based essentially on the writings of Soviet academic specialists on the United States as they have appeared in a number of books published by the USA Institute and in the pages of *SSha: ekonomika, politika, ideologiya* (*USA: Economics, Politics, Ideology*), the journal of the institute, published between 1970 and 1976 (hereinafter cited as

SShA).[8] Its focus, therefore, is neither on the expressed views of the top Party leadership nor on those of the Soviet government agencies responsible for foreign policy—the Ministry of Foreign Affairs or the Ministry of Defense.

Thus, in some measure, the materials used are not representative, in the sense that they often differ considerably from the accounts on the same subject appearing in the Soviet media. The writings of the Soviet Amerikanisty are both richer in detail and more sophisticated in analysis.[9] And to the extent that we are searching for evidence of innovation the analytic focus of the study will tend to be distorted in favor of the most imaginative aspects of official Soviet writings on the United States. Also, by the very nature of the enterprise, there is a tendency to give these findings a coherence and thereby a collective weight which, in fact, they rarely have.

To control for overevaluation and excessive enthusiasm, the reader should try to keep in mind that the materials cited are often only isolated nuggets buried in a vast field of orthodox Party formulations. They are, most typically, unevenly distributed, and in many cases hard to find. We should also be aware that we are dealing with mere words, which should not always be taken at face value. As the Soviet political analyst, Alexander Bovin, has reminded us: "The verbal expression of policy can play a dual role: it either reflects real political interests and intentions, or, conversely, is called upon to conceal these interests and intentions."[10] Nevertheless, the importance of innovation in Soviet public discourse should not be minimized. Given the rigorous demands of a Party leadership highly intolerant of unorthodox formulations and views, even occasional hints that Soviet perceptions of the United States may be changing must be considered as politically significant, and perhaps carry with them important policy implications. We shall return to this last point in our final section.

The research on which this study is based was supported by a research contract jointly funded by the U.S. Department of State and the United States Information Agency, and grants from the Committee on Research of the Academic Senate, University of California, Riverside.

1

ECONOMY AND SOCIETY

S oviet attitudes toward the American socio-economic system reveal an odd mixture of respect and contempt. The Soviet leaders strive at once to "catch up" with the United States and to "bury it." As Paul Hollander has noted, this country is seen both as model and adversary.[1] The slogan "catching up with America" reflects the Kremlin's long-standing admiration for the productivity, organizational efficiency and technological sophistication of American industry and agriculture.[2] While urging Soviet workers to "overtake and surpass" the United States, the Soviet leaders refer to American culture and society with profound contempt. Soviet revulsion is founded on the conviction that a society built on the institution of private property must, inevitably, give rise to an unjust socio-economic system, one which generates ruthless exploitation, enormous inequalities of wealth, fierce competitiveness, commercialization of relationships, and general moral decadence.

Capitalism, especially in its American incarnation, produces economic deprivation and massive social injustice. To document these judgements Soviet publishing of American literature through the 1950s focused readers' attention on such writers as Steinbeck, Sinclair Lewis, Caldwell and Dreiser, who were presented as though they portrayed life as it was really lived in the United States. While the details of *The Grapes of Wrath*, *Babbitt* and *Tobacco Road* were admitted to be somewhat dated, and some economic improvement

7

was acknowledged, social relationships under capitalism were unchanging. As Friedberg has written:

> portrayal of the United States as a land of robber barons and long lines of
> the unemployed, of bloated merchants and impoverished share croppers,
> of decadent southern gentry and of blacks always threatened with lynching,
> of a country devoid of spiritual values, to say nothing of cultural ones,
> remains—according to Soviet critics—*essentially true*. [Italics in the
> original.][3]

More recently, Soviet criticism and publishing of American literature has shifted emphasis. It is occasionally admitted that the material conditions confronting most Americans are less grim than before. Nonetheless, they still lead miserable lives. Now, however, their afflictions are ethical and psychological rather than economic. Contemporary capitalism, the Soviet reader is told, produces loneliness, alienation, dissatisfaction and ethical conflict. Such writers as Cheever, Bellow, Albee and Updike are presented as on-the-scene witnesses to this country's "allegedly all-pervasive atmosphere of futility, drift, impotent anger and, above all, isolation and loneliness."[4]

Thus for Khrushchev, as for many others among the Party faithful, "Capitalism is not simply an unjust economic system. It is a way of life that leads to a corruption of important values."[5] And the Soviet leader remained convinced that, for all its economic strength, capitalism in the United States is fated by history to decline. Hence his belief that a socialist USSR will "bury" or outlive "capitalist America."

Such pronouncements, while revealing much about Soviet self-images,[6] tell us rather little regarding the forces and factors which in their estimation shape American foreign policy. Much more useful, in this regard, are the recent discussions of major trends in the American economy.

The American Economy

Orthodox Marxist theorists make two judgements about the character and future of the American economic system which have a direct bearing on foreign policy. First, it is a verity of orthodox Marxist doctrine that when "mature," the capitalist economy—as a result of its "internal contradictions"—will just shrink and then collapse, a fact which would of course have ruinous implications for both internal stability and America's world role. Second, even before its historically unavoidable demise, the "social nature" of the American socioeconomic system is said to engender pressure to resolve both domestic and foreign policy problems by imperialist, i.e. aggressive, military means. Although both formulations are frequently referred to in the popular press, Soviet Americanists have offered strikingly unconventional interpretations of these basic dogmas.

Soviet officials have long held American technological achievements in high regard. Stalin himself was an admirer of American economic efficiency—which he hoped to combine with "Russian revolutionary sweep." Despite his respect for its accomplishments, he believed that growth rates in American industry were, save for abnormal wartime situations, on the decline. Under Khrushchev, Stalin's stagnation theory was repudiated. Quoting Lenin, Khrushchev said at the 20th Party Congress: "It would be a mistake to believe that [the] tendency to decay precludes the rapid growth of capitalism."[7] Traditional predictions regarding the increasing severity of capitalist economic cycles were quietly abandoned. As one official noted, "Soviet economists have long cast aside former ideas of an automatic collapse or shrinkage of capitalism. On the contrary, they appreciate its ability to develop productive forces and to control, to some extent, its cyclical movements."[8]

The measure of respect accorded the American economy is reflected in the highly complimentary—though still sharply critical— article by Nikolai N. Inozemtsev, director of the *Institut mirovaya ekonomika i mezhdunarodnye otnosheniya* (*IMEMO*) (Institute for World Economy and International Relations), in the first issue of *SShA*. The United States, writes Inozemtsev, possesses "the mightiest and most highly-organized production mechanism" in the capitalist world. In 1968, he notes, it was the source of 44.2 percent of the industrial production of the capitalist economies, with second-ranked Germany producing only 8.8 percent. The United States, he goes on, was capitalism's largest exporter, especially strong in power equipment, nuclear reactors, aircraft, wheat, corn and foreign investment capital. "No capitalist country," in Inozemtsev's judgement "can count on reaching a par with the U.S.A. in economic indices in the near future."[9] This enormous economic power is of particular concern, of course, because of its implications for American military power. "In this respect too," notes Inozemtsev, "the USA holds a special place." Which leads him to conclude that "thanks to its economic and military might, the position of the U.S.A. . . . is that of a kind of 'superpower.'"[10]

Although Inozemtsev is quick to point out periodic slumps in U.S. industrial production, "deformations" such as unemployment, enormous wasting of resources, and "very acute" social and political problems—the anti-war movement, the civil rights struggle, and "various manifestations of social protest," there is little expectation of serious economic problems ahead. In fact he regards numerous features of American industrial processes—such as the use of computers in supply and marketing systems and the modernization of management systems on the basis of programming and production forecasting—as of "considerable interest" to the USSR. An economy this mighty and this advanced is hardly about to expire.

More recent Soviet analyses, as one would have expected, have paid considerable attention to the 1974–76 economic recession in the United States. The sharpness of the slump, the intractability of the dual problems of inflation and unemployment, and the energy crisis are all cited as new symptoms of the fundamental illness of contemporary capitalism, further indication of its "deepening contractions." S. A. Dalin, venerable observer of the American economic scene, characterized the crisis as "the most intense and the longest in postwar history."[11] According to Y. I. Bobrakov, leading economist at the USA Institute, it was "the deepest and most severe crisis since the 'Great Depression' of the 1930s." At the nadir of the crisis in April 1975, he observes, industrial production was almost 15 percent below pre-crisis levels, GNP was down 7.8 percent, unemployment was up 8.9 percent. Furthermore, the "combination of recession and inflation created exceptionally difficult problems."[12]

Despite the intense economic difficulties, Soviet analysts were very cautious in their judgements about long-term consequences. While there was some comment at the height of the crisis that the "sharp aggravation" of economic problems was "fraught with 'dangerous' socio-political consequences,"[13] traditional Marxist predictions regarding the imminent collapse of the West were scarce. There were, of course, detailed reports in the daily Soviet press of unemployment, skyrocketing prices, long lines in front of gas pumps during the oil embargo, and New York City's economic woes. Such items have long been the usual fare of Soviet media coverage of the West. Nonetheless, the Amerikanisty showed considerable reluctance to see profound implications in the West's economic difficulties.

Though other factors were involved (including their concern that depression in the West would jeopardize détente by endangering such prospects as then existed for economic cooperation with the West), the reticence of Soviet analysts reflected their continued confidence in the durability of the American economy. Thus, in the summer of 1975, Dalin would note that "the present crisis is not chronic. The crisis is cyclical and, therefore, temporary." Forces "contributing towards recovery," he noted, were already making themselves felt.[14] In the fall of 1976, Inozemtsev told an interviewer that "the capitalist countries were getting over what he called a 'crisis of over-production' and were heading for more balanced growth." He said "growth rates would pick up in the next year or two."[15]

Typical of the basic Soviet position on this matter is the comment of Valentin Zorin. In an article devoted to the "acute" domestic, especially economic problems confronting the United States in the 1970s, he suggests that

> it would, of course, be incorrect to assume that the American bourgeoisie has exhausted all of its potentialities and reserves and that, therefore, there is nothing left for it but to sag under the weight of its vices and sicknesses. The United States is the most powerful and richest capitalist country which still possesses considerable economic and political reserves.[16]

Though published in mid-1971, i.e., before the economy began seriously to falter, this comment remains characteristic of more recent Soviet views. In language similar to that employed by Zorin, A. I. Shapiro, a ranking Soviet economist, writes in January 1976 that

> The economic potentials of contemporary American capitalism are far from exhausted. Because of its highly-organized production system, its vast natural resources and its reserves of qualified manpower, it still has possibilities for economic growth. The American monopolies still have enough power and inertia of movement to continue operating for a certain amount of time, achieving further expansion of their supremacy and accelerated development of their productive forces.[17]

11

Perhaps the most significant index of Soviet continued respect for the American economy is the fact that, despite its travails, the United States is still very much the model of comparison for Soviet economists. Thus, in an article published in September 1975, near the height of the economic recession, V. M. Kudrov, *IMEMO* Department head, notes that labor productivity in the USSR is only 55 percent of that in the United States, that the Soviets lag behind the United States in terms of efficiency of machinery and capital utilization, that housing in the USSR is in terms of living space "twelve times lower" than in the U.S., that national income in the Soviet Union is 66 percent of that in the U.S., and that in terms of the quality of their diet and the availability of consumer durables the lot of Soviet consumers compares poorly with that of their American counterparts. Clearly, despite occasional difficulties, the productivity of the American economy is very highly regarded; it is the United States which sets the standards which are to be "overtaken and surpassed."[18]

The sources of this abiding confidence in the vitality of the American economy are several. First, as we have already seen, Soviet analysts are most impressed with its great wealth and its "highly-organized productive forces." In addition they place enormous store in American scientific and technological capabilities. For example, in an article on the "scientific and technical revolution," Georgi Arbatov, USA Institute director, notes that the United States has long played a major role in this arena. "The United States unquestionably has very strong positions in this sphere, primarily by virtue of its great economic possibilities which are so important for creating a mighty scientific and technical potential."[19] This is a matter of considerable significance, notes Arbatov, for today science has become "a direct productive force." It is, in his view, "the source of the continuously accelerating and widening stream of innovations in all spheres."[20]

While insisting that American technological preeminence is only transitory,[21] Arbatov underscores the fact that "competition with the United States is an extremely complex matter." He ends on a somewhat ominous note:

States which cannot create a sufficiently powerful scientific and technical potential of their own are faced with a difficult dilemma under such

12

conditions. They have a choice: either they fall seriously behind . . . or they tie themselves firmly to a country which possesses such a potential.[22]

Scientific and technological advantage, therefore, may well have serious political implications. It may result, as Arbatov noted in 1974, in the "binding" of other nations to the United States, in establishing "relationships of domination and subjugation." It could result in "economic slavery," that is to say, in a less advanced country "losing some part of its economic, yes, and even its political independence."[23] Though Arbatov was specifically referring to relations between the United States and "other capitalist countries," he may well have had his own country's interests in mind as well.[24]

Thus while the advantage may be only "fleeting," as Arbatov suggests, "he who is in front can derive certain—sometimes sub-stantial—economic, military or political benefit" from his techno-logical mastery.[25] As numerous Soviet economists have observed, it has been precisely this phenomenon, the so-called "technological gap," which has aided the American penetration of European mar-kets and allowed the United States to maintain its economic pri-macy. As a result of its technological superiority the United States is recognized as having achieved a dominant position in the "latest fields," viz., semiconductors, digital control systems, production of automation equipment, information systems, turbo-jet engines, and numerous others. American companies are acknowledged to occupy a near-monopoly in the production of electronic computers. Accord-ing to one group of Soviet economists, IBM and other such giant American firms "control approximately 95 percent of the world's production of computers."[26] Another source concludes that the United States

occupies the leading position . . . in the export of capital, in international scientific and technical relations and in other spheres whose significance is rapidly increasing. The United States remains the major, if not the only, supplier of many types of the most scientifically and technologically complex products to the world market.[27]

Thus, although in quantitative terms the economic power of the European countries and Japan—and the Soviet Union—has been increasing rapidly, "the 'technological gap' between the United States and its competitors is growing wide."[28]

American technological capabilities, therefore, are seen to be an enormous reserve of economic strength. Thus the problem of "raw material shortages," which looms so large in the thinking of Western economists, is in the Soviet view not a terribly serious one. First of all, according to a resource analyst for *Ekonomicheskaya gazeta*, "the United States has colossal natural reserves of the majority of raw materials which are quite suitable for industrial development."[29] In addition Inozemtsev suggests that "scientific and technical progress itself continuously creates qualitatively new possibilities for developing energy supplies, replacing natural raw materials with synthetic, man-made ones."[30] The combination of advanced technology and economic wealth puts the United States in a very advantageous position to deal with both resource and environmental problems, and simultaneously to promote economic recovery. As Dalin has observed,

> Technical progress will continue and, on this basis, fixed capital will be replaced and expanded and industrial investments will increase. The energy crisis has already led to an increase in coal mining, the search for new technical methods for converting it to gas and energy, the accelerated construction of atomic power stations, off-shore drilling for oil, and the construction of pipelines of great diameter and length. Enormous expenditures will be required in the fight against environmental pollution.[31]

Given the reverence which Soviet analysts have for the "scientific and technological revolution," they seem to believe that problems which would strain the economy of a lesser nation are soluble for the United States.

A second major source of American economic strength, in the Soviet view, has been the introduction of Keynesian practices— what Soviet economists like to refer to as "state-monopoly regulation of the economy." The Johnson administration's "new economics," note Soviet observers, led to "the active utilization . . . of the state mechanism for insuring steady and higher rates of growth." Thus, in the view of Bobrakov,

> The significant increase in the American economy during the period 1961–68, when the adjusted GNP increased almost 1.5 times, was due not

14

only to favorable economic conditions, but, in many respects, also to the purposeful utilization of state resources to support and stimulate the national economy.[32]

Such policies, note the Amerikanisty, are not restricted to the Democrats. Though by tradition opposed to such practices, the Republicans under Richard Nixon also recognized the indispensability of extensive government intervention in the economy. "Squeezed in a vise of problems," the Republicans in the early 1970s found it "necessary to forget for a time about old beliefs" about private property and classical free enterprise. Thus in 1970 the Nixon administration sought to stimulate economic growth by means of the strategy of a planned deficit in the federal budget. In January of the following year Nixon admitted to a television audience: "I have become a Keynesian in economics." "The Republicans 'apostasy' reached its apotheosis," comments a Soviet analyst, when in 1971, as inflation became increasingly severe, the government resorted to a wage-price freeze, an action unprecedented in peacetime.[33]

For a time, notes one source, the use of Keynesian measures to stimulate economic activity "engendered a certain fetishism with regard to the capabilities of the bourgeois state." These methods ultimately failed however; the "anarchic forces of the capitalist system" proved impossible to regulate.[34] Thus, writing in August 1975, Dalin concluded that the 1974–75 economic crisis demonstrated the utter bankruptcy of Keynesian ideas.

It is hard to imagine a greater failure than the one experienced by the theory of the 'New Economics.' . . . Instead of full employment, the seventies are marked by a rise of unemployment; instead of high growth rates, their decline and a new economic crisis; instead of price stability, their rise in leaps and bounds.[35]

As Bobrakov has observed, "The economic upheavals of recent years have dealt a severe blow to bourgeois ideas of 'crisis-free growth' and 'stable prosperity.'[36]

Despite the disenchantment of some with the effectiveness of American efforts to deal with the combined problems of recession and inflation, others retain their faith. They argue that as economic difficulties have mounted new methods of controlling the economy are being employed—including national economic planning! American economists, writes A. V. Anikin, head of *IMEMO*'s Department of the U.S. Economy, are now "actively debating" a "capitalist state plan." "Plan or perish . . . or, in any case, at least 'plan or fall behind'" has become the slogan.[37] This shift to a more "systematic approach," to "long-term projections and prognostications" is seen as promising. "Naturally," writes Bobrakov,

> no amount of programming can eliminate the inherent contradictions of capitalism. . . . However it would be erroneous to discount the ability of modern state monopoly capitalism in the United States to exert a rational effect upon the production process, stimulate economic growth and accelerate its tempo.[38]

The 1974–76 economic decline, it is suggested, further intensified interest in planning. Though previously regarded as anathema, anti-American and "communistic," government planning is now seen as one means of preserving the economy. This ideological turnaround, according to Bobrakov, attests to the "depth of America's present economic problem and the intensity of the crisis."[39] Government planning—by a "Capitalist 'Gosplan'"—has, of course, nothing in common with "socialist planning."* It was proposed "by rather far-sighted representatives of bourgeois scholarship precisely in order to strengthen the capitalist system," i.e., to mitigate economic crises and better control internal conflict.[40]

Thus to ensure continued economic growth U.S. "state-monopoly capitalism" is resorting to "unaccustomed methods of regulation." "For the sake of maintaining the position of capitalism as a whole," writes Anikin, "the State is forced to inject itself to a heretofore unthinkable extent" into the private sector of the economy.[41] We shall have occasion to meet this formulation—introduction of "unaccustomed methods" for the sake of "the system as a whole"—again.

In the judgement of Soviet analysts, then, the United States has still not exhausted its economic potential. Though carefully watching for economic "difficulties," "fluctuations," and "contradictions," they

---

Gosplan is the acronym for the USSR State Planning Committee, the offical Soviet planning agency.

are wary of overstating them. "Be careful," Arbatov warned an Italian Communist newspaperman in May 1974, "the U.S. economy remains very strong: it is still 40 percent of the entire world capitalist economy."[42] Soviet respect for this country's "possibilities" has been such that, in contrast to the Stalin period—when there was "wide acceptance of the thesis that the volume of production in capitalist countries would decline"—Inozemtsev now feels obliged to warn his colleagues that "imperialism's strength and possibilities should not be exaggerated."[43]

Clearly the United States is considered an economic power with great resources and—within the limits of their ideological commitments—an imaginative and flexible leadership. This country, notes Igor Geyevsky, head of the USA Institute's Section on U.S. Mass Social Movements, is "still the most advanced capitalist nation." As such, it has enormous and ever-growing funds "which can be used for 'social maneuvering,' " i.e., to "ease the acuteness of problems temporarily and quell the wave of dissatisfaction of particular concerned groups." The American leaders, he grudgingly admits, have used these resources with some success. They have "managed to achieve certain results (the problems of mass hunger used to be acute, access of workers' children to higher education institutions was expanded somewhat, etc.)."[44] Given its resources and talent for "social maneuvering," a major economic collapse does not, in the view of Soviet analysts, appear imminent—or likely. And those—like the American Black Panther Party—who base their political strategy on such an unlikely turn of events—are chided for their "underestimation of the capabilities of state-monopoly regulation."[45]

While the economy of American capitalism is viewed as essentially durable, what of its "aggressive" character? Here, even more dramatically, orthodox stereotypes have been significantly modified.

Party doctrine, as noted earlier, has traditionally held the view that the capitalist socio-economic system is, by nature, predatory. Domestic conflict and contradictions are said to "force the ruling circles of the imperialist countries to search for an outlet in foreign adventures and in the aggravation of international tension."[46] The rulers of "monopoly capitalism" deliberately encourage "military gambles" in order to secure overseas markets and investments and, at the same time, to promote militarization of the economy—both of which generate enormous super-profits.[47]

The child and prime beneficiary of this system is the infamous "military-industrial complex," the "monopoly weapons manufacturers . . . top military brass . . . and the bureaucrats and scientists specializing in weapons design." This "reactionary alliance," writes G. A. Trofimenko, head of the USA Institute's Foreign Policy Department, is "the most bellicose grouping" in the capitalist system, whose "vested interest in the arms race . . . [has] sharply intensified" the bourgeoisie's "general class aspirations toward militarism." Thus the "military-industrial complex" is seen to play the role of a "constant catalyst of militarist processes and military adventures."[48] The main objectives of this unwholesome gang are "an increase in the share of the national budget earmarked for military purposes—the creation and retention on a permanent basis of a wartime economy and wartime business conditions." Given these purposes, "tension and world conflicts play into the hands of the military-state monopoly grouping."[49]

It is not, however, the "military-industrial complex" alone which profits from an aggressive foreign policy. As a Soviet textbook notes:

> An increase in state military orders sometimes acts as a lever for increasing overall production, including goods for civilian use. It can also *temporarily* promote a certain increase in wages, particularly of those employed in war industry.[50] [Italics in the original.]

High levels of military spending, therefore, bring benefits to all sectors, not just those corporations with defense contracts. The capitalist economy as a whole is thus believed to have a vested interest in international tension and the arms race.

The orthodox position may be put thus: "Imperialism gives rise to militarism and militarism under contemporary state-monopoly capitalist conditions inevitably leads to the creation of a military-state-monopoly grouping," which in turn "further urges on and intensifies the process of militarization and militarism." This "sinister spiral," according to Tsagolov, is "one of the most dangerous and vicious, although perfectly natural manifestations" of American capitalism.[51]

As an illustration of this "perfectly natural" connection between "state-monopoly capitalism" and the arms race, Anatoly Gromyko points to the first military budget of the Kennedy administration. In the early 1960s, Gromyko writes, "economic indicators increasingly demonstrated that the United States was entering a period of critical decline in production . . . [A]s in earlier situations of this nature, great hopes were placed in the arms race and military expenditures as measures to combat the crisis. . . . The new president did not break with tradition."[52] In the view of Gromyko and other militants, therefore, it is the "predatory nature of capitalist society" which "forms the basis of the foreign policy and diplomacy" of the United States. "No smoothing over or prettifying up of imperialist diplomacy is capable of changing its entirely negative essence."[53]

In the more recent scholarly literature this view has been distinctively modified. The arms race, militarism and even an aggressive foreign policy are no longer seen as automatically working to the advantage of the American socio-economic system. In fact, as analysts argue at great length in the pages of *SShA* and elsewhere, significant segments of the business and political leadership of the United States have come to regard high levels of military spending as economically — and politically — dangerous.

The most articulate spokesman for this position is the institute's director, Georgi Arbatov. "Until recently," Arbatov noted in a lecture at the University of Michigan, "considerable numbers of Americans saw the arms race as an instrument for preventing economic slumps and depressions in their country." Now, he went on, "the situation has started to change. It has started to become increasingly obvious that colossal military expenditure in no way stimulates prosperity but, on the contrary, has a destructive effect on the U.S. economy." Soviet analysts, he suggests, have long held such views. What is critical is that "this fact is finding ever wider acceptance in the United States."[54]

What explains this dramatic turnabout? The main factor, according to Arbatov, has been "the enormous economic costs of the modern arms race," the result largely of "the accelerating obsolescence of weapons" (the "logic" of unchecked scientific and technical progress "forcing one again and again to replace improved type weapons by yesterday's standards with ever more modern ones"). And with each

19

new generation of weapons costs rise in "truly geometric progression." The impact of these developments on the economy is striking. Arbatov writes:

> The military economy has grown from a relatively small sector, which the ruling class even regarded as a useful "balance wheel"—enabling the state to regulate economic fluctuations by softening the impact of cyclical crises—into an enormous unproductive part of the economy, disturbing the normal operation of the economic mechanism.[55]

Spiraling weapons costs, Arbatov notes, have had severe economic consequences. Huge U.S. military expenditures in the postwar period (which, he states, totalled $1.2 trillion) resulted in "inflation, rising taxes, a shrinking domestic market, the undermining of the USA's competitive position and the exacerbation of domestic problems."[56] In light of these conditions ever larger numbers of Americans are now aware that even "such a rich country as the United States" cannot "provide both 'guns and butter' at the same time."[57]

What Arbatov is suggesting is that the postwar arms race, which consumed enormous resources, significantly overstrained and destabilized the American economy. The "bankruptcy" of traditional American policy became apparent during the war in Vietnam when "the interests of the military-industrial monopolies came into definite conflict with the interests of other more numerous and also highly influential groupings of monopoly capital." Underlying this "conflict of interests," according to Arbatov, was the fact that "of the 500 largest corporations from which the Dow-Jones average is compiled, only approximately 50 are connected with military matters."[58] The latter clearly benefited from the Vietnam war. As Trofimenko notes: "The lion's share of the funds allotted for military purchases is to be found lying in the safes of aerospace and electronics industry monopolies and firms producing conventional arms and ammunition."[59] The great majority of firms, however, clearly suffered as corporate profits fell sharply, as did the value of stocks, while taxes doubled. Thus, as Geyevsky writes, "the war in Vietnam and the militarization of the economy had a negative effect upon the incomes of a considerable part of the American bourgeoisie."[60] Many U.S. companies, especially those oriented toward the consumer market, "believe that they could have earned much larger profits if part of federal military expenditures had been switched over to finance domestic social programs."[61]

The economic impact of the Vietnam war was, therefore, unevenly felt. For the fifty corporations directly participating in military contracts—the "nucleus of the military-industrial complex"—it was enormously profitable and to the bitter end they urged its continuation. For the remainder Vietnam was a great burden, which they grew to loath and to oppose. As Yuri A. Shvedkov, a leading foreign policy analyst at the USA Institute, has noted, the "global strategy" of American foreign policy "no longer suited U.S. monopoly circles. For just this reason . . . representatives of certain very large banks and industrial monopolies in the USA began to come out in criticism of Washington's foreign policy and with demands for getting out of the war in Vietnam." To help achieve this end, they organized themselves into "Businessmen Against the War in Vietnam."[62]

It was precisely this divergence in economic interests which led to serious splits in the American political elite, especially regarding the war in Vietnam and the U.S. military budget. According to Arbatov, "The economic interests of a considerable part of the ruling bourgeoisie began to collide with the old political line."[63] The American government was pressured to modify its policies. "The discontent of business circles," he writes, was "one of the chief factors forcing President Johnson in 1968 to abandon plans for escalating the war (after the Tet Offensive) and to abandon the presidency."[64] And to help deal with increasingly severe economic and social problems, the size of the military budget had to be brought down. As Soviet analysts have reported, the proportion of the U.S. Federal budget devoted to military expenditures has declined from 44.6 percent in FY 1970 to 33 percent in FY 1974, and by 1978 should amount to 30 percent. While they stress that "the absolute amounts of military expenditures . . . are continuing to grow,"[65] the trend towards greater spending on social welfare and economic programs has been duly noted. As part of a much larger anti-war movement—of which more shortly—U.S. business interests sought to persuade the Nixon administration to withdraw from Vietnam. And, more recently, "definite moods" have appeared among business circles "which could bring pressure to bear on official Washington, pushing it toward some further steps in limiting the arms race."[66]

The above analysis suggests a clear departure from the traditional interpretation. While the orthodox Leninist view assumes a direct

21

causal link between "monopoly capital" on the one hand and an aggressive, militaristic foreign policy on the other, contemporary analysts now recognize that the two do not always necessarily go together. The American business community is now seen as internally divided between a relatively small group of major corporations — about 10 percent of the total according to Arbatov's figures — who have an immediate stake in international tension and a stepping-up of the arms race — and a large number from the non-military sector of the economy, who regard high levels of defense spending with considerable misgivings. Thus whereas earlier writers identified the whole of the business community with the "military-industrial complex" — on the grounds that defense orders bring direct or indirect benefit to virtually all branches of the economy — economist A. G. Mileikovsky now argues that this view is "a mistake," since "not all of the big corporations gain access to this privileged market." Moreover, "militarization and its fellow traveller, inflation, represent a clear blow to the interests of a significant part of the corporations."[67] Given the fact that "the positions of various capitalist groups are determined by their real interests,"[68] it is not surprising that on matters of foreign and defense policy their views sharply differ.

The point is not merely, however, that U.S. business corporations do not share equally in defense contracts. Previous writers have noted this.[69] What is significant is the fact that now for the first time "influential groups of monopoly capitalists" have come to understand that militarization and war are no longer a reliable stimulus for economic development. While the "military-industrial complex" is believed to retain a political influence "much greater than its economic share,"[70] other segments of the American business community — especially the vastly larger multinational corporations[71] — are increasingly challenging both its policies and its political influence.

Traditional views regarding the "predatory nature" of capitalist society have, therefore, been revised. Soviet Americanists have concluded that the majority of American corporations do not have a stake in continued international tension and a prolonged arms race. The American "ruling circles," they write, "have stopped seeing the arms race as an absolute blessing."[72] From the orthodox view that the U.S.

economy rests on its arms expenditures, it has now come to be held that continued economic health depends on a curtailment of military spending. Thus, once regarded as the motive force behind the aggressive policies of the United States, the class interests of American big business are now seen to be behind Washington's more moderate stance.

One final point. In the view of Soviet Americanists, U.S. policy makers no longer rely on military expenditures to control business cycles, as they are believed to have traditionally done. Defense spending, as was noted by Arbatov, has been transformed from a "balance wheel" to a "disturber" of economic activity. Furthermore, as is now recognized, decisions regarding military spending often take place independently of business conditions. A major reason why intervention in Vietnam produced such serious consequences for the American economy, according to one writer, was its poor timing. In World War II and the Korean war military production began during periods of economic recession—and therefore had a stimulating effect on the economy as a whole—but U.S. industrial production levels in the mid-1960s were already high. In these conditions the extensive development of military spending inevitably resulted in an "overheated" economy. [73]

In the case of Vietnam, then, increased military budgets were adopted independent of business-cycle calculations. Decisions relating to defense spending are not, therefore, exclusively economic. This point is recognized by Arbatov, who notes that "poor relations between states always spur on the arms race, serving as a justification for very large military appropriations, even under conditions of various economic difficulties." [74] While American policy makers cannot shape policy in total disregard of economic factors—the "arrogant" assumption that this was possible has, in the Soviet view, created many of the economic difficulties currently facing this country— basic decisions regarding defense spending are considered to be essentially political.

The Crisis of Bourgeois Society

Soviet accounts of socio-political developments in the United States in the late 1960s and early 1970s take a predictable turn. The

23

tumultuous events of this decade—racial violence, student unrest, assassination of major political figures, presidential instability—along with the more traditional symptoms of "social pathology"— unemployment, poverty, crime, drug abuse, pornography—were seen as further testimony of the crisis-ridden nature of capitalist society. When in the latter 1960s the anti-Vietnam war protest movement turned from sit-ins to massive demonstrations, American society was seen to be in serious disarray. Increasingly acute socio-economic crises were turning into a political and even spiritual crisis.

The importance attributed to the "increasing aggravation of domestic contradictions" in American society reflects, in some measure, the enthusiasm with which the newly-formed USA Institute approached its task. Many of its leading analysts, never having been in the United States before (Arbatov himself, as he told me in California in February 1969, was then on his first visit), could not but be fascinated by the "conflicts" and "tensions" of capitalist society, many of which were played out before their very eyes. Their analyses, in some cases, were smug and self-satisfied. For example, in his account of the "constantly growing difficulties which have befallen the citadel of capitalism," veteran Americanist Valentin Zorin writes:

> For a time the leaders of the American bourgeoisie, self-satisfied and haughty, believed that they had succeeded in controlling the historical process and in finding a panacea for the troubles and evils of capitalist society. [They were] blinded by the rapid growth of the American economy, [and] lulled by the songs of the troubadors of bourgeois science, who asserted that the means had been found of ensuring the continuous and crisis-free development of American society.[75]

For Zorin the disturbances and social unrest of the late 1960s were clear and gratifying evidence that capitalism's "general crisis" had not bypassed the United States.

While many may have shared Zorin's sense of pleasure, the social and political turmoil of the late sixties and early seventies were approached with the utmost seriousness. Some gave voice to the view—one also held by many American commentators—that the mounting demonstrations, and especially the increasing levels of violence, were "tearing our society apart." The problem was seen to be "extremely serious." The key question confronting the United States

24

according to one analyst was: "will it succeed in guiding protest along the harmless channels of parliamentarianism or will it take forms which are more resolute and formidable for the social system?"[76] The threat of major social upheaval—even revolution—was not beyond mention.

Critically important in the Soviet view was the reaction of the American "ruling circles" to these deeply disturbing events. This was a "very critical period," writes Arbatov in mid-1971. Spreading "negro riots," the "very acute" problem of youth alienation (often referred to as the "disillusionment of the most sensitive elements in American bourgeois society"), the "rapid increase" in crime, drug addiction, immorality and pornography, the problems of the "sick" American economy, (declining growth rates, inflation, growing unemployment) were mounting in intensity. Even more significant he writes, was the "increasingly organic interlacing of those difficulties" with the opposition to the continued war in Vietnam, a war which many considered "immoral and criminal." Americans are losing faith, notes Arbatov, "not only the broad public but also the ruling circles."

> Growing uneasiness, doubt with respect to the correctness of the policy that is being pursued and anxiety concerning the fact that the USA in entering a period of profound and dangerous internal convulsions became characteristic of a significant number of them during these years.[77]

The situation was seen as serious; worsening socio-economic crises were believed by Geyevsky to be "dangerously undermining the stability and shaking the foundations of bourgeois society."[78]

The "organic interlacing" of domestic problems and the anti-war movement produced what some analysts regarded as "a political crisis of unparalleled intensity," one which threatened the political stability of the United States. The American leadership was losing its self-confidence, wrote Zorin in 1971. A speech given by President Nixon at Colorado Springs in September 1969 is quoted: "We are encountering a collapse of confidence in the very government of the United States, a growing lack of confidence in all authority." Zorin observes that "a great deal had to happen for the president of the United States to make such a statement publicly." In his view we were then facing "what may perhaps be called a 'crisis at the summit.'"[79] Others saw the situation similarly. Increasingly concerned about declining corporate profits, the American "ruling circles," according to Arbatov and Vitaly Zhurkin (1972), were also deeply worried about "the more indirect threats to their omnipotence which result from the aggravation of economic and social problems . . . and the increase in oppositional attitudes engendered by these difficulties."[80] Official Washington was clearly alarmed. By 1970, at the height of the anti-war movement, writes Trofimenko, the question for the American leadership had become, in the words of then Vice-President Agnew: "Will the government of this country remain in the hands of its elected officials or will it descend to the street."[81]

In response to this growing political crisis, Washington policy makers began a review of America's "national priorities." To help find a way out of their increasingly acute crises, writes Geyevsky, "real searches are taking place in the [American] ruling camp for a new and more effective social strategy."[82] This high-level policy review was seen to have had two major consequences: it was decided, first of all, "to put our own house in order" by giving greater attention and resources to domestic needs. This decision and the increasingly obvious failure of the war in Vietnam led, secondly, to an overall reappraisal of the course of U.S. foreign policy.

As a result of the "deepening crisis" of American capitalism, notes Geyevsky, the decision was taken by the Nixon administration to give "priority to domestic needs in the distribution of budgetary appropriations. . . . This is witnessed, in particular, by the increase — absolute and relative — in federal expenditures for social needs." Though the amounts "look impressive," he comments, they are of course only "modest palliatives," the "most minimal concessions" designed to "reduce the acuteness of the most explosive problems and push back the wave of mass demonstrations." Nevertheless, this new policy decision is significant, especially since it "of course, results in great pressure on the federal budget, including on those items which were regarded as inviolable, military items." While the decline in expenditures for military purposes is "not in itself" an indication of a basic change in U.S. defense policy — especially since the absolute level of military spending remains the same — Geyevsky quotes President Nixon's 1972 budget message statement that "for the first time in 20 years we have spent more to satisfy the needs of man than we have for defense needs." "Statements of this kind," he comments, "were entirely inconceivable several years ago."[83]

Thus extremely tense social and political crises, compounded by serious economic difficulties, compelled the "ruling circles" of the United States to divert increasing funds to domestic social programs and, proportionally, away from the military budget. Writing in 1975, one Soviet analyst reported that

> The proportion of expenditures [in the federal budget] in the category of "national security" has been reduced from 45 percent in the 1967/68 fiscal year to 29.3 percent in 1973/74. Simultaneously . . . the total expenditures on such goals as the training of the work force, education, public health and social security have increased . . . and in the 1973/74 fiscal year they amount to more than 40 percent of all federal spending. . . . In 1967/68 they were about 30 percent.[84]

Though a rise in defense expenditures has more recently been noted,[85] Soviet analysts are persuaded that the "serious threat" to domestic stability compelled a reduction, rather than an increase, in American military budgeting.

Equally important in Soviet eyes was the impact of our domestic travails on the American spiritual climate. The events of the 1960s, writes Arbatov, have "thoroughly shaken" the faith of many in the United States in "the superiority of 'the American way of life.'" The effect of social turmoil and violence was shattering, raising serious doubts not only about "the superiority of American economic, social and political institutions" but also about what he labels as America's self-proclaimed "right to implant its 'ideals' throughout the world." Quoting from Andrew Hacker's *The End of the American Era*, Arbatov remarks: "A growing number [of Americans] are convinced that the quality of life [they] have in this country can hardly serve as a pattern for export."[86]

The traumas of the 1960s are therefore seen as having weakened the ideological underpinnings of U.S. foreign policy. With the loss of confidence in the infallibility of American society, the "myth of the 'American era'" was discredited. The "nobility" of Washington's "mission . . . to 'defend' freedom and democracy" around the world was called into doubt, according to Arbatov. Faith in traditional

27

policies was further damaged by the futile war in Vietnam. "Millions of Americans," he writes, including "a significant segment of the ruling circles," are now asking: "Should and, most important, can their country continue to spend vast sums of money and manpower on the arms race and foreign-policy problems?"[87]

Thus, under the combined impact of domestic socio-economic crises and the war in Vietnam, "definite changes" began to occur in the foreign-policy view of the American leadership. They began to "understand and admit the need for change," to raise questions

about the bankruptcy of old political precepts, about the need to take a new approach to many traditional policy concepts such as national security and national power and to recognize that the strength and international influence of the USA requires first of all concern for the stability of its own rear.

And it is precisely this change of views which is identified as the basis of the Nixon administration's decision to move from an "era of confrontation to an era of negotiations" in its relations with the Soviet Union.[88]

The implications of this analysis for the Soviet image of the American political system are most striking. Rather than assert, as many doctrinal Party spokesmen still do, that the "ruling circles of the monopoly bourgeoisie" seek a way out of internal crises in foreign-policy adventures to divert attention from domestic social ills, Soviet authors are now suggesting that anxiety regarding their "unreliable home front" (Zorin) has led American policy makers toward a more moderate foreign-policy position. As in the case of the economy, the "vested interests" of the "ruling circles" are now considered to be poorly served by a policy of expansion and international tension.

This argument is spelled out by Zhurkin. Only quite recently, he suggests, "international conflicts and the chauvinist feelings they gave rise to were regarded in the United States [and in the Soviet Union] as an important means of mobilizing public opinion." However, as the crises in France during the early 1960s (over the wars in Algeria and Indochina) indicate, international conflicts are increasingly "becoming a stimulus for the development of domestic political and social crisis in the country which has instigated the aggressive actions. . . . The genuine split of American society over

28

the issue of the Indochina war may serve as the most vivid illustration of this." Thus, rather than serving as a means to encourage "social peace," wars are now considered "one of the chief causes of domestic conflict."[89]

The adoption by the United States of the policy of détente, it is held, is a result of such calculations. According to a group of foreign-policy specialists at the USA Institute meeting in 1975, Washington endorsed the "reduction of international tension" as one of its "main goals (interests)" precisely in order to help "maintain the socio-economic stability of the American social system."[90] This same view is set forth by V. M. Berezhkov, editor of *SShA*, when he writes that at

> the beginning of the seventies, past experience made the U.S. ruling circles abandon their unsuccessful attempts to resolve urgent domestic problems by all kinds of international adventures and an unrestrained arms race. In recent years, the understanding has grown that one cannot embark on the practical resolution of domestic problems without a favorable atmosphere in the world arena.[91]

In a stunning reversal of form, the social stability of "monopoly capitalism" in the United States—as well as its economic well-being— is now believed to require a tranquil international environment.

Two additional points. Although the USA Institute clearly regarded the tumultuous developments of the 1960s as highly important—at least in terms of their impact on foreign policy—at no point were they regarded as seriously threatening the political stability of the United States. This was for three reasons. First, in the view of most Soviet analysts, such potential for oppositional activity as may then have existed was weakened by internal divisions within the ranks of the system's adversaries. According to Geyevsky, for example, "the black liberation movement" was torn by "certain ideological and political differences, different points of view on practical action, on ultimate goals, and on the ways and means of achieving these goals."[92] Similarly, Shvedkov observes that while "preconditions arose for uniting the many democratic movements which had developed . . . on a common anti-imperialist, anti-war platform," these were "only partially realized." The "organizational weakness" of these forces, "their lack of communication, a certain weakness in the progressive forces resulting from many years of persecution and repression," all stood in the way of their effective mobilization.[93] Little, clearly, was to be expected from the CPUSA.

The "democratic protest movements" were also the victim of revolutionary romanticism. "One of the main errors of the American radicals of the sixties," writes a close student of their activities, "was that of underestimating the capabilities of the contemporary state-monopoly capitalism in the United States." This lack of realism, he suggests, had serious consequences. It "gave rise at first to unjustified hopes of a rapid overthrow of American imperialism, but that was followed by disillusionment."[94] The political opposition of the 1960s had failed to take into account the ability of the U.S. leadership to engage in "social maneuvering." Their revolutionary hopes therefore went unfulfilled. Soviet analysts, ever more sober, had few dreams to begin with.

Finally, Soviet authors take an equally dim view of the revolutionary potential of the American people. The traditional benchmarks of a revolutionary consciousness—class hatred of the oppressor, burning social resentment, a passionate sense of the intolerability of the present—are hardly to be found among the broad masses of Americans. Even the American working class is devoid of proletarian militancy. Betrayed by the "reactionary" trade union "bosses" of the AFL-CIO, the worker has apparently also been seduced by the "consumer society," (capitalism's strategy of ensuring social peace by means of overt bribery of the working class.) The American worker, notes Mileikovsky, has received "a marked increase in wages," improved housing, cars and other consumer durables, all of which has meant a real improvement in living standards. As he recognizes, fear of impoverishment no longer spurs American workers to militant action. All Mileikovsky can find comfort in is the recent concern for the "quality of life" and the growing consumer movement, which he sees as evidence of a new militant spirit aimed against the ideals of the "consumer society."[95] For all its "profound spiritual crisis," the American working class is still a long way from the barricades.

Thus Soviet judgements continue to be influenced by their high regard for American social and economic capabilities. As in the case of the economy, Soviet Americanists were confident of the "system's" ability to ride out the social convulsions of the late sixties and early seventies. In a symposium at the USA Institute in October 1972, for example, in the context of a discussion of the "very severe crisis" then confronting the United States, one commentator observed that "during its almost two centuries-old history, the American federal system has more than once demonstrated its ability to adapt to changing conditions."[96] Aside from noting for the record that "this capacity for adaptation . . . is not unlimited"—especially in "a socio-economic system which has historically outlived its time"—nothing said by this speaker, or any other symposium participant, indicated that they expected to celebrate the collapse of the American system in the foreseeable future.

And perhaps just as well, for they seem far from certain that a severe capitalist crisis would work to Soviet advantage. As Arbatov told Giuseppe Boffa of L'Unita, "we are well aware that every crisis in bourgeois society may have various results. The crisis of the 'thirties' produced Roosevelt and his 'New Deal' in the United States and Hitler, fascism, and war in Germany."[97] Eminent Soviet commentators—Arbatov, Inozemtsev, Zorin, and many others—have repeatedly warned that harsh economic and socio-political crises lead to the activization of "rightist" and "the most reactionary groups." Thus writes Zorin, "the deepening crisis of American society" has given rise to a marked increase in the danger from the right. The experience of history indicates that movements of a fascist type arise when there is a worsening of social and economic contradictions.[98] And as recently as February 1976 a leading Party specialist on the United States (its ranking member on the editorial board of SShA) wrote that although there is no imminent threat of a fascist takeover in the United States, "it is necessary in the long-term perspective to keep the fascist threat in mind."[99]

Obviously memories of the grim experiences of the thirties persist. Soviet analysts still fear that economic instability will give rise to political instability, which could well work to the benefit of conservative, right-wing elements. The ultimate dread is that economic collapse will result in fascism. When economic pressures intensify, Soviet observers fear, the "longing" of certain groups for "a 'strong hand' capable of coming down on the working people" increases.[100] The risk of fascism, however small, is not to be treated lightly. As

31

Soviet Party Secretary Boris Ponomarev has observed, "in the nuclear age, the strengthening of fascist forces and, even more, a fascist seizure of state power, would be even more dangerous . . . than on the eve of World War II."[101] Thus the fact that the United States emerged essentially unscathed from its recent travails is undoubtedly a greater source of comfort than Soviet spokesmen would openly admit. The ultimate horror—a new Hitler with access to the American nuclear arsenal—is not, thankfully, a very likely prospect.

2

THE AMERICAN POLITICAL SYSTEM

In their attempt to understand the American political system, Soviet analysts suffer from a variety of disabilities. They have been burdened, as we have seen, by the constraints of rigid ideological preconceptions and, until recently, limited personal contact with the United States. They also lack the benefit of useful historical guidance; Tsarist Russia never produced a Tocqueville or a Bryce.* There is another, even more serious obstacle, however. They are attempting to comprehend a democratic political system, one whose institutions and processes neither they nor their countrymen have ever had any experience with. (The feeble efforts of the last Tsars and the Provisional Government hardly qualify.) While there are at least folk memories and socio-economic histories available concerning life in the emergent capitalism of pre-1914 Russia — for whatever value they may hold — there is virtually nothing to guide the Russians'

---

*As S. Frederick Starr has reminded us, the ancien régime did produce one brilliant Americanist, Moisei Ostrogorsky, whose two-volume *Democracy and the Organization of Political Parties* is recognized to be a major contribution to the study of American politics. Ostrogorsky's "profound insights," suggests Starr, "justify his being ranked after Alexis de Tocqueville and Sir James Bryce as the most sensitive foreign observer of this country" ("The Russian View of America," *The Wilson Quarterly* 1, no. 2 [Winter 1977]: 110). Curiously, however, though originally published in English in 1902, and in French the following year, this work has never been published in the Russian language. (See Seymour Martin Lipset's introduction to the 1964 Anchor Books edition.)

efforts to make sense out of the Senate Foreign Relations Committee, the *Washington Post*, Senator Henry Jackson, public opinion polls and the American legal system.

The USA Institute has, as one of its major tasks, the responsibility of filling this intellectual and informational void. And its researchers have spent long hours pouring through the American press and magazines, professional journals and transcripts of congressional hearings, reading American history and biography, interviewing U.S. government officials and political leaders. Given the handicaps with which they began—and the constraints which domestic political considerations still impose—the results have been surprisingly good. There are, to be sure, blind spots and rigidities, as we shall explain. It must be recognized, however, that Soviet perceptions of the American political system have notably improved.

Both to indicate the degree to which Soviet thinking has changed and as groundwork for a later discussion of American political dynamics, a brief sortie into political-economic doctrine seems useful.

"State-Monopoly Capitalism"

The basic character of the U.S. political system, according to orthodox Party doctrine, is shaped by its class nature, especially by the special relationship which is seen to exist between major American corporate interests and the federal government. According to this view, the power of large "monopolies" is united with that of the state, hence the label "state-monopoly capitalism." Thus, states a recent text, "The essence of state-monopoly capitalism . . . is the direct union of the power of the capitalist monopolies with the enormous power of the state. In this union the state occupies not an independent but a subordinate position."[1] This last point is crucial; the function of the political mechanism is to promote the interests of major corporations—to help them enrich themselves (via government contracts, tax privileges, credits), to safeguard them from economic crises and foreign competition and to protect their political dominance from adversaries, domestic and foreign.

The state, in this view, is the tool and the servant of the dominant economic interests, to whose purposes the machinery and processes of government—and society as a whole—are bent. Following Lenin's

34

notion of a "personal union" between the banks, industry and the state, it is argued that

> To utilize state power more effectively, the tycoons of finance capital had themselves appointed as ministers, heads of important departments, ambassadors and prominent officials. The state machinery and the monopolies are so intertwined that it is often difficult to determine the boundary between them.[2]

All agencies and processes of the democratic state—government office, parties, the press, the legislature—are at best trappings serving to obscure the dominance of big business. In the United States, Lenin wrote, "The stock exchange is everything, while parliament and elections are marionettes."[3]

Lenin, as we shall see, did speak of divisions and disagreement within the ruling circles of capitalism, a condition which gave rise on occasion to serious debate over questions of foreign policy. This observation admitted at least the possibility of some meaningful political life under capitalism. It was the prevailing wisdom of the Stalin period, however, that capitalist governments were dominated by an essentially united oligarchy of finance capitalists—Wall Street. Stalin thus denied the possibility of autonomy to the sphere of politics or to the state itself. In his view the capitalist state was in the hands of the corporate interests and not vice versa.

The orthodox view, therefore, is based on crude economic determinism, according to which the economic base (dominated by big business) determines the political superstructure, whose prime purpose it is to strengthen the base. Thus the agencies of the federal government, the Congress, the courts as well as the political parties, elections, and the media are all seen to be mere pawns serving the interests of their bourgeois masters. There are, in this view, no politically significant differences or conflicts either among the major corporations or within the state apparatus subordinated to them.

This system of dictatorial class rule is seen to be essentially reactionary and aggressive. Operating under direct instructions from monopoly capital, the American government is viewed as inherently hostile. The imperialist elite, recognizing the threat which socialism poses to its class interests, seeks to use the state to wage total war against the Soviet Union. The essence of this position was ably captured in the title of a book published in Moscow in 1951: *Amerikanskiye imperialisty: zleishiye vragi mira, demokratii i sotsializma* (*American Imperialists: The Worst Enemies of Peace, Democracy and Socialism*). And in this view Soviet diplomacy is largely powerless to temper such deeply-rooted hostility.[4]

Since the death of Stalin such primitive formulations have been significantly modified. As earlier studies have indicated,[5] Soviet analysts have in the past two decades moved considerably beyond these crude interpretations. It must be noted, however, that such views are not completely absent. They are frequently found in the popular press and, on occasion, even in the writings of eminent Soviet Americanists. Thus, for example, Anatoly Gromyko has written that

the interests of the large monopolies are the very compass by which the United States government is guided in its activities. The president of the United States, the venerable senators, the smartest members of the House of Representatives and the entire bureaucratic apparatus are, in fact, in the service of the monopolists. Monopoly capital is the main and decisive force which controls American foreign policy.[6]

Gromyko goes on to say that it is perfectly natural that leading American diplomats "are close in their views to those of their bosses, the American monopolists. Frequently they are offended when they are called 'servants of capital' . . . they even get indignant. . . . Facts, however, are stubborn things."[7] In a similar vein, another Soviet analyst (writing in 1972) asserts that "all eight postwar secretaries of state have been appointed mainly on the basis of their ties with the business world." They are all, he insists, either directly or through their law firms, "proteges of the most influential financial groups on Wall Street."[8] Given Henry Kissinger's association with the Rockefeller Brothers' Fund, and Cyrus Vance's legal ties,* the number now is undoubtedly "all ten."

In a major study Shvedkov states the case in sweeping terms, writing that

American monopolies exert a constant influence on the government apparatus that is intertwined with them along an infinite number of channels at various levels. . . . Many government departments operating

---

*Before joining the Carter Administration, Secretary of State Vance was a partner in the Wall Street law firm of Simpson, Thatcher and Bartlett.

in the field of economic policy have become so intertwined with private organizations of monopolies that it is quite impossible to establish where the line between them runs.[9]

Corporate influence on government policy, he writes, is also transmitted directly. By means of connections at the very top—through participation in special presidential commissions and task-forces or, less formally, by their presence at unofficial dinners and meetings at the White House—corporate executives "convey the main pulses from the principal groupings of monopoly capital that affect government policy as a whole."

The persistence of such views in the writings of Soviet Americanists has led some to conclude that, for all their awareness of fact and detail, their findings are nothing more than old wine in new bottles. Such is not the case. Though the language often remains unchanged, the specific interpretation given to "state-monopoly capitalism" indicates a far better appreciation of contemporary American politics than such rhetoric would seem to allow. While analysts still remain loyal to basic doctrinal formulations, which they must, they have managed to cast them in a new, far less inhibiting light.

Though the rhetoric of "state-monopoly capitalism" is retained, its dynamics are today understood quite differently than during the heyday of Stalinist dogmatism. A cardinal difference relates to the degree of internal cohesion thought to exist within the American ruling elite. Once regarded as essentially united, both in terms of views and interests, the American leadership is now seen to be internally divided. As one Soviet analyst has observed:

> various classes and even different groups within classes interpret the development of different events in different ways and place a different evaluation on it. . . . [A]s the ruling class becomes divided and various social groups and political factions begin to grow within it, there is a broader struggle not only between the ideologies of different classes, but also within the prevalent ideology within the society. This is precisely the present state of affairs within the United States.[10]

Thus the leadership of "state-monopoly capitalism" is now considered to be at odds with itself. Arbatov notes, for example, the existence of a considerable "struggle of opinion" in Washington regarding Soviet-American relations. There are, he suggests, three groups, viz., "hard-headed anti-communists," those who adopt "more 'flexible'" though equally hostile methods and, finally, "those who look on things more realistically." The proponents of each of these views, suggests Arbatov, "have of course not ceased being convinced adherents of capitalism and opponents of communism." They all, he argues, "first of all have American interests in view." Policy disagreements among these groupings are explained by the fact that "these interests are understood by them differently."[11]

Clearly the dogmatic assumptions of the Stalin period are no longer accepted. As Soviet analysts frequently note, though all of the major political actors in the United States are committed to the existing socio-economic system, this unity of "class interest" does not eliminate differences—sometimes very significant ones—regarding the ways and means by which individual groups seek to achieve their purposes. As we saw in the previous chapter, attitudes on both domestic and foreign (especially defense) policy have become increasingly differentiated. Various segments of the American leadership have taken differing positions on such policy issues as "reordering national priorities," economic planning, Vietnam, and the arms race. According to another source, "internal instability" in the United States in recent years has generated "differences of opinion" within the American leadership regarding the best ways to overcome these "multifaceted" crises. The "prevailing view" is said to be "one which holds that the best way lies in 'tightening the screws.' . . . At the same time," this writer notes, "there is a certain revival of reformist currents."[12]

Although the groups composing the American leadership are seen to be guided by the interests of their own class, they interpret these interests differently. Nothing less than a "fierce struggle" is said to have been "going on for a long time" within the American leadership regarding jurisdiction over the continental shelf, the underseas territory immediately adjacent to the U.S. coast. The dispute "has mainly been between military circles wishing to keep these boundaries close to the mainland and the oil monopolies taking the opposite position," that is, "in favor of a 'large shelf.'"[13] Common "class interests," therefore, are no longer assumed to explain policy positions among an increasingly heterogeneous "ruling class." Conflicts and disputes emerge from different interests and assessments.

38

In these circumstances, the role of the bourgeois state is significantly different from what it was earlier conceived to be. In a June
1974 article on "U.S. Corporations in the Context of Détente,"
N. D. Turkatenko, deputy editor of *SShA*, notes that

> The state itself performs the function of coordinator of "streams of influ-
> ence" originating from the corporations, and carries out legislative,
> economic, diplomatic, or military measures proceeding from the pre-
> vailing—either immediate or long-run—general interests of state
> monopoly capital as a whole. [14]

Turkatenko's formulation focuses attention on the political sphere.
Noting the existence of internal divergences and even conflicts of
interest—hence the need for a "coordinator"—questions naturally
arise regarding the various interests involved, alternative interpretations and leaderships, and the factors influencing policy choices,
i.e., political questions.

In contrast to the Stalinist "subordination" thesis, which held
that the bourgeois state cannot act against the interests of the
monopolists, who were themselves said to have maintained tight
control of the state apparatus, Turkatenko recognizes the role of
government as an autonomous political force. If the function of the
state is to protect the "long-term," "general" interests of the system "as
a whole," the political leadership can embark on a course which
conflicts with the "short-term," "narrow," interests of specific corporate groups. The president, argues Petrovsky,

> As the spokesman of the political will of the whole of monopoly capi-
> tal . . . can himself influence the activities of individual monopoly groups
> and, when necessary, act against some monopolies that further their own
> selfish interests to the detriment of the common interests of monopoly
> capital [as a whole]. [15]

Soviet writers cite numerous examples of such presidential
autonomy. In 1961, for example, President Kennedy forced a rollback
in steel prices—despite bitter opposition from the heads of the steel
industry—out of concern for the impact of the price rise on the rest of
the American economy. For actions such as this, it is noted, Kennedy
was in fact considered to be an "anti-business President," very much
like President Roosevelt, who in his time was regarded as a "traitor to

his class."[16] According to a Soviet historian, President Kennedy was "a flexible figure who sometimes spoke out against certain groups of monopoly capital in order to defend the interests of the ruling class as a whole."[17]

Similar views are expressed concerning several other recent presidents—Woodrow Wilson, FDR, and Richard Nixon (who, as we have seen, substantially modified the course of American defense and foreign policy, despite opposition from the "military-industrial complex"). In the words of N. N. Yakovlev, such leaders "imposed strict discipline and sacrifice that was sometimes considerable for the sake of the higher interests of the capitalist class."[18]

The role of the political leadership is now considered to be clearly of prime importance. Though Presidents Wilson, Roosevelt, Kennedy and Nixon were all "guided by the interests of their class," they held distinctive views as to how these interests could best be served and were in a position to act on their beliefs. The particular policy orientation of individual political leaders, therefore, can be decisive.

Such non-dogmatic assessments, viz., analyses which recognize the existence of divergent, even conflicting, views regarding the interests of the "ruling class," the possibility that disagreements could arise between economic, political and military elites, and the autonomous role of the state in determining official policy, relatively independent of narrow economic considerations, are not, it should be noted, unique to the present. A number of scholars have convincingly demonstrated that many of the basic notions extant today regarding "state-monopoly capitalism" had their origin in earlier periods. Lenin himself, as indicated previously, recognized divisions and disagreements within the ruling circles of capitalism. He saw, in particular, the existence of several tendencies within Western leadership circles. In addition to hard-line anti-Soviet groups of various hues there were those elements interested mainly in improving world trade. Finally, in all bourgeois countries, a pacifist, liberal tendency was seen to be present. Soviet diplomacy, he urged, could not afford to ignore such differences within the adversary camp.[19] Lenin also saw the state as somewhat independent of the will of the financial oligarchy. He viewed the Tsarist state as "balancing between opposing interests representing to a certain degree a self-sufficient politically organized force."[20]

40

Though Stalin consistently placed his main emphasis on the "subordination thesis," which insisted that the bourgeois state is subordinate to the most powerful economic interests, namely the omnipotent financial oligarchy, a number of Soviet analysts in the early postwar period revived the Leninist interpretation. Led by the ranking economist, Evgenii Varga, they pointed to the existence of disagreements within, for example, the Japanese ruling class (between the military and financial interests). Varga argued that the state often acts in the interests of the bourgeoisie as a whole. Referring to the experience of Western governments during World War II, he suggested that, in order to ensure victory, the capitalist state had to take measures directed against some monopolist groupings. "The bourgeois state as the organization of the entire bourgeoisie as a whole was forced to use coercion in its attempt to subordinate the private interests of particular enterprises and particular persons to the interests of conducting the war."[21]

Such interpretations of "state-monopoly capitalism" and their advocates did not fare well. Hewing close to Stalin's rigid formulas, militant elements in the Communist Party in the late 1940s and early 1950s denounced Varga and his colleagues. However, during the Khrushchev period and since, such analyses have received renewed attention. As we noted earlier, primitive views are still to be found in the Soviet literature on the United States. Nonetheless, "state-monopoly capitalism" is now being interpreted in relatively sophisticated terms.

Though the evolution of Soviet thinking described briefly here can be seen as a return to earlier modes of thought, more is involved. To the extent that they have again become aware that, in Arbatov's phrase, "the superstructure can have a relatively independent role,"[22] Soviet analysts at the USA Institute have studied its operations with considerable care. Their judgements and understanding of this "superstructure," the institutions and processes of the U.S. political system, are in many ways a considerable advance of previous notions. It is to these that we now turn.

The American President

In contrast to the formulations of the Stalin era, which saw American policy as the product of a cabal, worked out in the board rooms of Wall Street financial houses and the executive offices of the National Association of Manufacturers, current Soviet conceptions explicitly reject a crudely conspiratorial model of American politics. It would be naive to assume, writes Arbatov, that there exists "as in the military sphere . . . a kind of political General Staff which draws up a common plan and issues orders in accordance with which various campaigns are launched."[23] Recent analytic focus, especially in the sphere of foreign policy, is on the office of the president. In the formation of American foreign policy, writes Inozemtsev, a "big role" is played by "individual statesmen at the highest levels of the official hierarchy (this applies especially to the president, who . . . is vested with very important powers.)"[24] Or, in the words of Foreign Minister Gromyko, "responsibility for policy is borne by people — primarily those who are invested with authority and stand at the helm of state rule."[25]

While the constitutional authority of the president is recognized, it is not seen to be without constraints. And, in the judgment of Yuri Shvedkov, they are considerable. The problem in his view is essentially bureaucratic, i.e., the management of the gigantic apparatus of government. This phenomenon, he writes, has made the job of implementing foreign policy "increasingly difficult." The president, he notes, has "become a captive of the cumbersome bureaucratic machine. . . . Frequently, implementation of decisions taken becomes bogged down in interdepartmental labyrinths." More specifically, presidential decisions are seen to be the victim of bureaucratic inertia. Also at times they are met with open defiance by some governmental departments which, because of alliances with powerful forces on Capitol Hill — and elsewhere — have been able to attain "a certain autonomy." Quoting Roger Hilsman (at some length), Shvedkov concludes that because of "uninterrupted internal struggles within the government apparatus and outside it . . . 'the president is hardly able to govern in a sphere which is supposedly almost entirely within his authority.' "[26]

In his analysis of the Kennedy administration, Anatoly Gromyko cites numerous instances of bureaucratic opposition and resistance to presidential authority. The Department of Defense, the Joint Chiefs of Staff, and the State Department were all seen as having attempted to force a hard line on the administration on a host of issues—military doctrine (the strategy of "flexible response"), the Bay of Pigs, the Cuban missile crisis, Berlin. Nevertheless, throughout his analysis, Gromyko stresses that ultimate authority to make decisions was in the hands of the president, that nothing happened without his approval and that he always had to be persuaded and was never dictated to. That there was intense pressure brought to bear on him by "militaristic" groups only reinforces this point. Though Kennedy's decision not to allow American forces directly to participate in the Bay of Pigs invasion "aroused strong resentment within the CIA and the Pentagon," his orders were carried out.[27] Again, "despite the military who wanted to force a confrontation" during the missile crisis, Kennedy remained determined to avoid one. When an American U-2 plane was shot down, "the supporters for war again demanded the implementation of an air attack on Cuba followed by an invasion. Kennedy again rejected their demands."[28]

The president, in Gromyko's view, is in control. Once Kennedy had firmly decided that a certain course was the correct one, regardless of the pressure to the contrary, he stood fast and, more importantly, his decision was implemented. (Shvedkov points out that Kennedy's decision to withdraw medium-range American missiles from Turkey "was not implemented for several months because of delays by the State Department and the Department of Defense."[29] Gromyko does not mention the Turkish bases.) Despite considerable opposition and counterpressure, Kennedy decided to meet with "the head of the Soviet government" in Vienna. (In a striking display of Soviet political etiquette, Gromyko avoids direct reference to the former Soviet leader. Having been removed from office in disgrace, Khrushchev became a "non-person.") Kennedy also ignored internal critics when he agreed to accept a coalition government in Laos and to sign the Partial Test-Ban agreement. The president, in Gromyko's judgement, has overwhelming independent power.

The generally accepted view of the scope of presidential authority is set forth in an earlier work by Gromyko, *Diplomacy of Contemporary Imperialism*. Here he writes that, as chief of state and head of government, the president must "unconditionally be given first place" as an influence on foreign policy. He "possesses such great powers" that he "frequently . . . operates practically on his own initiative . . . in the making of individual decisions." However, he goes on, the situation "is rather different when developing the overall strategic . . . policy. . . . In this process dozens, if not hundreds, of people and numerous state institutions take part." Basic policy lines are set as a result of "hundreds of decisions arising from deep within the political and state machinery."[30]

The president, it would seem, can exercise considerable initiatives only in particular instances. He has especially great authority in periods of great crisis. According to Zhurkin, "the last word in making decisions in international crisis situations rests with the president. The old rule that 'crisis is the president's show' still holds."[31] (It has been noted, though, that during the 1973 Yom Kippur War in the Middle East, "The president himself and the U.S. secretary of state were largely operating under the influence of the administration's weakened domestic positions," i.e., Watergate.)[32] Nonetheless, in terms of day-to-day operations and the shaping of the basic directions of U.S. foreign policy, the president has "behind him hundreds of people and forces"[33]—bureaucratic, political, and economic.

Having asserted this as a general rule, Soviet writers again and again come back to the exceptional cases—FDR, Kennedy and Nixon—presidents who were able to surmount bureaucratic and economic pressures and take independent, i.e. favorable, policy decisions. Roosevelt, writes Ernst Genri,

> was incomparably more far-sighted than his diplomats and subordinate officials. . . . He, of course, nourished no special sympathy for Soviet or socialist ideas. At no time did Roosevelt stand apart from the bourgeois society in which he was born and raised. But the democratic traditions of T. Jefferson and A. Lincoln were alive in him; he sincerely hated fascism and understood that a victory by Hitler would threaten the world.[34]

FDR's "farsightedness," his "instinctive presentiment of the future" led him to support a "realistic" foreign policy, i.e., one which recognized the importance of good relations with the USSR. "Roosevelt's merit," suggests N. N. Yakovlev, "lies in the fact that he was able to overcome a certain inertia among U.S. ruling circles and put realism before ideological prejudices."[35]

Soviet treatment of the Kennedy Administration is of the same cloth. Kennedy was mistrusted by many, writes Gromyko, precisely because they feared that he "might become a new Roosevelt. . . . The 'ghost of Roosevelt' has always frightened" those on the "right" both for his domestic policies and because he normalized relations with the Soviet Union. They feared Kennedy would seek to do the same.[36] Kennedy did move in a "realistic" direction, as we have seen, and he often acted with caution. Furthermore, unlike "Truman, Eisenhower and Johnson [who] preferred in general not to go against the current," Kennedy proposed numerous measures which "were to a considerable degree at variance with the ideas prevailing in the State Department, the Pentagon and the CIA."[37] "More than any of its predecessors," writes Trofimenko, the Kennedy administration "seems to have tended towards changes in U.S.-Soviet relations and a certain restraint in the policy of military confrontation." Such "restraint" was particularly notable, according to Trofimenko, during the "second phase" of the 1962 Cuban missile crisis. Though "confronted with mounting pressure from the U.S. military and political establishment calling for a military solution," President Kennedy "finally overcame his [earlier] vacillations and committed himself to a settlement by political and diplomatic means."[38]

Reactions to the foreign policies of the Nixon administration have been even more positive. Though initially apprehensive—and at times deeply troubled, as we shall see—Soviet analysts became increasingly enthusiastic after the 1972 Moscow summit. Since then President Nixon has been described (quoting an American source) as "the first president since Franklin Roosevelt to have recognized the legitimate interests of the USSR,"[39] as having understood that, quoting Nixon himself, "every confrontation means coming into contact with the potential nuclear destruction of all civilized countries,"[40] and in general for helping break the ice of the cold war, opening up broad prospects for Soviet-American relations and contributing to an improvement of the whole international atmosphere.[41] The "realistic" policy of the Nixon Administration was "conditioned by objective factors," writes Yakovlev. Nonetheless, it "bore to a certain extent (and, of necessity) the character of the president's 'personal course.'"[42]

Though at times somewhat muted—out of deference to American sensibilities regarding Watergate—the Americanists' high regard for the policies of the 1972–74 period is unmistakable.

What this literature suggests is that Soviet analysts place a great deal of weight on the personal qualities of individual presidents. They point out, to be sure, that other elements—such as conservative circles within the governmental apparatus (of which more in a moment) and pressure from "right wing" forces in and outside the government—seek by various means, both fair and foul, to resist the moderate policies of thoughtful presidents. In 1947, for example, "reactionary circles" attempted to restrict the authority of future presidents to make policy decisions at their own discretion. Fearful of another FDR, Shvedkov writes, they sought to tie the hands of all presidents:

> The idea of setting up the National Security Council had something in common with the law limiting the president of the United States to an 8-year term of office adopted by the Congress at the same time. All of this reflected the desire of reactionary circles to prevent a man of independent views and broad capability . . . from occupying the chief political post in the government.[43]

The fact remains, however, that despite the efforts of such unenlightened elements, "sober," "realistic" political figures do manage somehow to emerge at the helm of the U.S. government, a fact which may lead to significant changes in U.S. foreign policy. While the resistance and counterpressures they face are often considerable, Soviet observers continue to search for—and to find—American presidents who, by personal inclination and character, "exceed the bounds."[44]

The United States Congress

While responsive, even sympathetic, to individual presidents, Soviet analysts have as a whole been less understanding of other basic features of the American political system. They do not seem able to understand, for example, the principle of limited government, the rule of law, the separation of powers and majority rule. They have difficulty even conceptualizing the value we place on individual liberty, freedom of speech and the press, or the concern we have

46

regarding the morality of our public leaders. Soviet obtuseness regarding fundamental American political principles is easily demonstrated. In a revealing article printed in the *New York Times*, the deputy procurator general of the USSR, Sergei I. Gusev, suggests that, according to the U.S. Criminal Code, were Soviet dissident Andrei Sakharov an American citizen, "he might well find himself behind bars" for advocating and abetting the destruction of the regime. Even a leading Soviet jurist seems incapable of understanding that political criticism and dissent are not everywhere seen to be the same as treason.[45] Obviously Soviet comprehension of the American political process is severely hampered by their truncated political preconceptions. As Marshall Shulman perceptively suggests, "it is difficult to grasp the workings of pluralistic power hierarchies if one has only experienced, and if the history of one's country has only known, autocracy."[46]

Soviet Americanists have made substantial attempts to understand the role of the U.S. Congress. As a result of these efforts they have become impressively knowledgeable, especially regarding the shifting moods of opinion on Capitol Hill. Nonetheless, such knowledge as they have acquired reflects more an awareness of the specific ways various parts of the congressional machinery can affect particular policies than an appreciation of the legislative process itself. Congress as a whole is thought of primarily in terms of whether or not it supports—or opposes—"détente," with little mind to its place in the American political system.

Soviet writers have become familiar, as one would expect, with the mechanics of congressional operations—the committee structure of both houses, areas of competence, hearings, voting procedures, vetoes and overrides and, recently, the impeachment procedure. There is on occasion evidence of some degree of understanding of the functions of Congress. Thus, for example, commenting on the Senate Foreign Relations Committee, V. A. Shvetsov stresses the important role of congressional hearings. He writes: "Exercising the right to hold hearings and conduct inquiries, the committee has broad opportunities for a comprehensive discussion of foreign-policy problems." The committee, it is noted, has in recent years held hearings on a variety of important issues—the Partial Test-Ban Treaty, relations with Western Europe, China, Vietnam, etc. "Because of the critical attitude towards the administration's line taken by many of those who appear," writes Shvetsov, "these hearings have aroused considerable interest on the part of the American public."[47]

A thoughtful account was given of Senate hearings (February–March 1974) on the Pentagon's proposal to enlarge its facilities at Diego Garcia in the Indian Ocean, with fairly good coverage of the presentation made by the Defense Department. Attention was, however, focused on the testimony of those opposed including, incidentally, CIA Director William Colby. "During the hearings," writes A. D. Portnyagin, Colby

> declared that ". . . despite the Pentagon's uneasiness, the Soviet Union will hardly build up its fleet in the Indian Ocean substantially if the United States does not first begin building its own fleet there." Thus, even the chief of U.S. intelligence cast doubt on the Pentagon's assertions.

The author concludes on a positive note: as a result of the "stormy debates" in Congress in 1974, advocates of the construction of an enlarged base on Diego Garcia "were defeated." However, he warned, "the Pentagon had not abandoned its plans."[48]

Other Soviet commentary on congressional hearings, however, has been less enthusiastic. V. S. Anichkina, for example, points out that as part of his campaign against normalizing relations with the USSR, Senator Jackson's Subcommittee on Investigations held hearings in the spring and summer of 1973 to which "violent opponents of the Soviet Union and well-known 'cold war' ideologues British 'Sovietologists' W. Laqueur and L. Labedz" were invited. Similarly ill-intentioned hearings were held by the House Internal Security Committee that November in which "notorious opponents of improved relations . . . appeared as 'witnesses.' "[49]

Soviet regard for congressional hearings quite obviously depends on their thrust. When testimony and committee questioning run parallel to Soviet policy positions, e.g., on Vietnam, ABM deployment, bases in the Indian Ocean, they are considered to be significant. When they take a contrary view, they are condemned as a tool of reaction. At best, however, even when supportive of "realistic" policies, congressional hearings have been seen as nothing more than a lightning rod, a device to distract an angered public. Critical congressional hearings and even debates within Congress itself, writes Shvetsov, are used "to steer deep public dissatisfaction in a definite channel, to open valves so as to alleviate pressure from the dissatisfaction seizing the masses."[50] Legislative debate, therefore, is a ruse, a mechanism to beguile and deceive.

Soviet disdain for parliamentary processes is clearly demonstrated in SShA discussions of the issue of presidential war powers. Soviet analysts have, of course, endorsed congressional efforts "to restrict the uncontrolled activity of the president and to return to the Congress the role it has lost in matters concerning the use of armed forces abroad."[51] The passage in 1971 of the Cooper-Church Amendment (which banned congressional financing of combat operations by U.S. ground forces in Cambodia) and, in late 1973, the override by Congress of President Nixon's veto of the War Powers Bill, a more blanket restriction on presidential authority, were both hailed. The latter, in particular, was seen as having "significantly reduced the capacity of the executive to conduct undeclared wars or conflicts not sanctioned by Congress."[52]

In light of their political heritage and the absence of any tradition of shared power, the basic constitutional issue underlying this legislation, i.e., the challenge by the Congress to what is seen to be an abuse of executive authority, is at best dimly perceived. For Soviet Americanists, the only point of interest is the "reduced capacity"—for whatever technical reason—of the power of the president to employ military force. The question, in their mind, is political—what its policy implications are for the USSR—not constitutional.

Given Soviet policy concerns, the Americanists virtually ignored the Case Amendment (1972). In much the same spirit as the Cooper-Church Amendment and the War Powers Bill, Senator Clifford Case (R.-N.J.) sought to have Congress require that the president inform the legislature of the details of all executive agreements within sixty days of their conclusion. Such information, hitherto often unavailable, would strengthen the legislature's power over foreign policy. Since many of the understandings signed by President Nixon

49

at the 1972 summit conference were in the form of executive agreements, however, Soviet sources were distinctly uninterested in seeing new congressional initiatives which might result in having these agreements overturned. Commenting on the Case Amendment, one Soviet analyst stressed that the Senate's concern to limit the president's authority did not call into question the legitimacy of executive agreements as such. This form of international obligation, he argued, "has become firmly established in American diplomatic usage."[53]

The same logic, not surprisingly, characterized the Soviet response to the Jackson Amendment. Moscow was deeply displeased when, in December 1974, Congress imposed constraints on the implementation of the 1972 US-USSR Trade Agreement. (A congressional majority, organized by Senator Henry Jackson [D.-Wash.], appended a number of amendments to the 1974 Trade Reform Act, which made the granting of preferential trade status to the USSR, promised by President Nixon in 1972, conditional upon the easing of restrictions on the emigration of Soviet Jews. Congress at the same time placed a limit upon credits available to the Soviet Union to purchase American equipment and technology.) Though he endorsed, in principle, its reemergence as an important influence shaping U.S. foreign policy, these limitations introduced by the Congress were condemned by Ye. S. Shershnev, deputy director of the institute, as "irresponsible."[54] The essence of the Soviet position is reflected in the following comment:

> The U.S. Congress, decisively supporting the shift from "cold war" to détente by voting approval of the strategic arms limitations agreements and by the passage of bills putting an end to the financing of U.S. military operations in Cambodia and limiting the power of the president to wage "undeclared wars," became bogged down in the nets of the "cold war" on the question of the abrogation of discriminatory trade restrictions against the Soviet Union.[55]

The issue here is hardly one of "presidential usurpation" but, more importantly, "is it good for the Soviet Union?"

Soviet obsession with their own policy interests helps explain their confusion regarding the Watergate affair and the resignation of President Nixon. Though applauding the constraints imposed by

Congress on the president's foreign-policy authority, the Amerikanisty never saw these initiatives in terms of a constitutional confrontation. The growth of congressional restiveness in the face of an "imperial presidency" was generally ignored. Soviet analysts tended to the view that "The president and the Congress are indeed not competitors but rather partners working in one and the same direction."[56] Throughout 1973 and well into 1974 the mounting tension over Watergate went unnoticed. Soviet analysts refused to take seriously investigations by Senate and House committees (headed by Senator Sam Ervin and Congressman Peter Rodino) into presidential misdeeds. The possibility of presidential impeachment was hardly mentioned. Mr. Nixon's resignation, itself, though noted, was not explained by Soviet commentators; attention was focused on President Ford and his pledges to continue the Nixon policy of détente.

The reluctance throughout the crisis of Soviet observers, including those at the USA Institute, to deal with the basic issues involved in the Watergate affair persists to this day. Not one article has yet appeared in SShA directly focusing on the most extraordinary event in modern American political history, the resignation of the president of the United States.

Two factors help explain this rather curious behavior. First, the Soviet leadership was undoubtedly shaken by the fall of Mr. Nixon, a man who was and remains much admired. Former Ambassador W. Averell Harriman reported in September 1976, after a visit to Moscow, that Soviet Party leader Leonid Brezhnev still thinks well of the former president and "doesn't understand what Nixon did in [relation to] Watergate" that forced his resignation. "[Mr. Brezhnev] only thinks of the progress they made together."[57] Despite their stress on the primacy of the "objective factors" underlying détente, of which more later, Soviet analysts, as we have already seen, tend to personalize diplomatic relations. With the demise of the main symbol of America's support for détente, they have been acutely worried that the policy itself may be in jeopardy. Much as the death of Roosevelt in 1945 coincided with the end of wartime cordiality in Soviet-American relations, so it has been feared that the fall of President Nixon symbolized a more difficult period ahead. (Develop-

51

ments during the 1976 campaign and since undoubtedly lent further credence to such gloomy views.) To avoid facing the implications of such an unpleasant contingency, they try to ignore it.

Another source of difficulty lies in the fact that Soviet officials, as Mr. Brezhnev indicated, are simply unable to understand what the former president did, or could have done, that compelled him to resign. Soviet incomprehension on this issue reflects their own rather distinctive political assumptions. By historical tradition and political ideology the Soviet people share an understanding of the concept of power and authority singularly different from that held in the United States. As Philip E. Mosely perceptively observed:

> One feature which strikes every foreigner who stays in the Soviet Union for a substantial length of time is the great respect, even awe, that is generally felt for power, for authority. Neither word exactly expresses the Russian word *vlast'* which means power so great that one cannot oppose it. It can, if one is skillful, be placated; if one is lucky, it can be hoodwinked; but it cannot be resisted, for there is no ground on which the isolated individual can take his stand.[58]

Thus, in contrast to the American tradition, where "power is multiple, fragmented, temporary, limited and comprehensible," the Soviet people share a "notion of overarching power that is both absolute and legitimate."

The notion of power that is by nature absolute does not fit well with that of constitutional constraints. In the USSR the very concept of abuse of executive authority is virtually a contradiction in terms. It was only after his death that Stalin could be charged with somehow having exceeded his power. Even now, after the "illegal repressions" of the Stalin era have been repudiated, there remains, as Hedrick Smith points out, a considerable nostalgia for Stalin as the *krepkii khozyain*, the strong boss.[59] To suggest to the bearers of this tradition that the chief executive does not have legal authority to engage in covert operations, to "cover up," "bug," "stonewall," draw up "enemies' lists," or to use intelligence agencies for his own political purposes is to suggest something totally alien and unnatural.

Little wonder, then, that Soviet sources find it difficult to understand Watergate. Nothing in their political philosophy, historical tradition or practical experience has prepared them to explain such a mysterious event. Even where they try to do so, confusion abounds. Some seek to interpret Watergate in traditional ideological terms, emphasizing conflict among competing monopoly interests. According to Zorin, for example, the president is "closely connected with one of the competing monopoly groupings," a fact which creates "definite advantages" for it. The Congress, on the other hand, "is much more evenly balanced. Each of the leading groups of American monopolies is suitably represented" there. Conflict between the two institutions is therefore inevitable. This clash of economic interests, suggests Zorin, has played "a not insignificant part in the tendency in recent years to limit the power of the presidency." Watergate is therefore seen to be a part of "a corrective process in the distribution of power" among competing monopoly groupings.[60]

There are, it should be noted, analysts who report more perceptively. For example, S. B. Chetverikov holds that the affair was "not merely a case of the Democratic Party seeking to extract maximum political advantage" from Republican misdeeds. The real source of Watergate, in his view, is "the autocratic tendency" in American politics, i.e., the trend towards concentrating "real power and administrative authority in the hands of the president and his close associates in the White House." He notes, however, that "the constitutional system of the separation of powers and, also, the two-party system of rule create a number of serious obstacles to the strengthening of the power of the president." Watergate thus became "a political scandal of enormous proportions," i.e., led to the resignation of the president, because, in the words of a Soviet reviewer, "constitutional principles . . . continue to play a role in the mechanism governing the everyday functioning of the executive system."[61]

Some among Moscow's Americanists do seem to understand the significance of the Watergate affair. For most, however, the Soviet political heritage has not been one to sensitize them to the dangers emanating from "the autocratic tendency" and the potential benefits of constitutional and political arrangements which could be used to protect against undesirable concentrations of power. They have insisted, even in private conversations, that President Nixon was the victim of a political cabal of disgruntled Democrats, ultra-right, anti-Soviet elements, newspaper publishers and other inveterate Nixon haters. Constitutional notions regarding the separation of powers and the principles of limited government remain, with rare exceptions, very much a mystery.*

The USA Institute approaches congressional "bipartisanship" in foreign policy much the same way as it does constitutional processes. Previously condemned as the attempt by "reactionary Democratic and Republican leaders" to promote continuity in policy during changes of administration, an approach which led to congressional "passivity," and a willingness "to follow the decisions of the president obediently,"[62] "bipartisanship" is today very much in favor. When Congress failed to close ranks and unite, in the best bipartisan tradition, in support of the administration's trade bill, it was denounced, as we have just seen, for having become "bogged down in the nets of the cold war." More recently, when Senator Church predicted "strong bipartisan support in Congress" for the Vladivostok agreement signed in November 1974, his remarks were quoted approvingly.[63] Clearly, on "bipartisanship," as on "presidential usurpation," and all other American political traditions and practices, the sole concern is whether it helps the cause.

Seen in these terms, what is the overall balance of forces in the Congress? Assessing the political equilibrium on Capitol Hill and predicting voting behavior is approached with some degree of caution. As Soviet analysts are quick to recognize, neither party in Congress is "monolithic," i.e., neither adheres to an agreed-upon ideology nor supports a unified policy. As a result of their decentralized organizational structure and lack of internal political discipline, each party is seen to include several blocs and "independent ideological enclaves." Voting in Congress thus tends to take place not along party lines but according to groupings, with temporary blocs occasionally joining together on specific questions.[64]

---

*Characteristic of the Russian attitude towards Watergate was the view expressed by the Soviet first deputy procurator general, Mikhail P. Malyrov: "It is calculated just for show. . . . All Nixon has to do is show a little firmness and the whole thing will come to nothing." Others, more sympathetic to America, were horrified at the political turmoil then prevailing in the United States. An American correspondent was asked by an incredulous Russian: "What are you people doing to your President? . . . What are you people doing to your country?" (Hedrick Smith, *The Russians* [New York: Quadrangle/The New York Times Book Co., 1976], pp. 242, 244).

While emphasizing the diffuseness of the political dividing lines between the parties, Soviet analysts have placed considerable stress in recent years on the role of "moderate" and "liberal" elements in Congress. Conservative figures, to be sure, still play an important role. Led by Senators Jackson and Goldwater, congressional conservatives reflect the "very considerable" influence of "the most reactionary forces."[65] The power of this group is "very strong" as a result of their "long service in Congress and the seniority system." Their prestige is seen to be so great that in some instances, they "can openly ignore the official leadership of their own party."[66]

However, noted Lebedev in 1973, it is the "moderate bloc which remains the most influential" in both houses of Congress. "These men"—Mike Mansfield, Carl Albert, Thomas O'Neill, Edward Kennedy, Hubert Humphrey and Edmund Muskie—"lean towards compromise and behind-the-scenes maneuvers. Practically all important leadership posts in the Democratic party organization . . . are held by adherents of this line."[67] By 1976 Soviet analysts had begun to stress the prominent role being played by "liberal" elements in Congress, especially in the Democratic party. "In both House and Senate," writes Shimanovsky,

> The liberal bloc, consisting of representatives of the Democratic and Republican parties, constitutes an increasingly effective opposition to the conservative bloc of southern Democrats and right-wing Republicans who, only ten years ago, still felt secure in their domination of the Congress.[68]

The attention increasingly granted to moderates and liberals reflects Moscow's appreciation of their increased political importance. As Shimanovsky suggests, liberal circles "constitute one of the most active political forces in American society." Not only are they "active," liberals are seen to be increasingly effective. "Operating through the government mechanisms [the federal bureaucracy], the Congress, the press, and public organizations," he writes, "they exert significant influence upon the formulation of the nation's foreign and domestic policy."[69] He notes, for example, that "they launched the call for the review of the role of nuclear weapons and military power in general, within the framework of America's foreign policy," they "exerted significant opposition to Washington's policy in Southeast Asia," and "have been in the forefront" in urging the normalization of Soviet-American relations.[70] Although their support for détente is seen to be somewhat mixed and inconsistent—because of "their chronic anti-Communism"[71]—liberals are also recognized as having taken "a critical stand with respect to the growth of expenditures for military purposes" and "have been actively advocating a revision of America's national priorities" i.e., shifting attention and resources from foreign and military to domestic policy. These initiatives, it is noted, are being "increasingly reflected in the congressional struggle over issues of federal appropriations."[72]

Soviet attention to the role of moderate/liberal elements on Capitol Hill has been accompanied, especially since 1975, by a new sensitivity to the role of Congress itself. Prior to 1975 Soviet analysts tended to downplay its importance in the formulation of American foreign policy. Thus the majority of the members of Congress, especially in the House of Representatives, it was suggested, "as a rule act too indecisively and vaguely." Though they claim to favor détente, they assumed "a passive-conservative position" on the Jackson Amendment to the administration's 1974 trade bill; despite their proclaimed opposition to the arms race, they continue to "avoid specific action" to reduce the size of the U.S. military budget.[73] Even as late as early 1975, an analyst reported that although Senate "liberals" tried to cut back defense spending during 1973 and 1974, their efforts failed, largely because of an unstable and vacillating group of "centrist" Senators.[74]

The Congress, clearly, was viewed as an uncertain force. Though the size of the "liberal" bloc in the Senate had grown, it too was considered unstable and could—as Popova reported it did in 1974—lose strength.[75] It was this very lack of focus, this amorphousness and unpredictability that in the Soviet view explains the weakness of Congress. It simply cannot compete with the better-organized executive departments. As Shvetsov pointed out in 1972, "The apparatus of the executive branch has a better developed bureaucratic organization compared to the diffuseness . . . of responsibility and lack of proper coordination in the activities of congressional bodies."[76] As a result of its many weaknesses, Congress' "direct influence on the foreign strategy of the administration is, of course, limited."[77]

The renewed activity of the Congress during the Vietnam war attracted increased Soviet attention. As we have seen, the Americanists were very much interested in the Cooper-Church Amendment and especially in the 1973 War Powers Bill. It was not until 1974, however, that they began to view Congress seriously. The key role of Senate and House committees in the Watergate investigations and especially adoption of the "irresponsible" Jackson Amendment, which led to Moscow's cancellation of the 1972 Soviet-American Trade Agreement, were a sharp reminder to Soviet Americanists— and not only to them—that the Congress was indeed a force to reckon with.

Evidence of renewed Soviet respect is considerable: in early 1975 Dolgolopova notes that the process of financing military spending in the Congress has become "more complicated." Until recently, "this was essentially a formality and a brief procedure sometimes ending up with the Pentagon receiving more than it has requested; now the situation has changed in a direction clearly not in favor of the military."[78] Similarly Mosin reports in July of that year that both conservatives and liberals in the Congress are increasingly critical regarding presidential requests for foreign aid financing. He reports, with obvious sympathy, Secretary Kissinger's warning that manipulation of military and economic aid appropriations should not be used to "pressure" foreign nations. With obvious allusion to the Jackson Amendment, Mosin suggests, paraphrasing Kissinger, that such attempts "impose a challenge to the receiving countries' sovereignty" and end up causing "such an adverse reaction that it becomes a more important factor than the matters under dispute themselves."[79] Though wary of such unwarranted congressional intrusions upon executive initiatives, he clearly endorses careful congressional scrutiny—and curtailment—of the American foreign aid programs.[80]

Much in the same vein, Linnik reports in October 1975 that its efforts to investigate the Central Intelligence Agency were part and parcel of the concern of the 94th Congress "to restore its constitutional powers in the sphere of the formulation and implementation of foreign policy."[81] In December two Soviet analysts report on the efforts of the Congress to limit "personal diplomacy" by members of the administration. Fearful that the United States would secretly take on undesirable "new commitments" as part of its responsibilities under the 1975 Sinai Agreement (which provided for stationing of American civilian specialists in the buffer zone between Egyptian and Israeli forces in the Sinai desert), Congress insisted that all documents concerning the Sinai Agreement (including those which had been stamped "secret" by the State Department) be published. The fear in the Congress, note Kislov and Osipova, was that the decision to send 200 U.S. technical specialists bore "a striking resemblance to the initial stage of U.S. 'involvement' in South Vietnam." Congressional misgivings about the U.S. role in the Sinai were, in no small part, therefore, a reflection of "the so-called 'post-Vietnam syndrome'" in the United States and a general suspicion by the Congress of the executive as a consequence of the "Watergate affair."[82]

Congressional approval in early 1976 of the Tunney Amendment, which blocked financing of American military aid to political forces in Angola, was also hailed as evidence of congressional assertiveness vis-à-vis the executive branch. As a result of congressional actions, "the government was legally deprived of funds to continue its intervention in Angola." Here, too, "the United States' sad experience in Vietnam has had a significant effect." Passage of the Tunney Amendment was seen to be "a decisive attempt by the legislators to reject those principles of American foreign policy which led to . . . Vietnam."[83]

The point is clear. The power of Capitol Hill in the formulation and, especially, the implementation of U.S. foreign policy has been recognized. It is now well understood, in the words of the USA Institute's chief congressional analyst, that the Congress

can limit or increase appropriations in spite of the will of the administration, can reject or call into question the nominations of the head of the government, can deliberately delay or even set aside the adoption of this or that piece of legislation—all of which creates a situation whereby Capitol Hill is able to intervene in the plans of the White House and even frustrate them.[84]

Having themselves been the victims of such an intervention, Soviet observers regard Congress with considerable respect.

Instances can be cited, to be sure, where Congress is seen to be "dominated by the burden of the cold war," and where it is concluded

that "old traditions and 'mental inertia' are still strong."[85] Commenting on congressional approval of a record $104 billion military budget,
a ranking institute official wrote anxiously in the Red Army newspaper
in August 1976 that "whereas only 2–3 years ago Congress sometimes
took a critical approach to the Pentagon's financial requests, now it is
again reverting to the practice of voting almost unanimously for the
enormous military expenditures proposed by the Pentagon." Such
trends, he observes, "are extremely unhealthy."[86]

Others tend to interpret conflict between the executive and the
legislature, and among different groups within the Congress, in the
framework of crude ideological stereotypes. Lebedev notes, for example, that differences between the Democratic and Republican parties
and other groups within the Congress "should not be overestimated."
Political conflict on Capitol Hill, he notes, is limited, for the competitors are "defending the interests of one and the same class." Their
differences therefore are essentially "tactical." "The struggle is held
within the framework of the two-party system and stays away from the
critical questions which the American people would like to see solved," i.e., presumably, advancement of the interests of the working
class.[87] Savel'yev suggests that when liberals adopt a "flexible approach" to policy issues, they do so solely out of narrow self-interest,
viz. their "understanding of the need to make concessions to the
workers in order to preserve the capitalist order."[88]

Despite such rigid formulations—whose function may be
primarily that of ideological protective covering, i.e., to make political analyses which deviate from standard doctrine on "state monopoly capitalism" more palatable to orthodox elements within the
leadership—Soviet assessments of the Congress have come a long
way. As a result of their bitter disappointment in the highly important
area of trade relations, they seem to have learned that even if primarily
concerned with the question "is it good for the USSR?" a simplistic
"class" analysis will not do. To understand and predict congressional
behavior accurately and to avoid surprise defeats (which the passage
of the Jackson Amendment obviously was) they have to be better
informed.

Thus after many years of inattention and even denigration of the
role of Congress—an attitude which USA Institute officials may
literally have learned from the Nixon White House—they have made

considerable efforts to study the Congress, to learn about its constitutional responsibilities to approve treaties and the nomination of am-
bassadors and cabinet and sub-cabinet level appointments, its role in
economic foreign policy, the power of the purse, its special role in the
area of arms control, and its power to initiate public debates through
committee hearings.[89] Soviet analysts not only know a great deal
more about the Congress but have become much more discerning
in their analyses of its activities. Recent articles are not simply better
informed, which they clearly are, but increasingly free of ideological
preconceptions. As early as October 1973, for example, a leading
Soviet observer of the Congress warned against "simplifying" the
problems of analyzing congressional behavior. Though class affilia-
tion and social origins of individual congressmen should not be
ignored, he stressed that "to a considerable degree a legislator's activity
is determined by his upbringing, education and traditions. It bears the
imprint of the character and inclinations of the particular individual."
Thus, "despite their not too high origins," Senators Everett Dirksen
and Margaret Chase Smith "have always been pillars of the establishment," which a "number of well-to-do patricians" like Senator Joseph
Clark have sharply opposed.[90] Much in the same vein, Shimanovsky
notes that although hard-line on foreign policy, Senator Jackson is
liberal on domestic issues.[91]

Similarly, Soviet coverage of recent developments in the
Congress—the downfall of Senator Fulbright in the 1974 elections,
congressional hearings on Diego Garcia, Senate debates on the military budget, discussion of the role of the congressional staff, of the
Senate Foreign Relations Committee under its new chairman,
Senator John Sparkman—while clearly partisan in its interests, is
largely accurate, temperate, based on a fair-minded reading of American sources (congressional testimony, public opinion data, roll-call
analysis), often thoughtful and, mercifully, increasingly free of the
stereotypes and polemics still characteristic of the popular media.[92]
Soviet analysts have learned that, in the words of Savel'yev, it is
impossible to analyze and forecast U.S. policy without taking the
"congressional factor" into account.[93]

3

THE FOREIGN-POLICY MECHANISM AND OTHER INFLUENCES

Whether from a more acute interest in the executive branch—the core of the foreign-policy-making system—or, more broadly, greater familiarity with organizational processes, Soviet Americanists seem strikingly comfortable in their treatment of the State and Defense Departments. Away from the wild terrain of legislative politics, where behavior is often unpredictable and surprises are frequent, they are much more self-confident when dealing with the bureaucracy. This, clearly, is the heart of politics in the Soviet view. In fact, it is only the belated recognition of the importance of "bureaucratic politics," (Halperin, Allison, et al.) writes Shvedkov, that has brought American analysts to a more realistic appreciation of their own political system.[1]

The "foreign-policy mechanism," in the Soviet view, is critically important. Whatever new policies the president may undertake, whatever treaties and accords the secretary of state may initial, all may be for naught unless they are properly implemented. As Chetverikov has written, "However thoroughly high-level decisions are thought out and substantiated, it is ultimately precisely the departmental apparatus which translates them into daily practice."[2] Fulfillment of new international agreements depends not only on "resolve to cooperate," but also concerns "the good will, frames of mind and the traditions of the administrative apparatus called upon to implement [their] specific provisions."[3] The government apparatus itself is thus seen to exercise an independent influence on foreign policy.

The State Department

In its responsibility for the implementation of policy, the State Department performs a critical task, upon whose fulfillment may rest the success or failure of high-level policy decisions. "Its role," writes Chetverikov "may be on the one hand, positive and constructive, or on the other, retrograde and inhibiting."[4] In the view of Soviet analysts, the State Department's role has generally been a negative one. That is to say, the "frames of mind" and "traditions" which have prevailed in the department are seen as having been hostile to the Soviet Union. This view is expressed most sharply by Anatoly Gromyko. "When John Kennedy assumed office," he writes, ". . . American foreign policy was trapped in the ice of the 'cold war.' The refrigerating plant of the 'State Department-Pentagon-CIA' corporation was generating at full capacity."[5] The majority of people at the State Department, he goes on, like those in the Defense Department and the CIA, regard the Soviet Union as the enemy of the United States, "increasingly pressuring us." Thus they believe "all means are justified."[6] The State Department, writes Gromyko, "never made any recommendations to the White House that might have aided the relaxation of tension." Moreover, many in the department "regarded the president's actions with apprehension. All this displeased Kennedy."[7]

In the current view, the situation has remained essentially unchanged. In an article in *Pravda*, Arbatov explains the existence of anti-Soviet attitudes among State Department officials in terms of their "vested interest" in the cold war. Among the "influential forces . . . stubbornly resisting . . . any shift towards détente," he writes, is "a rather substantial stratum of people from among bureaucrats, scientific personnel [i.e., academics] and journalists who, nurtured by the cold war and interested in its perpetuation, do not want to, and perhaps are unable to, think otherwise than in flagrantly anti-communist categories."[8] Chetverikov views "the obsolete traditions which had formed in the foreign policy departments" in much the same way. He writes: "Among the career bureaucrats there is a grouping composed of people who were brought up on the cold war and who are interested in perpetuating it. They, naturally, actively oppose changes which do not correspond to their views and interests."[9] Having thrived in the cold war, State Department officials are believed to have acquired a stake—professional and psychological— in its continuation. This would, presumably, be especially true for the Bureau of Intelligence and Research and the Bureau of Politico-Military Affairs, those divisions within the department whose size and function were "swollen" during the period of the cold war.[10]

The strength of such anti-communist, cold war sentiments is bolstered considerably, it is argued, by the bureaucratic inertia which pervades the department. Quoting from an essay by former Secretary Kissinger (published in 1969), Chetverikov observes that "the very nature of government structure introduces an element of inertia." He goes on to suggest that "many links of the bureaucratic mechanism which had mastered the old process of making and implementing policy" are reluctant to abandon it.[11] Clinging to the familiar—as much from inertia as from conviction—State Department officials are considered to be slow to change their old cold war views.

In the view of Soviet Americanists, then, the State Department is the captive of its cumbersome, sluggish, inflexible bureaucracy, whose career impulses encourage stereotyped, anti-communist, cold war habits and traditions. Such a situation, writes Shvedkov, "materially hindered . . . negotiations with countries having a different socio-political system."[12] Thus when the new Nixon Administration decided to "normalize" relations with the Soviet Union—and China—it had, somehow, to overcome the resistance of the State Department bureaucracy. To strengthen the hand of the president and protect his new policy course from being frustrated, the National Security Council system was revitalized.

Under the stewardship of Henry A. Kissinger, the National Security Council (NSC) became the dominant foreign policy agency of the Nixon Administration, superseding both State and Defense Departments as a source of influence on the president. This reform, argues Chetverikov, was of the utmost importance. It represented the "organizational registration and consolidation," the "institutionalization" of détente. Steps have been taken, he writes, which "take into account the key position of the executive apparatus," i.e., the White House, and which are "aimed . . . at improving the system of coordination and control primarily of the departmental apparatus." This new system of foreign-policy management attests "to the fact that the desire for détente has become deeply rooted in all the most important decisive spheres of American political life."[13]

The NSC system, therefore, was viewed as a means of overcoming the influence of a rigid immobile bureaucracy. Though "initially left by the wayside" by their resistance to the new foreign policy course, the State Department "began gradually to accept the changes."[14] With Henry Kissinger, one of the chief architects of the new policy, named to head the department in 1973, it had little alternative. Nevertheless, "obsolete traditions" and bureaucratic inertia have not been notably dissipated. Both "frames of mind" still persist and, as Arbatov noted, place State Department officials largely in the camp of the cold war traditionalists.

The main determinants of the State Department's policy orientation, it would seem, are largely political (high-level policy decisions) and organizational (bureaucratic interests, traditions and habits of mind), not economic. One still finds references to economic interests, of course. Chetverikov notes, for example, that "the apparatus of the state is linked by thousands of threads to the monopolies."[15] It is only in rather specific instances, however, that such assertions seem to be anything more than ritualistic. Even in the field of economic foreign policy, the significance of the "economic interests of the ruling classes" is not very clear. As we saw earlier, "contradictions have arisen between the monopolies oriented towards foreign and domestic markets"[16] as well as in respect to military industry. Thus, as Shvedkov observes, "even the influence of the leading businessman's organizations . . . is not unambiguous. . . . In the face of domestic problems and competition on foreign markets many of them are beginning to show a perceptible interest in expanding trade with the USSR . . . and in relieving world tension."[17] The best argument that the authors of "The Economic Levers" (in Shvedkov's volume, SShA:

64

Vneshnepoliticheskii mekhanizm [*USA: The Foreign-Policy Mechanism*]) can make is that "all units in the U.S. government mechanism" responsible for financial, trade, investment and aid policy "are bound up with one another because in the economic sphere they serve the single course . . . aimed at strengthening the dominant position of the United States."[18] Not a clear-cut policy guide, to say the least.

Within the department, the Bureau of Intelligence and Research is believed to be in a highly important position. The bureau is "the only departmental unit which processes information for all its other subdivisions. It receives the entire mass of information coming in from foreign points, it systematizes, analyzes and interprets it." The functions of analysis and interpretation have an especially important bearing on policy since they are, "as a rule . . . accompanied by a list of alternative political courses which inevitably predetermine the thinking of people making the decisions." The bureau, therefore, has unique access (within the department) to the information upon which policy is based, and is responsible for presenting policy recommendations, functions which give it—along with the CIA—a very important role in the formulation of policy.[19]

In the view of Soviet analysts, the State Department is far from monolithic. Its "internal structure," writes Bessmenykh, is "contradictory, unstable, complex and muddled." In addition to incessant conflicts between "career diplomats" and "political appointees" over key diplomatic assignments, the "broadly-trained" career officials are said to resent the recent influx of "specialists" (planners, economists, programmers, psychologists, propagandists, etc.) into the department. The "hostile reception given the newcomers" is due to (a) the "professional conservatism of the career diplomats," who have argued that foreign-policy decisions can and should be "based almost exclusively on knowledge obtained from experience, on an intuitive understanding of the processes taking place" rather than on "timely planning and forecasting," and (b) the fact that the new specialists "destroyed the 'elite' position which the diplomats previously enjoyed as members of a 'closed professional club.'"[20]

In addition to "professional incompatability" and "social dissociation," there are even cases of what are described as "disagreements on specific tactical matters." Thus not only does Arbatov note "serious disagreements" within the "power apparatus itself" at the time of the invasion of Cambodia, which provoked a protest from "250 State Department employees,"[21] but he has also commented on the fact that in the 1940s there was a policy disagreement between Secretary Acheson and Soviet experts within the State Department.[22]

As troubled as they may be by the internal strife, far more significant for the department's leadership is the sharp political struggle which pervades the whole executive branch. The entire foreign-policy apparatus, writes Bessmenykh, is torn by "intense, internecine conflict." The State Department is in continual conflict with the USIA, ACDA, and the Departments of the Treasury, Commerce, and Agriculture, not to speak of "the still more difficult relations" with the Defense Department and the CIA.[23] The "augmented role of the military and intelligence departments" has been a particular source of difficulty.

Though these "external factors" were seen to be "qualifying the role" of the State Department,[24] in the early 1970s the situation began to change. The creation of the new NSC system, Kissinger's role in the State Department, and especially his retention in the White House as head of the NSC after he became secretary of state, were all seen to reflect the administration's "desire to consolidate the system of levers of influence on the Pentagon."[25]

This bureaucratic competition is the heart of the policy process according to Shvedkov. He writes: "Policy is usually the result of various pressures on the government mechanism from outside, the complicated maneuvering of the agencies that comprise it, and the compromises concluded between them."[26] While corporate interests are seen to exert pressure "from outside," the focus of attention is on the mechanism itself. And though other agencies, especially the Defense Department, may well have some advantages, the State Department's position remains a central one.

The Defense Department (DOD)

The first and perhaps most important point made by Soviet analysts is that the Defense Department is "the largest and most expensive part of the government apparatus" dealing with the implementation of foreign policy. Not only is its yearly budget almost 10 percent of the annual American GNP, but it owns property worth more than $200 billion (three times greater than the combined properties of U.S. Steel, General Motors, Metropolitan Life Insurance Co., AT&T and Standard Oil of New Jersey), and is the country's largest single purchaser (signing more than 200,000 contracts a year, with more than 100,000 permanent suppliers). DOD is thus seen to be an enormous concentration of power, wealth and influence. "This position in the national structure makes it possible for the military complex to play a special role in U.S. domestic and foreign policy."[27]

The great size and wealth of DOD have enabled it to gain enormous political influence. Given its huge budget, it has been able to acquire "more up-to-date equipment for communications, data-processing and organization of management than the other government departments." This fact alone has magnified its power. While the "capabilities and intentions of men working in an organization" may affect its political role, "frequently the organization, particularly such a giant mechanism as the Pentagon, overpowers people and dictates their actions as if it had itself become an independent force."[28] The Pentagon's vast material resources have thus given it "a number of important advantages . . . in its constant rivalry with the State Department for influence over foreign policy."[29] Furthermore, writes Chetverikov, "since not one significant presidential decision is adopted without military factors being taken into account, the president is virtually constantly dependent on the Pentagon's information and recommendations . . . even when he has a certain mistrust of military people."[30]

In light of the Pentagon's central role in the formulation of foreign policy, the influence of the secretary of defense has since the end of World War II been very considerable. Under Presidents Kennedy and Johnson, writes Kulagin, "it was the secretary of defense rather than the secretary of state, who had the greatest influence." The military, along with the CIA, "played the most important role in planning and carrying out" the invasion at the Bay of Pigs. The policies of Secretary McNamara also "predetermined escalation" of the U.S. military involvement in Vietnam.[31] The role of his successor was believed to have been somewhat less important. Defense Secretary Laird was seen to fall "far short of a man like

McNamara in both energy and erudition." During the Nixon Administration, the importance of the defense secretary "declined somewhat."[32]

Another factor which has helped bolster the influence of the Pentagon over that of the State Department, according to Kulagin, is the relative advantages of military over political planning. "Military planning," he writes, "is based on a completely fixed material base: the size, structure, and deployment of armed forces, characteristics of weapons systems, the military capabilities of potential adversaries and allies, and so on." In contrast, the planning units of the State Department face an altogether different situation. "They have at their disposal only foggy projections, subjective guesses and proposals, facts and tendencies that are difficult to put in precise quantitative terms." The military can, therefore, engage in "concrete planning," which the State Department cannot. Its greater precision and concreteness, it is said, increases the influence of military over diplomatic planning estimates.[33]

The power of the Pentagon is increased still further by its vast political influence. Not only does it enjoy a symbiotic relationship with large military corporations, its powerful and wealthy allies in the "military-industrial complex," but DOD also has the firm support of a number of highly influential congressmen, viz., Senators Russell, Goldwater, Jackson, Thurmond, and Stennis.[34] Further, in order to ensure its continued influence on Capitol Hill, DOD employs the largest number of lobbyists of any department in the executive branch. "In 1969, it had 339 officials for relations with Congress, i.e., there were two Pentagon lobbyists for every three members of Congress."[35]

We are told, furthermore, that the scope of the "military-industrial complex" is much greater than the term itself implies. "It is essential to stress," wrote Trofimenko in 1972,

> . . . that the military-industrial complex is not only a bloc of military-industrial firms and the armed forces. The military-industrial complex is a concept which is far more capacious. It also includes large groups of scientists working on Pentagon assignments, journalists defending the viewpoint of the military on all questions of policy, trade union bosses . . . in a word, all those who are . . . interested, for reasons of "skimming off the cream of patriotism," in preserving the "cold war" situation.

The Pentagon's influence deeply permeates American society. Rather than speak of a "military-industrial complex" Trofimenko prefers the rubric "military-industrial-trade union-academic-scientific complex."[36]

The policy implications of this vast accumulation of power and influence by the Defense Department are essentially negative. As noted earlier, "the military-industrial complex" thrives in conditions of tension and world conflict. In order to protect its privileged bureaucratic position and enormous arms appropriations, the Pentagon strives to maintain constant nervous tension in the highest government circles. This inevitably places DOD in the anti-Soviet camp. As Oleshuk has written, the "military-industrial complex . . . based on its own strictly selfish interests," seeks to prevent improved relations with the Soviet Union.

> It is now a familiar story which is repeated from year to year: when the time comes to "push" new appropriations for military expenditures through the Congress, the Pentagon and the monopolies filling military orders inspire a routine noisy campaign on the subject of the "military threat" from the USSR. This helps force through Congress large appropriations for the armed forces.[37]

Such campaigns about "sinister Soviet intentions," writes Arbatov, "are whipped up with the inevitability of other seasonal phenomena (like the blossoming of the cherry trees in Washington)."[38]

So as to extort large appropriations, the Pentagon presents overstated appraisals of potential enemies. The influence of such practices is highly pernicious and serves to further aggravate Soviet-American relations. They lead, inevitably, to what Kulagin refers to as "the fabrications and myths that have intensified the atmosphere of cold war hysteria."[39] With its privileged power and status—and budget— dependent upon the continued primacy of national defense as a policy issue, the Pentagon has a definite stake in the cold war. In the case of the professional military men in the Pentagon, however, they tend towards aggressive behavior not merely because it is in their self-interest to do so; their political views and professional narrowness naturally bend them in this direction. Most American military officers, notes Kulagin, hold conservative or ultra-right wing views. Furthermore they tend to see only military answers to complex political issues. Thus, "in most cases the influence of professional military men on foreign policy is oriented toward the use of military means."[40] (General Gavin's criticism of U.S. Vietnam policy and Admiral La Rocque's opposition to high levels of military budgeting are among the exceptions noted.)

Though the Pentagon is enormously powerful, Soviet analysts do not view it to be uniformly evil. First, the Defense Department is not seen to be a tightly-knit, monolithic organization. In contrast to earlier writings, which tended to stress its vast size and pervasive influence, current Soviet writings recognize that DOD is a complex organization, which as often as not is at odds with itself. Trofimenko and his institute colleagues have noted, for example, the "fierce competition" which has existed between the three main military services since the end of World War II. The particular attitude taken by each branch to specific issues, they argue, is shaped by "purely egotistical considerations." That is to say, the position of the army, the navy and the air force on such matters as strategic doctrine ("massive retaliation," "flexible response") and weapons technology (ICBM, ABM, Polaris) is determined mainly by the implications of such policies for the budgetary and political position of each branch. Conflict over funds and influence, they point out, is rife within the Pentagon.[41]

While all branches seek ever larger defense appropriations—a circumstance which by itself helps stimulate the arms race—they respond in much the same "egotistical" fashion to the prospect of arms limitation. During the Strategic Arms Limitation Talks (SALT) with the USSR, notes Zhurkin, "fights" developed between the representatives of the various branches:

> The air force leaders suggested the limitation of anti-missile defense systems (belonging to the American land forces), but opposed the limitation of intercontinental ballistic missiles or strategic bombers; naval commanders suggested the limitation of intercontinental ballistic missiles and bombers, but would not agree to the limitation of nuclear submarines and submarine ballistic missile carriers. As for the commanders of the land forces, they favored the limitation of offensive strategic weapons (intercontinental ballistic missiles, submarine ballistic missile carriers and strategic bombers), but opposed the limitation of anti-missile defense systems.

All of which provides "further evidence of the fact that although the military-industrial complex rallies against common enemies, it still does not represent a unified whole and is being torn apart by acute internal conflict."[42]

"Fierce competition" and conflict within the American military is of considerable significance. Clearly the implications of some strategic doctrines and weapons systems may well be more ominous for Soviet security interests than others. This circumstance takes on additional significance in light of the fact that not all Pentagon leaders are seen to be equally hostile to the USSR. For example, even though he was severely condemned for U.S. policies in Vietnam, Secretary McNamara's reputation in Moscow is not wholly negative. Kulagin, as noted, regards him as a man of "energy and erudition." Trofimenko also views him with respect. He writes:

> One of the first U.S. leaders to be more or less realistically aware of the hopelessness of the "senseless inertia" of the arms race . . . was Robert McNamara. . . . He put forward the thesis of the "diminishing return" of capital investment in strategic arms systems under modern conditions. . . . "The country can reach a point," McNamara concluded in 1966, "when, in buying more military hardware, it is no longer buying more security for itself, and we have reached such a point."[43]

A recent study adopts a more critical posture. While recognizing his "sensible calculations," Trofimenko and his colleagues regard McNamara's policies with considerably less enthusiasm. Despite "all his sound judgments and evaluations," they write, "McNamara continued the strategic arms race even more zealously than his predecessors . . . increasing the American arsenal of 'overkill.' "[44]

Defense Secretary James Schlesinger, on the other hand, was at no time viewed positively. In the view of two prominant military analysts at the USA Institute, Mil'shteyn and Semeyko, Secretary Schlesinger's endorsement of the doctrine of "limited strategic war" was highly "dangerous," "runs counter to the trend towards détente . . . and gives ground for suspicion and distrust."[45] According to Arbatov, Schlesinger fell victim to "strategic scholasticism." His military doctrines were not only "completely divorced from reality" but, more dangerously, increased rather than reduced the threat of general nuclear war.[46]

71

Such militaristic views do not, however, go unchallenged. As we saw previously, "the sharp expansion" of the powers of the president's special assistant on national security affairs was, as Chetverikov writes, "a measure aimed at creating a balancing force to counter the military's influence in the NSC machinery."[47] These new arrangements, in the Soviet view, worked well. Mr. Kissinger was "'the president's man,' that is, the one who does not represent narrow departmental interests." He became, in effect, "deputy president on foreign policy matters."[48] Thus, though Defense Secretary Schlesinger was considered one of the "influential forces among the enemies of détente," he was constrained by the more powerful—and more moderate—forces in the White House.

There are, in addition, other forces for moderation. As previously noted, there is growing uncertainty within the business community regarding the wisdom of continued high levels of military spending. It would be simplifying too much, notes Semeyko, to suggest that American foreign policy is shaped by the interests of major war "businesses" and the military. The influence of such groups is restricted, among other things, by "the heterogeneity of interests among the war-oriented and other monopolies," i.e., the conflicting interests of the military and civilian sections of the economy.[49]

Furthermore, doubts regarding the desirability of large military budgets have spread, as we have seen, to Capitol Hill. There are in the Congress, writes Tsagolov, "many who actively oppose an increase in military spending and the continuation of the arms race, and their ranks have recently swelled."[50] The desire for constraint in the "arms sphere," writes Konovalov, "has been characteristic of both chambers . . . in recent years." For example, in the fall of 1974 Congress "made a cut of almost $5 billion" in the military budget requested by the Defense Department. He notes further than American "statesmen and military figures have themselves frequently stressed . . . the sober thesis . . . [that] the true security of the United States cannot be ensured by means of the endless spiralling of the arms race."[51]

The USA Institute's basic assessment remains, however, highly negative. The Defense Department is seen to be a powerful force in American political life, with a vital stake in the continuation of the arms build-up. This fact has critical implications. Any decision by the White House to negotiate arms control agreements with the USSR would, of necessity, jeopardize the power, influence, and economic position of the military. The basic interests of the Pentagon therefore demand that such decisions be opposed. This inbred hostility to arms control and, more generally, to détente inevitably generates what Soviet analysts see as "a certain inconsistency and dangerous zig-zags" in U.S. policy, which often "contradict the positions which have already been asserted" by the American political leadership.[52] The Pentagon—and its allies—remain in the Soviet view, a "complex" of enormous power and influence "which did not emerge yesterday and which will not depart the scene tomorrow."[53]

Special Interest Groups

Of the various other forces in U.S. political life which bear on foreign policy, Soviet analysts make particular note of three: special interest groups, public opinion, and the communications media. In dealing with the first, attention is focused on the worlds of business and of academia.

(a) Economic

As discussed in detail previously, Soviet analysts regard the American business community as internally divided in terms of its economic interests and, accordingly, having different foreign policy orientations. The weapons suppliers and their subcontractors, seeking an ever larger slice of the military pie, support an aggressive foreign-policy line. The far bigger non-military sector, concerned about inflation and economic stability, do not. For example, as Shvedkov points out, American oil companies opposed United States aid to Israel during the 1973 Yom Kippur War. Fearing Arab sanctions against their operations in the Middle East, the oil companies took what the Soviets saw to be a distinctly moderate stance.[54]

The one additional point worth further note is the interest shown recently in those segments of the American business community seeking improved relations with the Soviet Union. This, of course, is not a totally novel development. In the early 1920s, the newly-established Soviet regime hoped that "far-sighted [American] business leaders would see the advantage of commercial and diplomatic relations with Russia" and encouraged the Republican administration of President Warren Harding to pursue a friendly policy.[55] Soviet analysts and political leaders have placed similar faith in such business leaders as David Kendall, Armand Hammer, and David Rockefeller to promote trade and political relations between the U.S. and the USSR, with equally unimpressive results. (We shall return to this at a later point.)

(b) Academic

Soviet analysts are showing a growing interest in the American academic community. Once condemned as mere intellectual apologists paid to rationalize and justify the official government line, scholars in the United States are today regarded as an independent source of influence on policy. Government agencies, writes Gromyko, "have in recent years . . . been increasingly using the services of the academic community, turning for advice either to scholars who are experts on general problems of international relations, or to specialists on some particular country."[56]

To facilitate this relationship, a "fairly well organized system for exchanging ideas, understandings and mutual assistance" has been established between the U.S. government and the academic world. Although, as Gromyko writes, "primacy in the making of decisions belongs to the government and the last word remains, of course, with the president,"[57] academic influence is seen to be significant. For example, "the NSC staff regards scholarly research as an important instrument which makes it possible to outline more thoroughly possible alternatives of the U.S. position on the most important and complicated international problems before they are presented to the president."[58] This "approach" was used, Berezin notes, in putting together the American position in the SALT negotiations. After the conclusion of the first round of talks in Helsinki in November 1969, a special task force (headed by NSC weapons-system specialist Lawrence Lynn) including specialists from outside the government, prepared twelve studies for the American side.[59] Furthermore, as V. P. Lukin points out, scholars have played an important part in the shaping of U.S. policy in the Far East. He writes that "the actual content of the principal premises" of the Nixon Doctrine "evolved from debates over modern foreign-policy problems within scholarly research circles." In 1975, he notes, the Brookings Institution and other influential and "practically-minded research centers" published a number of studies which laid the foundation for creating a new "Pacific doctrine."[60] Thus, while not decisive, academic influence can be important.

Soviet analysts have made particular comment on three different segments of American academia—the "Arms Control Community," "think tanks" specializing in military and strategic problems, and Soviet specialists.

(1) THE "ARMS CONTROL COMMUNITY." The USA Institute has for some while been alert to the activity of those specialists working on questions of arms control, the so-called "Arms Control Community." During the "great strategic debates" in the United States on the adoption of an ABM system, notes Trofimenko, "eminent scholars and specialists . . . joined vigorously." Their role, he suggests, was positive. They opposed the ABM system as enormously expensive and basically ineffective. As a result in part of their writings and testimony before Congress, "a realistic line emerged victorious" when the president signed the 1972 SALT accords in Moscow, which limited ABM development.[61]

Soviet sources are unanimous in their conclusion that the Arms Control Community has grown into a considerable political force. "The strengthened influence of these sober scientists," writes another observer,

indisputably contributed toward official Washington's recognition of the principle of equivalency with the Soviet Union . . . and has already had a definite effect on the development and adoption of a number of proposals on arms control by the U.S. government and Congress, the most realistic of which have been recorded in treaties with the USSR.[62]

The critical role of the Arms Control Community is explained in part by the credentials of its members. The "eminent scholars and specialists" usually referred to—York, Kistiakowsky, Wiesner, Scoville, Rathjens, Chayes, Ruina, Panofsky—have all been high-level officials in previous administrations or served as government advisors. Their judgments, in the Soviet view, are authoritative; their criticism of Defense Department policy is, therefore, especially telling.[63]

75

USA Institute military analyst M. A. Mil'shteyn has observed a similar discussion regarding SALT-II. He writes: "There were continuous broad discussions at the most diverse levels in the United States around the questions which had to be solved at the second phase" of SALT—"in Congress, in government departments, at symposia and seminars . . . and particularly among the circles of people engaged in arms control questions (The Arms Control Community) [given in English]."[64] In this instance Mil'shteyn found the American discussion to be "unjustifiably pessimistic." Nonetheless he and Trofimenko clearly consider the "Arms Control Community" an influential group of "realistic" scholar-advocates who can frequently—though not always—be counted on to raise serious objections to the Pentagon's latest programs and contribute to the public and congressional discussions of arms control issues. Their influence, though not decisive, has at times been important.

(2) THE "THINK TANKS." Aware that, as Gromyko has written, the American position at SALT-II depends "upon the *entire* complex of forces . . . which take part in work on military-political problems,"[65] Soviet interest extends beyond the "Arms Control Community" to the research centers specializing in strategic analysis. The Soviet position on the strategic "think tanks" has turned 180°. Previously denounced for their "right-wing," militaristic attitudes, such organizations as the Institute for Defense Analysis and the Center for Strategic Studies of the Stanford Research Institute (SRI) are now openly courted— precisely because of their association with the Department of Defense. Such institutions, Gromyko notes with unusual candor,

> can significantly affect the process of government decision making if only because they are in a position "to shoot upward" their analytical and military-technical documentation and expertise, which may exert a very significant influence on responsible government officials.[66]

Thus even though "the interests of the military-industrial complex are deeply-embedded in these institutes," and "many on their staff take positions which coincide with the views of Senator Jackson," Mr. Gromyko managed to spend some time visiting with SRI's "energetic Richard Foster" (whose office, he notes, is "a ten-minute drive from the White House and right next to the Pentagon.")[67] And, presumably in the hope of "shooting upward" their own views on such matters,

ranking officials from the USA Institute and *IMEMO* have participated in a series of "research symposia" with SRI dealing with questions of military strategy and doctrine, Soviet-American trade, global
economic problems and political/strategic issues related to détente.[68]

(3) SOVIET SPECIALISTS. A special place in the Soviet pantheon of
the enemies of détente is reserved for American scholars specializing
in the Soviet Union. At best, according to USA Institute Director
Arbatov, the "well-known vices of Sovietology" include the following:

> empty thoughts, the deliberate complication of the most simple things,
> [and] persistent attempts to make great conclusions from facts of little
> significance (the method of "splitting hairs" or, as we say in Russia,
> attempts to "make an elephant out of a fly and then trade in ivory").[69]

Put less politely, academic specialists on the Soviet Union, like many
of their brethren in the State Department, are considered to be a
product—and a major beneficiary—of the cold war. Gromyko refers
to American Sovietology as "that product of the cold war which, in
turn, it did everything to stimulate."[70] Having made their career in
anti-Communism during the cold war, they seek to prolong its
existence. Thus, charges Arbatov, they disseminate false notions—
regarding an alleged "expansionist drive" in Soviet policy—"calculated to discourage any desire in the West to seek alternatives to the
cold war."[71]

Purveyors of ossified anti-communist dogmas, many of the
professional anti-Soviets are believed to have made a sizeable contribution to the cold war. In their time Zbigniew Brzezinski (long a
favorite bête noire) and numerous other lesser lights served in the State
Department, sowing the seeds of distrust and suspicion towards the
USSR. They appeal, in their writings, to liberal intellectuals and
students, "an impressionable and occasionally fickle and fashion-
conscious milieu."[72] Soviet scorn for Western liberalism is well captured in Arbatov's characterization of "liberal circles": "Like frivolous
young girls," he writes, "(although many of them are gray-haired),
they swing from one fashionable political trend to another."[73]

While numerous others—such as Walter Laqueur, Richard
Pipes, and Leopold Labedz—are also regarded as overt enemies of
détente, the picture is not all bleak. In a recent issue of *SShA*,
"political scientist"—a less ominous profession—Marshall Shulman

was mentioned without any abusive references and Zbigniew Brzezinski was seen to have begun to recognize reality.[74] Despite deep reservations about Jimmy Carter's choice of foreign-policy advisor, Soviet observers were diplomatic in their commentary during the 1976 election campaign. Though Mr. Brzezinski was identified as an "expert 'on Kremlin affairs' . . . well-known for his anti-Sovietism," his "positive" remarks regarding détente were cited in *Pravda* as "uniquely symptomatic" of the increasing support in the United States for a "sensible approach" to Soviet-American relations.[75]

Whatever influence they may have had in the past, "the prestige and authority of the so-called Sovietologists has declined sharply." The "new realities" of Soviet-American relations, writes Gromyko, ran counter to their "dire predictions." As a result, "the authority of these experts has now been shaken and their advice is listened to with an increasing amount of skepticism." According to Richard Barnett, reports Gromyko, "their analysis of the dynamics of the processes of development of Soviet foreign policy is now rejected by the government itself."[76] Just as détente enhances the authority of "far-sighted businessmen," it apparently "washes away" the positions of the "adherents of the cold war," America's Sovietologists.*

Public Opinion and the Media

Soviet accounts of the role of public opinion in U.S. political life are strikingly generous. *SShA* authors have observed that public sentiment has become so potent a force in recent years as to have compelled critically important changes—in both policy and personnel—on the U.S. government. In recognition of this vast power, official circles are striving to "manage" public opinion, i.e., to manipulate it and, it is hoped, render it harmless. It is to the accomplishment of this purpose, it is argued, that the activities of the

---

*As evidence of the current "crisis of 'Sovietology,' " of the fact that "the once-thriving specialists on the Soviet Union are going out of vogue," the Soviet press agency TASS points to the serious financial difficulties facing the Russian research centers at Harvard and Columbia Universities. Their fund-raising efforts, observes TASS, are to no avail. "Dollars . . . will not save the 'Sovietologists' possessed with the ideas of anti-Communism, falsifiers with or without academic degrees, who do not want to get rid of the burden of the past, do not want to heed sober voices in the United States itself," the agency said. (*FBIS*, 26 November 1976, pp. B2–3.)

communications media are directed. American newspapers, magazines and television have no function, therefore, save to serve the interests of the official leadership.

(a) Public Opinion

In an article in the August 1974 issue of *SShA*, Eduard Ivanyan, then the USA Institute's chief of section on U.S. public opinion, wrote that "there is every reason to assert that public pressure is objectively in a position to force a bourgeois government to take actions in foreign and domestic policy which might not have been considered in other times or under other circumstances." While stressing that public opinion is *"only one and not the only factor"* influencing its behavior, he underscores the fact that "position taken by broad circles of the American public was *one of the factors* along with a number of political economic and military factors, that influenced the decision of the U.S. government to withdraw its armed forces from Vietnam [emphasis in the original]."[77]

A similar position is taken by numerous others. Writing in early 1972, G. A. Trofimenko said that "the powerful popular protest against the war . . . with its nationwide 'Vietnam moratoria' of 1964–71 and with its long and stormy anti-war campaign of 1971 is the main factor forcing the Republican government toward the gradual withdrawal of American troop units from Vietnam." Furthermore, writes Trofimenko, it was this "grass roots" movement which "forced President Johnson, who was responsible for the escalation of aggression in Vietnam, to leave the White House in 1968."[78] Still more recently Geyevsky took the position that the anti-war movement was "one of the main factors which impelled Washington to sign the [Paris] peace agreements" ending the Vietnam war. Geyevsky, in fact, berates former student members of the anti-war movement for their political apathy. In his view they are "unable to understand the complex system of interrelationships between domestic and foreign policy" and unnecessarily "devalue the methods of mass struggle."[79]

The role of public opinion in the American political system is now clearly recognized. Thus popular "dissatisfaction" with CIA activities in Chile and its "systematic performance of police functions within the nation" is said to have led to an investigation and public exposure of its activities.[80] Further, "opposition to militarism" within the Congress is seen to be a result of changes in the public mood. "The necessity to listen" to the American people, writes Dolgolopova, "forces many members of the Congress more and more frequently to criticize the military-industrial complex and large military expenditures."[81] Most importantly, as just noted, U.S. policy in Vietnam was dramatically shaped by popular opposition. As Zhurkin recently observed, "It is difficult to over-estimate the significance of the anti-war movement in the United States . . . at the end of the sixties and beginning of the seventies. It was one of the main factors which caused the defeat of the U.S. intervention in Vietnam."[82] And having come to grief in Vietnam most "genuine Americans" now prefer to live by the principle of "live and let live." Such attitudes are said to have had "a most notable effect" on Washington. The public mood has been an "important factor" in the government's decision to abandon its "policy of confrontation," "insistently urging" the White House and Capitol Hill "to search for and find ways to develop and intensify détente."[83]

What explains this extraordinary turn of events? The orthodox Party interpretation argues that public opinion in bourgeois societies plays a negligible role, especially where foreign policy issues are involved. As Lenin wrote, "the most important questions—war, peace, diplomatic questions—are decided by a small handful of capitalists, who deceive not only the masses but very often parliament as well."[84] How is it conceivable, then, in the view of Soviet Americanists, for a popular protest movement to cost the political career of one American president and force his successor to abandon a major foreign policy commitment?

Ivanyan attempts to explain, but his answer is rather vague. "In formulating and implementing their domestic and foreign policies," he writes, "bourgeois governments are forced to recall that unless they ensure support for their chosen course from the country's public opinion, it is difficult to count on its successful realization."[85] What, precisely, the source of the difficulty is Ivanyan leaves unclear. Trofimenko provides a more discerning explanation. His reasoning runs as follows: whatever its public rhetoric, the United States government pays little attention to the view of the general public when formulating its foreign policy. On the contrary, its "optimum policy" is either to ignore public opinion completely, or, by manipulating public sentiment, to create an artificial climate of support for official policy. "However," he goes on,

> the possibilities for such manipulation are not infinite. Moments arise when the split between the sentiments and feelings of broad public circles and official policy proves so deep that a bourgeois government, wishing to remain in power, has either to correct official policy or to resign from power.[86]

Fearful that public wrath will result in their defeat at the polls, American politicians must mend their ways or leave the scene. "This, strictly speaking," writes Trofimenko in 1971, "happened in the United States in 1968, when public opposition . . . forced President Johnson to quit the White House." Similarly, the "present Republican administration must take account of the opinion of the overwhelming majority of voters."[87]

What Trofimenko refers to as "political reality" therefore demands that the U.S. government give some heed to the sentiments of "the broad mass of voters." Citing General Westmoreland, he refers to public opinion as the "Achilles' heel" of official policy. President Nixon admitted as much, notes Trofimenko, when he declared: "We do not have the authority to run matters as they used to be run in this country, and the enemy knows this." This declaration by the president, Trofimenko suggests, amounted to a recognition of "the power of public pressure on the administration."[88] Others take much the same view. At a November 1970 symposium at the USA Institute, Shvedkov noted that it "is not by accident" that the Nixon administration pays a great deal of attention to public moods. "The president must take into consideration the fact that twice during the postwar years, in 1952 and 1968, the American public's dissatisfaction with U.S. foreign policy has cost the ruling party dearly."[89] And later Shvedkov notes that "the dramatic and unprecedented refusal" of President Johnson to run in 1968 and the failure of Senator Humphrey to win the election "showed clearly the dimensions of the American voter's rage."[90]

American elections, therefore, traditionally denounced as nothing more than exercises in political casuistry—as Khrushchev declared in 1964, "a 'flowery screen' . . . .behind which capital is omnipotent and the workers are actually deprived of their rights"[91] —are seen to be an effective democratic political mechanism. An incumbent American administration must, in the current view, heed the changing popular mood, lest it lose public support at the polls. Such indeed happens at all levels of American political life—as demonstrated by the defeat of Senator Fulbright.[92] All elective officials, therefore, including the president and members of Congress, are seen to be subject to some degree of public influence.

Electoral considerations are seen to have a direct bearing on one particular area of U.S. foreign policy—the Middle East. This is true for two reasons. First, the distinctive distribution of Jewish voters—who are largely concentrated in five major states (New York, California, Pennsylvania, Illinois and Ohio)—is of considerable political importance. Their strategic location in these crucial states "which account for 165 electoral votes out of the 270 needed to elect a president," writes V. A. Kremenyuk, is "a fact capable of influencing the policy of the Washington administration." The views expressed by candidates of both parties on the Middle East during the 1972 campaign were influenced in considerable measure by this factor, that is to say by their desire "to attract to their own side the greatest number of Jewish voters." Thus "all prominent Democrats" and the Republican administration favored "decisive" and "active" support of Israel.[93]

The Jewish vote, though only 4 percent of the total electorate, is seen to have an influence well beyond its size. This is not only due to the pecularities of American electoral geography. Other factors are involved. While small, the Jewish vote is well-organized and led. Zionist groups in the United States, notes Ye. M. Primakov, deputy director of *IMEMO*, have considerable political influence. Quoting General George Brown, chairman of the U.S. joint chiefs of staff, he argues that "The Israeli lobby . . . is 'unbelievably powerful.' " Primakov writes:

> pro-Zionist elements occupy fairly strong positions in the American press, radio and television. . . . The compact Jewish community . . . , which takes an active part in elections, represents an important means of pressure on political leaders on Capitol Hill and in the White House. . . . Another important means of pressure is the fact that Jewish organizations make

large campaign contributions. . . . These organizations are responsible for more than half of the large contributions to the Democratic party's campaign fund.[94]

Given their domestic political leverage, Zionist groups in the United States are seen to exert considerable influence on official policy. They have, of course, a major impact on U.S. policy toward the Middle East. According to Primakov, "Domestic political considerations in general largely determine the development and implementation of the American course in the Middle East."[95] Their interests and influence extend to other issues as well. During the Nixon administration, writes A. K. Kislov, Zionist organizations pressed the White House to organize special Yiddish-language broadcasts to the USSR over the Voice of America (VOA). At the insistence of these groups, VOA "increased the volume of its radio broadcasts which slanderously depict the situation" of Soviet Jews. Further, just prior to the 1972 summit conference in Moscow, American Zionists "persistently made demands to include provocative questions [regarding easing of restrictions on the emigration of Soviet Jews] on the agenda of the Soviet-American negotiations which were, by design, deliberately intended to complicate these negotiations. . . . In order to 'calm' Zionist circles," prominent members of the Nixon administration "repeatedly . . . stated that they were devoting 'a great deal of attention' to the problems 'facing Soviet Jews.'"[96]

Clearly electoral considerations are now believed to have a significant influence on U.S. foreign policy. This factor, according to Pakhomov, played a key role in the passage by the Congress of the Tunney Amendment which cut off U.S. military aid to Angola. The fact that 1976 was an election year, he writes, a period "when public opinion is of 'great significance' for the politicians" had "a serious influence on the decision adopted by the legislators."[97] Soviet analysts have apparently learned that, whatever the teachings of Party doctrine, the formal requirement of winning periodic elections can and often does affect the behavior of U.S. government officials.

Elections, however, are not the only channel through which public opinion can make its influence felt. As the institute's Deputy Director, V. V. Zhurkin has recently observed, "the public . . . has no few opportunities to exert a sobering influence" on U.S. foreign policy. "This was very graphically revealed," he notes, "during the mass movement against aggression in Vietnam which unfolded in the United States during the late sixties and early seventies."[98]

The anti-war movement, writes Zhurkin, had a major impact on American political life. "This was, in terms of scale, the most powerful campaign for stopping aggression in the history of the United States."[99] It united practically all the major anti-war organizations into a broad public front and directed their activity toward one goal—ending the war. It successfully coordinated its efforts with anti-war campaigns in other countries. Further, it developed many new "means of struggle"—the "teach-in," the "sit-in," mass burnings of draft cards, boycotts of corporations which "profitted" from the war, etc. As a result of these efforts, the anti-war campaign was by 1967–68 transformed into a nationwide movement. Between 1969 and 1971 millions participated in mass protests against U.S. "interventional" policies in Southeast Asia.[100]

These nationwide demonstrations, notes Zhurkin, had a profound effect on the American government. They "gave rise to growing anxiety" within U.S. leadership circles and "split their ranks." Further, "they prodded Congress into putting forth more decisive demands to stop the war and compelled official Washington to maneuver, to seek a compromise." *The Pentagon Papers*, suggests Zhurkin, provides evidence from "the inside" which shows "how in practice the anti-war movement exerted influence on the leadership of the military and the whole U.S. state machine." As the authors of the report indicate, "unhappiness with the war" and the growth of "public criticism" generated doubts within the government as to the wisdom of military escalation in Vietnam. Defense Secretary Clark Clifford, notes Zhurkin, in a secret memorandum of February 1968, "warned that continued escalation will lead to 'growing dissatisfaction,' 'evasion of military service and disorder in the cities' and in the end could lead to an 'internal crisis of unprecedented proportions.'" The contents of these secret documents, writes Zhurkin, "graphically demonstrate how powerful and effective was the pressure of social forces on the government."[101]

Thus it was fear of public indignation, he argues, which "forced" leading government officials to modify their policies. Not only did such public pressure compel President Johnson to quit the American political arena, and President Nixon to withdraw U.S. forces from Indochina and finally in January 1973 to sign the Paris Peace Agreement. It was dread of a new wave of public protest which, according to Zhurkin, deterred Washington from again resorting to force when in the fall of 1975 the Saigon regime in South Vietnam collapsed.[102]

On the basis of this experience, Zhurkin concludes that "the public now represents one of the decisive factors in diminishing and preventing international confict." The position of American public opinion, he writes, "which clearly demonstrated its potentialities during the struggle to end the aggression in Indochina . . . serves today and can serve in the future as a serious means to contain the aggressive schemes of the lovers of military adventures." The worldwide struggles against the war in Vietnam, he suggests, "embody and reflect the enormous potential" of the anti-war movement.[103]

Though obviously impressed with the anti-war movement in the United States, seen by some to be evidence of "the exceptional capacity of democratic forces to exercise an influence on government foreign policy,"[104] Soviet enthusiasm regarding the political role of public opinion is decidedly mixed. First, there is the problem of its staying power. The "mass struggle" against the Vietnam war was by all accounts a unique phenomenon. Zhurkin notes repeatedly that in terms of numbers of people, scope of activities and political effectiveness, the peace movement was unprecedented in American history. Soviet analysts recognize that the political climate in the United States during other periods of military conflict has been rather different. Most Americans during the Korean war, notes Kremenyuk, were not bitterly critical of government policy. It was only with the war in Vietnam that an end was put to the "apathy of the ordinary American in foreign policy matters."[105] Whether the future will give rise to unprecedented circumstances and once more turn public opinion into "a factor whose influence has proven impossible to nullify" must be in considerable doubt.

Second, and more important, Soviet observers have little faith in the basic political instincts and judgment of the American public. As a matter of fundamental political doctrine, Moscow holds that rank-and-file Americans, like "ordinary people" everywhere, are by their very nature democratic, peace-loving and basically progressive. Recently, however, Soviet analysts have been giving voice to rather harsher views. Soviet commentators, especially since early 1976, have been depicting "the average American" as one "who still has not quite understood the nature of the changes occurring in the world and who has become accustomed to America's predominant role" in world affairs.[106] Trofimenko finds most Americans afflicted with "illusions . . . regarding American omnipotence and American superiority, the certainty that the United States could decide everything unilaterally."[107] Institute Director Arbatov puts the matter still more sharply when he warns against "emotions still lurking deep in the minds of many people" in the United States—"national superiority, jingoism, suspicion and enmity to everything that is unusual and alien."[108]

Even the traditionally hallowed working class is regarded with some misgivings. The "thick-skulled policies" of the "right-wing" AFL-CIO leadership aside, Popov warns against underestimating "the force of conservatism in the American labor movement." Not only does the ideology of the trade unions in the United States accept the existing capitalist system, but its policies are very much influenced by a "strong conservative nucleus." Furthermore, "most ordinary workers" are believed to have "a passive attitude toward matters of foreign policy." Living in "a nation surrounded by oceans," they are not concerned with questions of foreign policy "unless there is a war going on." American unionists are also seen to be victimized by anti-communism ("the trade unions as a whole are freeing themselves of the burden of militant anti-communism more slowly than other groups in American society") and "fairly strong feelings of jingoism and chauvinism . . . combined with racism."[109]

Given the persistence of such unenlightened attitudes, it is not surprising to find, as Berezhkov reported, that 57 percent of American "blue-collar workers" supported Nixon over McGovern in the 1972 presidential elections. The workers rejected the Democratic candidate, according to Berezhkov, because he was seen as too radical. They feared McGovern's social program would have meant additional tax burdens for them. They opposed many of his other programs such as his endorsement of amnesty for those who evaded the draft during the Vietnam war, racial quotas in trade unions and school busing

86

to promote racial integration. They were offended by his image—cultivated by the Republicans—as a defender of hippies, a proponent of drugs, sexual license and other vices. "It must be admitted," writes Berezhkov, "that on the whole American workers are still very conservative and such propaganda as accused McGovern of 'dangerous radicalism' played a certain role" in his defeat.[110]

The public as a whole, including its "leading detachment," the American worker, is regarded with considerable suspicion. The distinctly conservative even chauvinistic views of many Americans—a significant number of whom are acknowledged to be advocates of a "new conservatism" (calling for the decentralization of power and restrictions on "big government")[111]—are potentially a negative influence on Washington, allowing in given circumstances for a turn towards the political right. During the 1976 election campaign, for example, "some statesmen" were seen to be compelled by "the drive for votes . . . to flirt with reactionaries."[112] Arbatov notes that "the entry of the extreme right-wing figure of R. Reagan into the fray managed to shift the election battle far to the right, forcing some other candidates to try to prove that they would be even more orthodox than he."[113] Fearful of being outflanked by Reagan's appeal to the country's conservative voters, President Ford was forced "to make particularly great concessions to right-wing circles," i.e., by publicly jettisoning use of the term détente. Furthermore, while the political attitudes of the American public can become a powerful constraint on government policy (as in the case of Vietnam), they can also prove helpful to more aggressive elements. Thus, suggests Trofimenko, "Conceptions of power, falling on the fertile soil of Yankee chauvinism, rooted in the century-old tradition of 'the American dream,' still, apparently, hypnotize . . . the ordinary citizen" and lead him to support the claims and policies of the Pentagon. It was this tendency in American politics, he writes, which led the leaders of both parties during the 1976 campaign to stress the importance of America's "position of strength" even though "it was precisely such intoxication with strength which led U.S. foreign policy into the blind alley" of Vietnam.[114]

In sum, the American people are seen to be an uncertain, sometimes even negative influence on U.S. foreign policy. As a measure of Moscow's exasperation with public opinion in the United

States and its willingness to endorse "conservative" and "jingoistic" policies, Soviet sources frequently judge the average American to be "politically naive," "lacking information" and "misinformed."[115] Whatever its potential—via elections or more direct action—the American public is obviously not considered a steadfast or reliable political force.

(b) The Media

The communications media are the most poorly understood feature of American political life. Paul Hollander has remarked on the striking tendency of Soviet judgments on American society "to project upon it characteristics of the Soviet social-political environment. . . . Time and again Soviet spokesmen credit American society with political conditions which actually exist . . . in the Soviet Union."[116] Nowhere is this more clearly the case than in the Soviet treatment of American newspapers.

The starting point in the Soviet interpretation stems from their analysis of public opinion. Ivanyan puts it simply. He writes: "Bourgeois states would violate their nature if they were not to at least try to halt or retard the . . . awakening of class consciousness and the political activity of the popular masses."[117] Such concerns explain the role of public opinion surveys in American political life. U. S. government officials are interested in opinion polls, writes Ivanyan,

> not so much because they want to take into account the attitude of the public in the formulation of government policy as because they want to try to obtain information about how they should conduct their propaganda work in order to alter tendencies in public opinion that are unfavorable to the country's ruling circles.[118]

Thus if public opinion cannot simply be ignored, then it can be transformed. It is to this end, that is to say the management of public opinion, that the media are directed.

The role of the media is described simply as that of a tool of the ruling clases to ensure continued public support. The "powerful mass media" make it possible for the ruling classes "who exercise control over them, to constantly and vigorously exert an effect" on American public opinion "and thereby to artificially implant ways of thinking that are necessary to these circles."[119] Competition between various segments of the media—newspapers, magazines, radio and television—can be found. Such competition reflects, however, not freedom of the press but a struggle between the owners of different media for the advertising dollar. And "even though commeecial competition does exist, it does not prevent all mass media from working as a united front when it is a case of brainwashing the public. . . . In such a case, there is complete unity between them notwithstanding tactical differences stemming from the political sympathies and convictions of the individual owners."[120]

The picture is one of endless manipulation and pervasive government control. The following comments give some sense of the tone of Soviet commentary: "There is a rather clearly defined distribution of duties and demarcation of spheres of penetration between the mass media. Each has its target." "In the overwhelming majority of cases, newspaper owners permit official Washington . . . to use newspapers and journals to implement its domestic and foreign policies and to influence public opinion." "Government power and the capital press corps" are "linked . . . by transmission belts[!] (press conferences, briefings), that make the latter a 'quasi-official branch of the government.'"[121] "Very strict censorship has for a long time prevailed over the speeches . . . made by any employee of the federal government on matters of foreign policy"—"rigid control . . . exercised over the news media . . . is constant."[122]

The USA Institute's handling of the publication of *The Pentagon Papers* by the *New York Times*, the *Washington Post* and other leading newspapers in June 1971 reflects the basic Soviet attitudes towards the press. In a lead article appearing in its September issue, *SShA* reported the following:

> Newspaper corporations in the USA are a great force closely linked to the banks and industrial monopolies. If the most powerful and influential newspapers in the country publish documents of the military establishment against the will of the government and most of the members of the Supreme Court support them for doing so, this means that someone's patience has reached its limit on the American Mount Olympus.[123]

Trofimenko argues similarly. The "close connections" between American "business circles" and the media, he writes, explain such "seemingly paradoxical actions as the publication by bourgeois press organs of exposés" like *The Pentagon Papers* "despite government opposition."

It can be said that a certain section of the U. S. ruling classes has grown tired of the war. Having suffered commercially from the war, they . . . are therefore prepared to resort to powerful "shocking" eruptions within the "establishment" itself to achieve a speedier end to the protracted and fruitless adventure.[124]

In deciding to publish *The Pentagon Papers*, therefore, Katharine Graham, Arthur Ochs Sulzberger and the other publishers involved were responding not to any journalistic notions of public service; their main concern, like that of the non-military sector of the "ruling class," was the interests of "coffers and commerce" (Trofimenko).

The only other explanation offered for the "paradoxical actions" of the media, i.e., the publication or broadcast of material hostile to the interests of government policy, is a bureaucratic one. Such "scandalous exposures of Washington's policies" as the publication of *The Pentagon Papers* or the release by Columnist Jack Anderson of the minutes of the NSC's Washington Special Action Group meetings during December 1971, at the height of the Indo-Pakistani crisis, writes Shvedkov, "are by no means random initiatives by individual persons." These " 'bureaucratic scandals' are above all the result of the keen rivalry in the ruling clique in Washington, a result of the struggle for power and influence." The "real reason" behind these "leaks," he writes, was the effort by Defense Secretary Laird to discredit Henry Kissinger and the NSC system. Resentful of the White House's "administrative innovations," Laird, with the support of allies at the State Department, sought to sabotage his chief rival.[125]

The media, therefore, have no independent role; they are, at once, the tool of the business world and the foil of Washington bureaucrats. While occasional kindly remarks are made about individual "realistic" journalists (e.g., Walter Lippmann), and "authoritative" newspaper columnists (e.g., James Reston) are quoted, Soviet Americanists view their publishers in the grimmest light. As for "investigative reporting," this is seen to be nothing more than "an attempt to calm the American public by suggesting the idea that it ought not be particularly troubled and dissatisfied with the present state of affairs because the press is 'on guard' to protect its interests."[126] Like the American muckrakers of the early 1900s, Jack Anderson, Ralph Nader, Robert Sherrill, Seymour Hersh et al. are considered to be agents of the establishment, employed "to distract the masses" and allow dissatisfied elements "to let off steam."[127] Thus "the hullaballoo in the press" concerning Watergate "fully corresponds to the traditions of the American two-party system . . . [of] using passing scandals to distract the public's attention from the really fundamental social problems of society.' "[128] So much for the efforts of Bob Woodward and Carl Bernstein, and their colleagues at the *Washington Post*.

In terms of Moscow's political calculus the media are a hostile force. According to V. A. Kremenyuk, "the American press, or in any case, the overwhelming majority of its most influential organs, such as the *New York Times*, the *Washington Post*, and magazines such as *Time* and *Newsweek* . . . all function as mouthpieces of pro-Israeli circles."[129] The major media, furthermore, are considered to be anti-Soviet. "They do everything to present life in the Soviet Union in the most gloomy terms," observes Berezhkov, "and make people mistrust the Soviet Union's policies and to renew cold war fears about the so-called Communist menace." They adopt such policies for predictable reasons. "The owners of the mass media," notes the editor-in-chief of *SShA*, seek "to stir up the old fears and are trying to make it seem as though the Soviet Union presents a threat to the United States. They thereby hope to divert the people's attention away from the flaws and diseases of American society."[130]

In pursuit of this mission, the media are said by Berezhkov to be carrying on a "persistent fight against the policy of easing tension." To this end no efforts are spared. According to Berezhkov's deputy, N. D. Turkatenko, the opponents of détente "use all means, including the most base. One of their favorites includes personal attacks on precisely those people who in one way or another are connected to the policy of détente." According to Turketenko, the screening of the film, *All The President's Men*, based on the book by Woodward and Bernstein on the Watergate affair, and the simultaneous publication of *The Last Days* by the same authors, were nothing more than "salvos" in the campaign against détente.[131] The publishing and film industries, apparently, made common cause with the *Washington Post* in a campaign to defame President Nixon and his foreign policy — using methods "most base."

Soviet treatment of the American media is especially undistinguished. The most compelling explanation of their abyssmal lack of understanding reflects both an ignorance of such institutions and, relatedly, a tendency to engage in mirror-image thinking. First, as observed earlier, the Soviets have difficulty conceptualizing what they have never experienced. In the USSR the press and other means of communication have always been considered agents of the official leadership, whose prime function it is to elucidate and legitimize the specific policy line of the moment. They can, and often do, reflect internal bureaucratic and political interests, but the possibility of a press independent—even critical—of official policy is totally unfamiliar and poorly understood. Furthermore, given their own distinctive conceptions of the media, Soviet analysts tend to have a mirror image of Western institutions. That is to say, they view the output of the *New York Times*, the *Washington Post*, *CBS* and *Time* much as they do *Pravda*, *Radio Moscow* and *New Times*, *viz.*, the products of a politically-sponsored campaign to defend the faith. Here, too, the notion of a free, uncommitted, critical press seems to be beyond their ken.

4

U. S. POLICY MAKERS

The personal qualities of specific leaders occupying the White House are, as we have seen, of considerable interest to Soviet analysts. The particular personality sitting in the Oval Office in the White House—be he a Roosevelt or a Truman, a Kennedy or a Johnson—can be of critical importance. Thus, though they continue to insist on the "the primacy of objective factors" (the "correlation of forces," levels of economic development, scientific-military factors, the "laws of historical development" and the like), these are seen to be "mere objective preconditions." Essential to the formation of U.S. foreign-policy strategy is the American leadership's "comprehension" of these factors, i.e., "how world realities are perceived—or how they may be perceived."[1]

The picture of the American political leadership presented in SShA is most striking. While not without its darker sides, the intellectual and moral qualities attributed to recent U.S. policy makers seem to have dramatically improved. From an anti-communist, expansionist, belligerent, at times even unstable band of essentially malevolent men, the key American decision makers have been characterized as considerably more cautious, flexible, perspicacious and realistic. Current Soviet views regarding the American leadership are perhaps best reflected in their assessment of three issues: (1) U.S. policy regarding the use of force, (2) Washington's "new realism," and (3) leadership attitudes toward the Soviet Union.

The Use of Force

"As is well known," write two major military analysts at the USA Institute

> military force has traditionally been regarded in the United States as the main instrument of foreign policy. This was reflected most vividly in the "positions of strength" policy whose pivot was based on the calculation that the solution of almost any foreign policy problem can be achieved with the aid of military force—by means of the threat of its use and when necessary by its direct use.[2]

The adoption of this militaristic stance, we are told, is a result of the "transient omnipotence" which the United States enjoyed after World War II. America, writes Shvedkov, was "the only world power which came out of the upheavals of war not only without having experienced disaster and destruction, but significantly enriched."[3] Furthermore, with "the appearance in their hands of the 'absolute weapon'—the atom bomb,"—U.S. political leaders became intoxicated with their own power. "Euphoric" regarding their own "omnipotence," they felt "anything goes" and sought by a policy of military diktat to achieve U.S. "world hegemony."[4]

As a result U.S. postwar diplomacy, it is said, "took on a hyper-trophied and monstrous form." Gromyko argues that "in the manner of an inveterate gambler," the American political leadership "undertook the risky game of inciting international tension." Thus, for the purpose of "of instilling fear," President Truman "used nuclear weapons on Japanese civilians so that everyone would understand the military capabilities of the United States." "Under the conditions of the temporary possession of the atomic monopoly the policy "of acting 'from a position of strength' became more and more fashionable on the banks of the Potomac."[5]

In pursuit of its "policy of strength," the United States is said to have engaged in three basic types of actions. "The first type," notes V. V. Zhurkin, deputy director of the institute and expert on U.S. "crisis behavior"

> was the demonstration of force to frighten, deter, blackmail, and sometimes also to bluff. In these cases, the use of armed force was either not envisioned at all or viewed as extremely undesirable. Clear examples of

such demonstrations were U.S. actions during the Berlin crises, the actions centering on Laos during 1961–1963 while Kennedy was president, and many others.

The second type was comparatively short actions, more or less limited in time, carried on with the active employment of armed forces. That is how it was during the U.S. intervention in Lebanon in 1958, in the Dominican Republic in 1965, and in a number of other cases.

Finally there is the third type, extended combat actions which are in fact what American military-political theoreticians call limited wars. This was the case in Vietnam.[6]

The point, clearly, is that U.S. political leaders are willing to resort to force to achieve their purposes. They employ the threat of force to "frighten, deter, blackmail and bluff" and actually use American power to engage in "military adventures"—in Lebanon, the Dominican Republic, Korea and Vietnam. President Kennedy is regarded as somewhat exceptional in this regard. According to Trofimenko, Kennedy recognized that, as he stated in November 1961, "the United States is not omnipotent and not omniscient."[7] The United States was becoming aware that its "chief potential adversary" possessed a weapons arsenal "sufficient to inflict an annihilating responsive nuclear missile strike against an aggressor. Such a situation, Kennedy stressed, called for caution, perspicacity, great realism and flexibility." Thus during the Cuban missile crisis he was able "to curb the 'hawks' straining for a fight and expressed readiness for a political, rather than a military solution." After the crisis he expressed readiness for negotiations with the Soviet Union, which led to the Partial Test-Ban Treaty and made "a fundamental decision to curtail American participation in the civil war in Vietnam."[8]

Kennedy was, therefore, seen to have dissociated himself from the use of military force, understanding that in the case of Vietnam "the tactic of military escalation . . . was not promising." In Zhurkin's view, Kennedy's "realism" was combined "in an eccentric manner with the basic one—the use of force." In any event Kennedy's successor was not so constrained and "the world was again witness to repetitions of the traditional policy of aggression"—in the Dominican Republic and especially in Vietnam.[9]

The experience of Vietnam, however—the lack of political and military success and the enormous cost (economic and social as well as human)—raised doubts about the wisdom of traditional policies. "The failure in Vietnam," writes Zhurkin, "gave rise to a sharp debate" in the United States in the course of which some

> even began to talk about a "post-Vietnam non-intervention syndrome" predicting that Washington would now show greater restraint in new international crises and conflicts, would strive to avoid involvement in some situations, and would soften its traditional principle of using force as the main instrument in conducting U.S. policy.[10]

The "fiasco in Vietnam" therefore served as a powerful catalyst impelling official Washington to reassess its basic policies. It had this effect, in addition, because the failure of U.S. strategy in Southeast Asia "fostered the coming to power . . . of a different party, the Republicans, and the logic of interparty struggle was obligated to a certain 'change of landmarks.'"[11] As Arbatov writes, "It is typical of the American political tradition for new leaders to attempt to formulate some kind of new foreign-policy line."[12] Furthermore, as Zhurkin observed, "the political interests of the new administration overlapped considerably with the moods and demands of the majority of Americans."[13] A repudiation of the discredited "interventionist policies" of the Johnson White House, he argued, would bolster the position of the incoming Nixon administration.

What lessons would the Republicans draw from Vietnam? The USA Institute was not especially sanguine regarding the outcome of their reassessment. Soviet pessimism was based on two factors. First, as Zhurkin has written, the "lessons" of Vietnam are more "complex and contradictory" than the unambiguous predictions about a "non-interventionist syndrome" believed. There is always the danger, he writes, of "attempts by an aggressor to take revenge for his failures by increasing the dimensions of a conflict." Such a course, he notes, was in fact considered in Vietnam in the second half of the 1960s. Actions of this kind, he somberly warns, could lead into "a descent into world nuclear missile conflict."[14] Yet another reaction to Vietnam, writes Zhurkin, could be the policy of *"faits accompli."* Fearful of becoming tied down in "new Vietnams," the United States might seek to achieve its goals by "rapid aggressive actions," i.e., to deliver quick strikes and withdraw, thus presenting U.S. and world opinion with "accomplished facts." Such a policy would be designed "to lessen the numerous negative consequences, domestic and foreign, which follow upon extended wars like that in Vietnam."[15]

While the threat of a vengeful U.S. nuclear weapons strike was felt to be small—Zhurkin notes that though U.S. military circles facing defeat had "frequently called for the use of nuclear weapons" (General McArthur in Korea in 1950 and 1951, Admiral Radford at Dienbienphu in 1954, and General Lemnitzer in Laos in 1961),[16] none of which requests were implemented—the policy of quick strikes could not be foreclosed. Additionally, although many in the United States were alert to the danger of "new Vietnams" and warned against future military involvement overseas, others, as Mil'shteyn later suggested, thought it urgent to continue pursuit of a strong American policy, one which would restore the faith of the average citizen in his nation's power and military might and prove that the defeat in Vietnam was "a transitory and accidental phenomenon."[17]

Which course would the new administration adopt? Much depended on its political character and judgment. Here, too, there was little in which to take comfort. The new president's political record was very well known in Moscow. While his "persistent declarations about an aspiration to switch 'from an era of confrontation to an era of negotiation' . . . inspired hopes that Washington's policy would promote a general relaxation of international tension,"[18] Nixon's previous anti-communist, anti-Soviet positions cast doubt as to their credibility. There is the question, wrote Arbatov, "whether his positions have really evolved from the right towards the center," that is, whether "the claims about a 'new Nixon' which were persistently advanced during the 1968 election campaign" were true. Noting Nixon's reputation as a "clever politician," Arbatov was dubious. He was also uncertain whether the president would "be able to display in his new position the qualities of a statesman which are essential, not so much for election to the position, as for running such a complex machine as the American ship of state."[19]

Doubts regarding the political style of the Nixon administration were not long lasting. By late 1970, at a symposium at the USA Institute, Arbatov concluded that though "declaring various new

97

principles of policy in relatively calm periods, in crisis situations the Nixon administration acts as before in the old 'classical' style."[20] What led to this judgment were Washington's policies toward Cambodia in the spring of 1970 and its response to the Jordanian civil war that September.

The new administration's decision to invade Cambodia in April 1970 was interesting to Soviet analysts on several grounds. This was the first major test of the operation of the new emergency decision-making machinery of the National Security Council, the Washington Special Actions Group (WASAG). The creation of WASAG, it should be noted, was seen to be a positive step. Fascinated with "bureaucratic rationality" and "orderly processes," Zhurkin viewed the establishment of a "permanent organ . . . for preparing decisions at the highest possible levels during crisis situations as a "very radical restructuring of the . . . decision-making process." Since the decision-making process during crises is of exceptionally great significance"—he notes that in such periods, "the U.S. president must make decisions in a matter of days (and sometimes hours) . . . on actions which may threaten the fate of entire countries, and possibly even the whole world"—the creation of WASAG was thought to be a step in the right direction.[21]

While enamoured of Washington's administrative innovations, Zhurkin was less than pleased with the results. The discussions in WASAG lasted ten days, 20–30 April 1970, during which a variety of alternatives were considered. "It is not possible to say," he writes, "that factors opposing the use of force were discounted completely." He notes in fact that "on April 24, Kissinger organized a political game with five of his staff assistants who had opposed new measures for broadening military actions in Indochina, giving them an opportunity to formulate their basic arguments."[22]

> The purpose of this game was to reveal the possible events and factors that would oppose such actions. . . . In particular, it was pointed out that this kind of action (especially if it involved American troops) would represent a serious escalation of the war in Indochina and that one could expect a real outburst of indignation in the USA and also negative consequences abroad.[23]

"However," notes Zhurkin, "all of these factors were in considerable measures analyzed one-sidedly, seeking to find ways of neutralizing them."[24]

Finally the decision was made to invade. While "practically all the alternative variants proposed" by WASAG "suggested the use of force," in the end "the toughest of all the proposed alternatives was selected," i.e., invasion by U.S. forces. The "only non-military alternative—to call a meeting of the international conference on Cambodia—was, so to speak, turned down from the outset."[25]

Washington's predisposition towards a military solution is explained in part by the fact that, according to Zhurkin (quoting *L'Express*), WASAG was "composed of the administration's hardliners." (It then included Presidential Assistant Kissinger; Undersecretary of State U. Alexis Johnson; Deputy Defense Secretary Packard; Chairman of the Joint Chiefs of Staff Admiral Moorer; and CIA Director Helms.) "Such a composition . . . cannot but be reflected in the character of the decisions taken." (He also notes that "the Nixon administration's political makeup is distinctly expressed in the selection of the WASAG membership.")[26] It also may reflect the fact that, as Zhurkin notes, precisely during crises "the influence of military circles and supporters of an assertive, aggressive policy" has been "particularly strong."[27] The decision to choose the toughest alternative, according to Shvedkov and Lesnoy, was taken "under the influence of the conclusions of the joint chiefs of staff."[28]

What this reflected about the administration's "style of action" was explained by Arbatov in the August 1970 issue of *SShA*. The decision to invade Cambodia, he writes, "produced an impression of unexpected and even convulsive action." Some, he claimed, suggested that "the administration even consciously sought to create such an impression in order, so to speak, to put the fear of God into the adversaries of the United States, to show them that it is ready for decisive, unexpected and risky actions." This "show of force" did not make "an impression" on the Soviet Union, says Arbatov. (He quotes a Brezhnev speech [13 June 1970] which scolds "shortsighted politicians" who seek to "amuse themselves with hopes that it is possible to scare the Soviet Union by any kind of show of force.") It does, however, raise doubts whether Washington can, "under the pressure of circumstances, in a crisis situation, control its emotions and maintain its composure and the necessary discretion."[29]

The Soviet Americanists seemed especially disappointed in the fact that the new decision-making machinery had produced such dismal results. The decision to invade, notes Zhurkin, "was comparatively carefully prepared under conditions when Washington had a certain freedom of action and sufficient time to analyze the situation."[30] The resort to force was a calculated one, whose purpose, therefore, was considered especially sinister. The American intervention in Cambodia "demonstrated that the old tendency in U.S. 'crisis policy'—reliance on force at critical moments, either the threat of force or its actual use—continued to operate."[31] Nevertheless, according to a study published in 1975, the White House was believed to have behaved with some caution during the Cambodian crisis. When it became evident that the invasion was not going well—not only was it unsuccessful in military terms but it generated "stormy protests" throughout the world, including the United States itself—"Washington began to back down and take steps aimed at withdrawing the American armed forces." And by 29 June 1970 U.S. ground troops were removed.[32] The "organizers of the American intervention" responded realistically to the dangerous consequences of their initiatives and backed off.

The crisis in the Middle East developed rather differently. The clashes between the army of King Hussein and "Palestinian guerrillas" which began in Amman on 16 September 1970, presented Washington "with a rapidly changing situation." "The mechanism of leadership," writes Zhurkin, "worked in extreme haste" (WASAG "sat almost continuously" between September 16 and 21) and depressingly "displayed a tendency to take spasmodic and extremely dangerous decisions in a critical and complex situation."[33] Zhurkin referred to the fact that at the time the crisis was unfolding Washington moved "large units of the U.S. Navy, including several aircraft carriers, to the region of the Mediterranean Sea," brought "American airborne units in the USA and West Germany to combat readiness," and so on. The purpose of this "massive demonstration of force," he writes, was "to use the situation which had come about in Jordan to weaken the front of the Arab countries, strengthen the position of Israel and generally change the situation in the Middle East in favor of imperialism."[34]

U.S. action in Jordan was even more ominous than that taken in Cambodia. Here, notes Zhurkin, "special efforts were made toward widely advertising Washington's 'resolution' to implement direct intervention. . . . Reports concerning the movement of ships and the quick mobilization of battalions and brigades to a state of combat readiness became the property of the mass information media." This was "an obvious and typical example of 'brinkmanship.' "[35]

Zhurkin's assessment of American policy during the Jordanian civil war is both stark and ominous. The crisis, he notes, "developed spasmodically and from time to time got out of control." Furthermore, "a new and extremely dangerous tendency was exposed in the behavior of Washington officials—the ability at moments of special tension to lose their heads and to set out upon patent adventures." (The reference here is to a decision, reportedly taken on September 21, that "in certain circumstances," i.e., if the "Palestinian partisans" began to gain victory over the king's army in Jordan and pose a threat to the authority of the king, the United States planned "to land American troops in Amman and for Israel to invade north Jordan.") "Moreover," he goes on, "according to the *New York Times*, it was in principle decided to use the U.S. Sixth Fleet against the forces of the UAR *or the Soviet Union*[!] should they come to the aid of the victims of aggression."[36] The United States, it would seem, had reverted to Dulles-like "brinkmanship" against the Soviet Union itself. As a result of U.S. policy during the crisis over Jordan, peace hung dangerously in the balance. According to Zhurkin, "the crisis threatened to become the most critical confrontation since the time of the Caribbean [i.e., Cuban missile] crisis in 1962."[37]

The Nixon administration, in his view, behaved recklessly. The American leaders took "extremely risky decisions" and, in critical moments, "lost the ability to appraise the consequences of their actions soberly." Furthermore, the belief is "now disseminated among the ruling circles in Washington that by playing with power, balancing on the edge of war, artificially heating up these and other acute crises situations Washington will be able to frighten its opponents." In fact, "some people are even considering the use of carefully-advertised recklessness in order to make their opponents more cautious and more yielding." These are "absurd calculations," he concludes, which can only sharpen international crisis situations and "heighten the threat of war."[38]*

Arbatov's analysis was quite different. He interpreted U.S. actions in Cambodia and the Middle East less in terms of aggressive adventurism than as an effort by the Nixon administration to shore up America's reputation as a world power. "On the one hand," he told his colleagues at the institute,

> the administration well understands that within the country there is a growing dissatisfaction with the foreign-policy adventures, the burdensome commitments, and the participation of the United States in aggressive wars. And the government cannot but take account of this dissatisfaction. It tries to show that it is responsible to public opinion.
>
> On the other hand the administration is experiencing a noticeable nervousness that other powers, particularly those whom the United States confronts in the world arena, will notice the complicated domestic situation in America and recognize that this limits Washington's freedom of action. This nervousness, apparently, pushes some American leaders to adventuristic actions in order to prove that the United States government as before has full freedom of action and in case of need is ready for any crisis and can, as the expression goes, "go all the way."[39]

Arbatov clearly feared that U.S. "adventuristic" behavior in 1970 was a case of an overreaction by the Nixon administration to domestic political difficulties. To prove that internal dissension had not paralyzed the United States, Washington resorted to a policy of "bluff" and "brinkmanship."

---

* Zhurkin was apparently close to the mark. According to Thomas L. Hughes, a former ranking official at the State Department, President Nixon placed great premium on impressing the Soviets with American irrationality. He reportedly told a group of newsmen during the Jordanian crisis that "the other side [the USSR] should not be confident of our response. They should be kept guessing about even an *irrational* response." Hughes also notes that during the 1972 "Christmas bombing" of North Vietnam the president expounded on the advantages of appearing mad. If the world thought him crazy for resuming the bombing, Nixon told a private audience, "so much the better. The Russians and the Chinese might think they were dealing with a madman and so had better force North Vietnam into a settlement before the world was consumed in a larger war." ("Foreign Policy: Men or Measures?," *The Atlantic* 234, no. 4, October 1974, pp. 55–56.) The former president believed, it would seem, that the virtues of unpredictability—useful, undoubtedly, to his much-fabled career playing poker in the U.S. Navy—were transferable to international diplomacy.

Though avoided by Arbatov himself, a similar interpretation was given to the U.S. military alert during the Yom Kippur war in October 1973. Alluding to the rising Watergate crisis then confronting President Nixon, the venerable French communist Jacques Duclos, writing in *Pravda,* observed that:

> In capitalist circles there are people capable of launching themselves on dangerous maneuvers in the international arena, proceeding, in particular, from domestic policy considerations, as though they were prompted by an awareness of the end of the regime — an awareness which was expressed on the eve of the great French bourgeois revolution in the phrase "après nous le déluge."[40]

Articles in *Pravda,* it should be noted, never simply express the personal views of their authors. There is good reason to believe, therefore, that this interpretation of the 1973 U.S. military alert was shared by important figures in the Soviet leadership.

The "general conclusion" reached by Soviet analysts was that the Nixon administration still "basically counted on the traditional application of force."[41] This conclusion was further corroborated by U.S. policy during the December 1971 Indo-Pakistani war when, a "group of ships from the U.S. Seventh Fleet, including the aircraft carrier Enterprise, the United States' most powerful warship, was brought into the Bay of Bengal . . . as a demonstration of force against India."[42] The "primary goal" of this action, according to Zhurkin, was "to exert pressure on India" by compelling it to withdraw ships and aircraft from the Pakistani front. "Moreover, clashes with India were not ruled out" nor was "the possibility of direct armed intervention" by the United States.[43]

Though sharply critical of their behavior, Soviet analysts, it should be noted, did not present a uniformly negative picture of U.S. policy makers on this crucial question. In fact there was, at least for a time, considerable support at the institute for the view that Washington was gradually abandoning its reliance upon military force. In early 1970, for example, Arbatov pointed out that, as the Vietnam war clearly demonstrated, even "the huge military power created by the United States has its limits." This view, he suggested, was shared by Washington. (As evidence of this, Arbatov frequently quoted an article published in 1968 in which Kissinger wrote the following: "The paradox of contemporary military strength is that a gargantuan increase in power has eroded its relationship to policy. . . . In other words power no longer automatically translates into influence.")[44] Furthermore, according to two military analysts, the enormous danger of nuclear war had made U.S. policy makers considerably more cautious. The "obvious realization of the hopelessness of a universal nuclear war," a war which "would inevitably lead to devastating consequences for the United States," write Mil'shteyn and Semeyko, ". . . contributed to a reassessment of views on the use of military force as the main instrument of foreign policy."[45]

Washington, at the very least, is frequently seen to be deeply divided regarding the wisdom of its traditional policies. Time and again it is torn by "sharp debates." For example, Zhurkin notes that during the 1970 Jordanian crisis, "various tendencies" were manifested in the Nixon administration. "On the one hand, there was the old inertia of the power approach. On the other, there was a certain readiness to back off at the right time."[46] Similarly Lukin observed that the endorsement by Defense Secretary Schlesinger in the spring of 1975 of the possible use of tactical nuclear weapons was sharply criticized by "other, fairly authoritative views" in Washington which regarded such a policy as "unrealistic and risky."[47] Further, in early 1976, "serious differences of opinion" were found to exist "on one of the most important principles of American foreign policy— intervention or non-intervention in foreign military conflicts." In voting for the Tunney Amendment (which curtailed financing American military aid to Angola), the Congress was seen to have made "a decisive attempt to reject those principles [i.e., "military interventionism"] . . . which led to the shameful aggression in Vietnam."[48]

Even so critical an observer as the institute's Deputy Director Zhurkin seems to have moderated earlier harsh judgments. In a book published at the beginning of 1975, he suggested that "realistically-thinking" political leaders in the United States had in the early 1970s begun "to reevaluate the possibilities of using or threatening the use of force—primarily military force—as the major tool of U.S. foreign policy."[49] As a result of their experience in Vietnam, he argued, U.S. policy makers acquired a greater appreciation of the dangers generated by their traditional policies of military interventionism. They have gained an "increased understanding of the threat presented by such crises to the security of the United States itself; the great military, economic, political, moral and other damage caused as a result of the intervention in Vietnam; and the domestic political, social and economic difficulties." This painful experience and the "increased understanding" which it produced, he notes, has led to "essential changes in the direction of restraint and realism in the U.S. approach toward international conflicts and crises."[50]

Reflecting the considerable optimism regarding détente then apparently shared by observers at the USA Institute, Zhurkin's analysis was especially enthusiastic. Although they "developed unevenly, with zigzags and deviations," he saw "certain extremely positive changes in the American foreign policy course."[51] As practical evidence of these developments, he pointed to the withdrawal of American troops from Vietnam, the reduction in the size of America's armed forces—by one million men, the four-power agreements on Berlin (1971), and the signing of "documents of universal significance" at the Brezhnev-Nixon summit conferences (1972–74).[52]

Trofimenko was equally impressed. In an article published in February 1975, he took particular note of the Soviet-American agreement on the prevention of nuclear war (1973). This accord was designed not only to exclude the possible outbreak of nuclear war between the Soviet Union and the United States, but sought to prevent local conflicts from escalating into nuclear wars. In signing this agreement, writes Trofimenko, the United States took a major step in the direction of "military détente." Back in the 1960s, he writes, Washington realized the dangerous nature of nuclear weapons and sought to avoid conflicts which might result in a direct confrontation with the Soviet Union. But at the same time it was believed that "mutual deterrence" on the nuclear level "allowed the United States to be 'bolder' and 'freer' to use conventional armed forces, which prompted it to unleash war against the Vietnam people."[53]

The understanding reached in the 1973 summit agreement, asserts Trofimenko, "testified to an extremely fundamental change of views [*svidetel'stvovala o ves'ma sushchestvennom izmenenii vzglyadov*] on the part of the American political and military leaders." This agreement, in which both sides pledged to refrain from the threat or use of force under any circumstances which might endanger international peace and security, "acknowledged the existence of a close tie between any conflict whatever and nuclear conflict." In so doing the American leaders are seen to have retreated from their previous views. That is to say, they "acknowledge the untenability of the theory that some kind of visible 'watershed' exists between conflict in general and nuclear conflict." Trofimenko argues that U.S. policy makers

> have in fact come to recognize that the most effective means of preventing nuclear war is not the artificial construction and fixing of one or another set of "thresholds" of military escalation, but the renunciation of the use and threats of force in any form. It was this change in attitude which made it possible to conclude the Soviet-American agreement on the prevention of nuclear war.[54]

Although most generous in their appreciation of the Nixon administration on this question, Soviet analysts have recently shifted back to a more negative appraisal. The United States, it is now generally believed, "has not fully renounced . . . the use of force for the achievement of this or that political aim. The old dogmas largely survive."[55] Throughout 1976 Soviet writers expressed growing doubts and reservations about the American leadership. In April Arbatov warned against Washington's traditional "inclination to see military power as the way to solve all problems." As for the cautionary effect of the Vietnam experience, the lesson had apparently not been learned. "The setbacks in U.S. foreign policy," he wrote, "particularly in Southeast Asia, have caused obvious relapses into thinking in cold war categories."[56]

By late 1976 Trofimenko retreated from his earlier optimistic assessment. Despite its positive diplomatic posture, the Nixon administration had pursued an ambiguous policy. Though the United States government had signed agreements accepting the principles of peaceful coexistence, these were "narrowly interpreted" to signify the obligation to show only "a certain restraint" in world affairs. In fact, argued Trofimenko, the United States "demonstrated restraint only where it must, i.e., in those situations where, for objective reasons, it was already impossible not to show it (for example, in Indochina)." He concluded that "despite the emergence of certain elements of realism," American foreign policy still has "far from rid itself of the burden of past unrealistic schemes based on military strength and hegemonistic illusions."[57]

These statements by leading Soviet Amerikanisty reflect their considerable disenchantment with the course of détente after President Nixon's resignation in August 1974. Not only had Defense Secretary Schlesinger been taking a forceful stand on matters of defense policy—his support of the possible use of tactical nuclear weapons was considered a direct violation of the spirit of détente—but in May 1975, in the *Mayaguez* affair, the United States again used its military forces in Southeast Asia (to rescue American merchant seamen captured by Cambodia). Further, in 1976, as a result largely of the election campaign, progress in Soviet-American relations ground to a halt. Negotiations on strategic arms limitations made no advance. In response to the entrance of the conservative figure of Ronald Reagan in the race for the Republican nomination, President Ford even abandoned the term "détente," preferring the more belligerent formulation "peace through strength."

Washington's "reassessment" of its policy regarding the use of force was, apparently, a casualty of Watergate. Or so it must have seemed to Moscow. In any event, "reliance on force," in the view of leading Americanists, remains a major characteristic of U.S. policy makers. As Zhurkin once told an Italian journalist, "let us not forget that in 1972 the port of Haiphong was mined, . . . that not long prior to the [1973] Paris agreements on Vietnam there were massive American bombing raids on Hanoi and that the Yom Kippur War broke out not long after that." In the judgment of the deputy director of the USA Institute, "anyone who follows American policy . . . knows that the Washington rulers . . . precede every diplomatic or political action with a threat or, if you prefer, by strong pressure. That is as a general rule."[58]

Thus, whether to intimidate adversaries, blackmail others into accepting American initiatives, or compensate for internal weakness, the Washington leadership is believed to place a premium on the "value of non-predictability" and to have easy resort to "unexpected," "convulsive," "risky," "adventuristic" military actions. As Zhurkin remarked, "We very well know with whom we have to deal. Détente is no picnic."[59]

The New Realism

Side by side with this dark assessment, recent American political leaders have generally received high marks for what is viewed as their "realistic," "sober," "sensible," "constructive" approach to U.S. foreign policy. While their policies were seen more in terms of necessity than virtue, Soviet Americanists had high personal regard for former President Nixon and especially for Secretary Kissinger.

Despite the initial suspicion with which they viewed his election in 1968, Richard Nixon's anti-Soviet past was not without its bright side. Thus in a November 1970 symposium Arbatov told his colleagues at the USA Institute about the argument heard in the United States which suggests that

> the fact that the people now in power enjoy a solid reputation as conservatives, figures of rigidly anti-communist convictions, has its positive aspects since people of that sort do not fear criticism from the right. They are free of that "inferiority complex" that has compelled some liberals to act in such a way as to demonstrate that they are "more Catholic than the Pope." In that case, the present leaders can go much further in the policy of the relaxation and normalization of the international situation.

Such suggestions, in Arbatov's judgment, contained a "certain logic, especially considering the 'service record' of certain of the more liberal predecessors of the present leaders of the United States."[60] Thus not only were "liberals" (presumably Democrats) seen to be frivolous and fainthearted, they were, paradoxically, always under suspicion of being "soft on communism." A Republican administration, especially one with impeccable anti-communist credentials, would be immune from charges of "selling out." His conservative flank protected, Nixon could, said Arbatov, "go much further" in negotiations with the Soviet Union.*

---

* A similar line of reasoning was applied by Berezhkov to the 1976 elections. As he told an Italian audience in late 1975, "The situation is complicated in the United States right now because of the elections next year and the tendency to win votes by adopting anti-communist stances. Nixon showed himself to be the most suitable person for bringing about a new phase in the relations between the [superpowers] because he knew no one could ever have accused him of being weak." Without a secure reputation as hard-line conservative, Berezhkov suggested, President Ford was much more vulnerable to internal pressure. As a result, he correctly forsaw, Soviet-American relations might well become more difficult. FBIS, 18 December 1975, p. B3.

Another factor attracting the attention of Soviet analysts was the new administration's interest in "new methods of foreign-policy management." Given the political complexion of the Nixon leadership, this came as something of a surprise. While Henry Kissinger "has himself always shown considerable interest in new methods of analyzing international situations" and recruited Charles Hermann, a specialist on simulation from Princeton University, to serve on his staff, the interest of the president in such matters was unexpected. According to Vitaly Zhurkin, a "serious attempt" to create an efficiently functioning decision-making system was being made "paradoxically . . . precisely under Nixon, a figure of conservative persuasion from whom it would seem that one could not expect special interest in scientific 'innovation' in the sphere of administration, analysis and so forth."[61] While "liberals" are frivolous, conservatives are conservative.

In any event the new NSC system, WASAG, political gaming (using during the Cambodian crisis) and other management reforms introduced by the new administration were seen to be efforts to systematize the process of decision making, i. e., to filter out irrelevant (bureaucratic) influences, and rationalize the method of presenting alternatives to the president for decision. Given the grave importance of the choices he must make, this well-ordered approach to the conduct of U. S. foreign policy was a potential, if somewhat surprising virtue of the new Washington leadership.[62]

The real source of interest, however, was less the organizational changes introduced by the Nixon administration than the modifications it was seen to have made in U. S. foreign policy. Here, clearly, the American policy makers received very high marks indeed. As Trofimenko noted, the adoption of the policy of détente by the United States "required a quite serious reexamination of the basic principles of its foreign policy and a very radical change in its practices."[63] It is this "radical," even "drastic" change in U. S. foreign-policy behavior which won the administration such great respect.

The contributions of the Nixon administration are said to be both practical and conceptual. Practically, the summit conferences—the personal meetings between the leaders of the Soviet Union and the United States—are considered to be of "exceptional importance."

During the cold war period, notes Trofimenko, the Soviet Union and the United States communicated with or "signalled" to each other "primarily by threats—direct or indirect." Despite the availability of extensive opportunities to do otherwise, "the two sides actually conducted their dialogue by means of various indirect 'signals'— ostentatious measures and countermeasures, actions and gestures in international forums—but in no way by direct contact." With the inauguration of the summit conferences, which began when President Nixon visited Moscow in May 1972, and especially as these meetings became yearly events, "the development of systematic contact at the highest diplomatic level" allowed for "frank and direct exchange of opinions." Such exchanges do not, of course, necessarily lead to elimination of differences. However, writes Trofimenko, they are a considerable improvement over the former system of "signalling." A frank discussion, he writes, is always useful "because it helps to get a better understanding of the intentions and interests of the other side and therefore provides an opportunity for . . . seeking solutions based on taking the interests of both sides into account."[64] For reasons to be explained shortly, the concern of the Nixon White House to learn about the intentions and interests of the Soviet Union and "to take them into account" is considered a marked improvement over the policies and attitudes of preceding administrations.

American willingness to negotiate regularly with the Soviet Union is based, in the view of Soviet analysts, on a prior modification of the American self-image. In the 1940s, Washington was seen to be inspired by a boundless faith in U.S. military and economic, hence political, supremacy, a cocky self-assurance which led it to pursue its cold war "positions-of-strength policy." The "Acheson concept of talks from a position of strength," writes Trofimenko (quoting historian Norman Graebner) "meant in practice no talks at all. . . . Diplomatic confrontations, as the secretary of state repeatedly said, should be used not for talks but to record Soviet diplomatic defeats. So long as Western superiority was not sufficient to ensure precisely such a result, Acheson preferred that the West avoid settlement."[65] Haughty with its own sense of omnipotence, the cold war "positions-of-strength" policy led to diplomatic bankruptcy.

The new American leadership, by contrast, took a modest and

restrained view of its own capabilities. Writing in 1972 one Soviet theorist suggested that Henry Kissinger is "among those American strategists to whom a sane view on certain problems is not alien. Evaluating the role and place of the United States in the contemporary world," he writes, Kissinger has noted its "limited capabilities."[66] Americans now recognized, as Kissinger openly admitted, that "we cannot do everything and achieve everything merely by the intensification of our own efforts."[67] In a speech to State Department employees, notes Chetverikov, Kissinger observed that "from the U.S. viewpoint, international relations are going through 'a critical transitional period.' This is expressed, above all, in the radical change in the world position of the United States. 'We no longer have,' he said, 'either an insuperable safety margin nor over-whelming predominance in resources.' "[68] The change in America's self-image was best symbolized, according to Svyatov, by comparing the statements of two U.S. presidents—made a decade apart:

> "Let every nation know, whether it wishes us well or ill, that we shall pay any price, bear any burden, meet any hardship, support any friend, oppose any foe, to assure the survival and success of freedom." (John Kennedy, 1961)
>
> "America cannot—and will not—conceive *all* the plans, design *all* the programs, execute *all* the decisions, and undertake *all* the defense of the free nations of the world." (Richard Nixon, 1970)[69]

Such declarations, in the Soviet view, implied a major change in official American thinking.

> The officially accepted slogan of "supremacy" in world affairs by means of achieving "superiority" in all of the means which make up the arsenal of foreign political and foreign economic coercion has been replaced by the expression "an important role in world affairs"; this has been a substantial departure from the view which was dominant during the first two postwar decades.[70]

This "substantial departure" from traditional "supremicist" views was the product of this country's recent political experiences. "Events," suggests Trofimenko, "especially the fiasco in Vietnam . . . made America recognize that it played a more humble role."[71] American analysts were forced to the conclusion, writes Kokoshin, that the United States "must take into greater consideration not only its own possibilities and desires but also the state of world affairs."[72] They were also led to understand "the inevitability and necessity of a dialogue with 'potential opponents,'" i.e., the USSR and China.[73]

Given a less inflated self-image, American policy makers are no longer so disdainful of diplomatic negotiations with the Soviet Union. Only with the acceptance of this more modest role, it is argued, could the American leaders recognize, as they did at the May 1972 summit, that the security of both the United States and the Soviet Union must be based on the principle of equality.[74] Previous assumptions regarding "supremacy" would not have permitted Washington policy makers to consider the interests of anyone save themselves. As significant, however, has been their willingness to recognize the need for negotiations, particularly in the sphere of strategic weaponry. Here, especially, what has proved to be of such great importance is the intellectual competence of the U.S. leadership. In the view of leading institute analysts, the Republican administration had a sound conceptual grasp of the strategic relationship between the Soviet Union and the United States. Writing in 1972, for example, Trofimenko saluted the American understanding of deterrence. "It should be said," he writes, "that in conditions of nuclear-missile standoff between the two great powers" not only are the military arsenals and strategies of each side important but "ever-increasing significance" is attached to the question of "what each side thinks of the capabilities and intentions of the other side. Thus," he continues, "H. Kissinger stressed that what a potential opponent believes about the intentions of the other side 'is substantially more important than the objective truth. Deterrence takes place above all in people's minds.'"[75]

This understanding, suggests Trofimenko, is the only basis for preserving the strategic stability between the Soviet Union and the United States. Each side must be convinced "that the other side does not intend to carry out a preventive nuclear attack against it." He goes on:

> This conviction will be strongest when it is based on a knowledge that the other side does not possess the physical capability of delivering a first (disarming) strike. In a situation of "mutual deterrence," such knowledge becomes a real deterrent force only when their opponent holds the same

views on this matter as they do, that is, when each of the sides believes that the other side will in all cases preserve its capability, will and readiness to deliver a crushing response in case a nuclear missile attack is undertaken against it.[76]

It is in terms of the essentially "psychological framework of deterrence," writes Trofimenko, that the concept of "sufficiency" introduced by the United States assumes significance. Thus, he notes, "President Nixon emphasized that one of the particular criteria of 'sufficiency' was the necessity of a deployment of U.S. strategic forces which the Soviet Union could not view as a provocation. 'Sufficiency,' Nixon stated, 'also signifies that the number, specifications, deployment of our forces will not provide the Soviet Union with grounds for interpreting them as an intention to threaten the USSR with attack in order to disarm it.'"[77] Washington, in his view, clearly knows what it is doing.

Furthermore, Trofimenko goes on, the United States understands that deterrence "is to some extent a closed circle. Any attempt unilaterally to change these established limits can only lead to a new turn in the spiral of the arms race . . . and create an atmosphere of increased nervousness in which the world is moved closer to the edge of global thermonuclear conflict." The White House, in the view of Soviet observers, is aware of the destabilizing effects of a continuing escalation of the arms race. For this reason, Kissinger has opposed those in the United States demanding "preservation of American nuclear superiority." In responding to their arguments, writes Trofimenko, the secretary of state takes the position that

the constant expansion of strategic weapons does not lead to an additional level of security. It only leads to a balance at higher levels of complexity and risk and, moreover, at the cost of colossal expenditures; this would engender an atmosphere of hostility and suspiciousness which would only make the emergence of political conflict more likely and would in time dispel the aspiration to create a calmer and more secure atmosphere in the world.[78]

The American leadership clearly recognizes, then, that effort to implement qualitative weapons improvements "destabilizes the existing balance to a particularly dangerous degree by creating a lack of confidence in the intentions of the other." This awareness, writes Trofimenko, was the basis of the SALT agreements.

The American leadership's understanding of this circumstance was reflected in the fact that it moved to conclude agreements with the Soviet Union to limit offensive and defensive weapons systems. The establishment of certain limits on the corresponding systems is very important on the level of "removing" the fears, whether real or illusory, of each side that the other side is nurturing the idea of a preventive "counterforce" strike.

Further testimony regarding the understanding by the ruling circles of the United States of the dangers involved in a nuclear "confrontation," including the psychological problem of incorrectly interpreting the intentions of one's opponent, is seen in the signing of the American-Soviet agreement on measures to reduce the dangers of nuclear war.[79]

For Trofimenko, then, Washington's "understanding" of the psychological dynamics of the arms race and, more broadly, of the need to take concrete measures to control international conflicts, prevent nuclear war and regularize and stabilize Soviet-American relations has been crucially important to the summit agreements signed since 1972.

The lack of movement in Soviet-American relations during the Ford presidency, as we have already seen, led to considerable disillusionment in Moscow. The stark contrast between the much-acclaimed achievements of 1972–74, on the one hand, and the stalemate and recriminations of 1975–76, especially regarding the renunciation of the trade agreement, on the other, could not but cast a pall on earlier enthusiasms.

Nowhere, perhaps, was Soviet disenchantment more apparent than in Trofimenko's commentary on the previously much-heralded achievements of the Nixon administration. He openly criticized Nixon for attempting to create what was, in effect, an "imperial presidency," an accusation till then assiduously ignored by Soviet Americanists. Writing in late 1976, Trofimenko charged that Nixon's organizational reforms were designed not, as had been claimed, to improve governmental efficiency; rather, they were "a maneuver to concentrate state power in the White House." As for the reorganization of the NSC under Henry Kissinger, this reform "led in point of fact to the creation of a barrier, isolating the president and his assistant for national security affairs from outside influences."[80] Despite the new procedures, concludes Trofimenko, the American foreign-policy apparatus produced "obviously ill-considered" programs. The results have been so abysmal, he writes, that "for many theorists and political leaders in the United States"—and the Soviet Union?—"even the old method of making decisions on the basis of 'bureaucratic compromises' within the ruling elite came to be seen as a blessing in comparison with the impulsive reactions of the 'reformed' foreign-policy mechanism."[81] Such "impulsive" actions as the U.S. military alert during the Yom Kippur War, the *Mayaguez* affair, and the administration's endorsement of military assistance to Angola apparently convinced Trofimenko that the new foreign-policy mechanism was, from the Soviet point of view, no improvement over those used by previous administrations.

While obviously disappointed—the intensity of their criticism may reflect the measure of their own earlier ardor—Soviet analysts continue to have high regard for Washington's "new realism." We have moved, in their eyes, a long way from the cold war. In April 1976, though concerned about the trend in Soviet-American relations, Arbatov, continues to place "a high value on the positive changes that, despite difficulties, have been achieved . . . in recent years" and sees the future as having "good prospects."[82]

The main elements of the "new realism" which still attract attention—and are the basis of the "good prospects"—relate to Washington's attitude towards the main political and psychological issues of the Soviet-American strategic relationship. Despite their recent uneasiness, the Americanists hold to the view that Washington still recognizes the urgent need to avoid nuclear war. Acceptance of peaceful coexistence in relations between the two nuclear powers, the USSR and the United States, according to a symposium at the USA Institute, is "the 'categorical imperative' of American foreign policy." Symposium participants generally agreed that "the avoidance of nuclear war will remain the foreign-policy goal of the ruling groups in the United States, regardless of changes in the present administration, during the whole period that this kind of warfare presents a danger."[83] Soviet analysts do note, however, that Americans differ as to "the ways and means of achieving this goal." While most agreed that "the present approach of the Washington administration" sought to achieve this objective by means of "normalizing relations" with the USSR, especially by freezing the arms race, others, especially those connected with the "military-industrial complex," sought to improve the quality of American strategic weaponry.[84] Thus, even though committed to a laudable goal, the U.S. leadership may shift its strategic orientation and adopt programs menacing to Soviet interests. Washington's policies therefore bear close and continual scrutiny.

A second aspect of the "new realism" which apparently still retains its vitality is the continued acceptance by the White House of the principle of military equality with the USSR. An essential feature of its policy of moving from "confrontation to a dialogue with 'potential adversaries,'" wrote Trofimenko, was the Nixon administration's understanding of "the impossibility of achieving a position of strategic military superiority over the USSR" and, in this connection, its willingness—"far greater than ever before shown"—to conduct "equitable negotiations" with the Soviet Union regarding the limitation of weapons, especially strategic ones.[85] Washington's "realism," on this question, he points out, was far from certain. Faced with a situation of nuclear balance, the Republican administration in 1969 confronted the question of which path to choose:

> to undertake new attempts to get ahead of the USSR or to stabilize the existing nuclear parity by means of mutually beneficial agreements . . . ? For the first time in the whole postwar period, the United States opted for the variant of equitable settlement and concluded the well-known agreements on strategic arms limitation which laid the cornerstone in the foundation of the normalization of Soviet-American relations, of détente.[86]

From the Soviet standpoint, American acceptance of the principle of "military parity" is crucial to their demand for "political parity." or equality. Only under conditions of equality are negotiations conceivable.

Here, too, Soviet analysts have some doubts. Trofimenko noted, for example, that "under pressure of right-wing forces and, perhaps, also under the influence of some kind of moods within the [Ford] administration, itself," views again were found which spoke of "the possibility of achieving superiority over the USSR."[87] Though in principle still committed to the principles of military parity and equal security, official Washington is seen to be under considerable pressure

116

to adopt a more assertive posture. The ability of "sober-minded circles" to persist in support of such realistic policies and stave off Pentagon pressure is in question. The power struggle for the soul of Washington must be carefully monitored.

Attitudes Toward the Soviet Union

Of the many indicators of Washington's "new realism," perhaps none is of greater psychological importance as far as Soviet analysts are concerned than the "sober" attitude recent U.S. policy makers have taken towards the Soviet Union. For a variety of historical and cultural reasons,[88] Soviet officials—and ordinary citizens as well—are highly sensitive to outside criticism. They are at the same time extraordinarily responsive to those, especially from the West, who recognize their country's historical role and achievements. FDR is remembered as much for having granted the Soviet Union diplomatic recognition in 1933, which several preceding administrations had refused, as for his leading role as one of the wartime Big Three. The concern by the Nixon administration to turn "from confrontation to negotiation," its "businesslike" policy towards the USSR, explains why the former president is treated with considerably greater regard in the Soviet Union than in the United States.

One of the chief "motive forces" of the cold war, it is argued in Moscow, is the profound animosity borne by the West toward the USSR. Many in the United States, Arbatov notes, have long regarded the socialist regime in the Soviet Union as "a kind of illegitimate child of history . . . a 'historical misunderstanding' which has to be ended in one way or another as quickly as possible." It was precisely this attitude which inspired the military intervention in Russia after World War I which sought to crush the Bolshevik revolution, "or, in Winston Churchill's words, 'to strangle the baby in the cradle.'" This also explains, he writes, why the United States delayed recognition of the Soviet Union for sixteen years—hoping thereby "that it would disappear from the face of the earth or maintaining the illusion that we really did not exist."[89]

Despite the profound resentment of such hostile behavior, some analysts demonstrate a curious understanding of the Western response

117

to the new Soviet regime. As Ivanyan told his colleagues at an institute symposium, the Bolshevik revolution "shook the foundations of international capitalism . . . [and] caused anxiety and confusion in financial and monopoly circles. . . . The October Revolution 'has started a fire in all of Europe and America. . . . They (the capitalists) have one thought: to prevent the sparks from our fire from falling on their roofs,' wrote V. I. Lenin."[90] Would not the bourgeois leaders have "violated their nature," not to speak of their self-interests, if they had not at least tried to put out the fire?

The emotions and fears born of this hostility, it is argued, lay at the heart of American postwar policy. Despite its leading role during the Second World War, the USSR's right to exist was still not accepted as legitimate and its policies were seen to menace the basic interests of the United States. As Davydov writes, American strategists in the 1940s

> proceeded from the notion . . . that the presence of the socialist camp, to say nothing of its expansion, was a direct threat to the very existence of the United States. As a result, official Washington declared that the sphere of American "national security" stretched to the borders of the socialist countries, and sometimes even further.[91]

This, it is believed, was the rationale for the American policy of "containment."

U.S. irreconcilability towards the Soviet Union, justified by an increasingly venomous anti-communist ideology, led to the creation of NATO, SEATO, and other military alliances. American hostility gave considerable impetus to the arms race which, as we have seen, further reinforced the aggressive cold war impulses of the American leadership. To secure ever greater funds for the protection of American "security interests," the military constantly harped on the danger of an external Soviet threat. The anti-communist animus was deep and abiding. Thus, writes Arbatov:

> Practically right up until the end of the sixties, all American policies vis-à-vis the socialist countries were regarded primarily as policies intended to influence their internal affairs. Both "containment" and "liberation" and even "bridge-building" were in the final analysis intended either to crush these countries by force or to promote the "internal transformation" of the socialist countries, their "softening up" and "erosion," that is, they constituted a policy aimed at interfering in their internal affairs.[92]

118

Central to the American cold war mentality, according to the institute director, was the "desire to assess any political step solely from the angle of how to harm the other side."[93] Thus the American aspiration for nuclear supremacy in the 1950s is explained as designed, in part, " 'to exhaust' the Soviet Union economically in the course of a new round in the nuclear-missile arms race."[94] The essence of the American approach to foreign policy during the cold war is set forth by Trofimenko. U.S. national interests at this time, he writes, were defined "by the 'obverse' method, that is, by counterposing them to the 'national interests' of the other side." This was the equivalent, he notes, of a "zero-sum" game. "On the basis of this kind of psychology, anything that was bad for one's opponent was always good for oneself, and vice versa."[95]

This approach, which by its very nature perpetuated confrontation and made even normal relations extremely difficult, began to fade in the late 1960s. The events of the past several years, wrote Arbatov in 1973, had increasingly revealed the "bankruptcy" of Washington's "primitive anti-communist stereotypes." Those who had built their policy on the crude notion that every misfortune America encountered was rooted in communism, he argued, found it increasingly difficult to attribute all changes in the world to a "communist conspiracy." The various difficulties confronting the United States— decline in American influence in the Third World, tension in relations with Western Europe and Japan, the growing bitterness of the competitive struggle for world markets—these and other problems could not be ascribed to the Soviet Union. "Even the most thick-witted representatives of U.S. imperialist circles could no longer see the 'hand of Moscow' in these dangers and threats or seek an answer to them in the build-up of armed forces and military adventures."[96]

Another factor undermining traditional anti-communist attitudes in Washington was the realization that the cold war had a deleterious effect on the United States itself. It became apparent to many that, as noted earlier, large-scale military spending associated with modern strategic weaponry, and especially the war in Vietnam, generated enormous pressure on the economy—causing serious inflation, declining productivity and profits—and exacerbated complex social and political problems within the United States. The profound internal crisis of the past several years, Arbatov argued, shook the messianic conviction in the infallibility of the American way of life. Further, it "taught the U.S. ruling class to realize that, in basing its policy wholly on a platform of bellicose anti-communism, the American bourgeoisie not only does not protect itself . . . but also can do substantial damage to its own class interests."[97]

Most important, perhaps, was the realization that the basic security interests of the United States were not being well protected by traditional cold war practices. Earlier, wrote Davydov, with the very existence of the USSR and its allies seen to present "a direct threat to the security of the United States, it followed that the threat could be finally removed only by liquidating them."[98] Changes in the nuclear arms balance, however, forced a shift in American thinking. With the development of Soviet strategic nuclear parity, he argues, the United States was confronted "for the first time in its history" with "a real threat of a retaliatory (and annihilating) military blow. As a result of the awareness of this new reality, the ideologists of the ruling classes concluded that the most important 'national interest' of the United States is the problem of 'surviving.' "[99] Long defined exclusively in terms of security from the Soviet Union, American national interests had to be reassessed. The main problem for Washington was now one of survival in an era of nuclear balance. This new awareness, concluded Davydov, "placed in doubt the correctness of a foreign-policy course aimed primarily at confrontation with the states of the socialist community."[100]

Under the pressure of "life itself," therefore, the doctrines and policies of the past began to lose their meaning. With the decline of "rabid anti-communism" in the American worldview, the "main objective" of postwar U.S. foreign policy—to oppose, at least to "contain," and ultimately to "crush" the Soviet Union once and for all—lost much of its former significance. Washington therefore abandoned its "black-white" view of the world. The United States, writes Arbatov, "no longer can base its foreign-policy assumptions on the premise that it has one and only one enemy in the shape of the USSR . . . and that any harm inflicted on that enemy automatically signifies an equivalent profit for the United States."[101] In brief, the

American policy makers no longer see the world in "zero-sum terms." This type of thinking—which sought to inflict the greatest possible damage on the Soviet Union—has, according to Trofimenko, been "finally overcome."[102]*

The decline in American anti-communism—what amounts to a secularization of U.S. foreign policy—was essential in the Soviet view to the recent détente in U.S.-USSR relations. Before serious negotiations could occur, before both sides could attempt to define spheres of cooperation in areas of mutual concern (especially in the prevention of nuclear conflict and controlling the strategic arms race), the United States had to acknowledge the legitimacy of Soviet diplomatic interests, a posture which it was believed previous administrations had refused to adopt. The summit agreements themselves demonstrated how far the U.S. leaders had come. For example, in the 1972 accord on the "Basic Principles of Mutual Relations" both sides agreed that "in the nuclear age, there is no alternative to conducting their mutual relations on the basis of peaceful coexistence." The development of "normal relations," they concurred, was to be "based on the principles of sovereignty, equality, noninterference in internal affairs and mutual advantage." Little wonder that Arbatov considers this agreement as having "the highest degree of significance." The Soviet Union is clearly no longer the "illegitimate child of history," at least not as far as the United States is concerned. Quite a change, he notes, from the period two decades ago "when the United States proclaimed as its official foreign-policy platform the doctrines of 'liberation' and the 'rollback' of communism, which in point of fact were the direct antipodes of the principle of the peaceful coexistence of states."[103]

---

* Soviet Americanists have explicitly disavowed the "zero-sum" approach to world politics. According to a member of the editorial board of SShA, this approach is "useless." He writes (in a lead article):

> Incidentally, the bookkeeping approach of profits and losses in which a plus in one column necessarily signifies a minus in the other is useless in international affairs. In other words . . . especially regarding issues of war and peace, a gain for one side does not necessarily imply a loss for the other. Here it frequently happens that either all sides win or all lose. (Georgiev, "Razryadka," p. 9.)

This rejection of the "bookkeeping approach" in favor of one which recognizes the existence of common interests, "especially regarding issues of war and peace," stands in marked contrast to earlier, more belligerent views. Soviet anti-Americanism, too, has faded to some degree.

In this and subsequent summit agreements the "special responsibility" of the Soviet Union (along with the United States) for preserving world peace, controlling international tension, and especially for lessening the danger of nuclear conflict, is emphasized. Arms limitation agreements, it is acknowledged, must be based on "the principle of equal security." Clearly, at least in principle, U.S. policy makers are seen as having recognized "once and for all, the viability, full equality and invincibility of the socialist system. . . . This is a very great gain for socialism."[104]

The political leadership of the United States has, therefore, clearly abandoned the "bellicose anti-communism" of the Acheson–Dulles era. Others, especially President Kennedy, were seen to be moving away from this tradition. In his third year in office, writes Anatoly Gromyko, Kennedy had come to recognize "the utter futility of his efforts to base American foreign policy exclusively upon 'cold war' dogmas. . . . He had begun to understand more clearly the need for peaceful coexistence. . . . He thus attempted to introduce a positive element into American foreign policy," attempts reflected in his American University speech and the U.S. signature on the Partial-Test Ban Treaty of 1963.[105]

It was not, however, until the presidency of Richard Nixon that the United States moved to a generally positive approach to relations with the Soviet Union. Despite his anti-Soviet, anti-communist past, Nixon was a "realist" who proved ready to "adapt" to changing conditions, domestic and international. He was furthermore assisted by Henry Kissinger, who even in the 1950s believed that bilateral talks between the two countries, "should be conducted with regard to Soviet interests," that the solution of the problem of limiting the arms race "depends precisely" on the USSR and the United States, and that "these two countries have a common interest" in avoiding nuclear war.[106] And, though recently criticized, Kissinger is still considered an opponent of "primitive anti-communism." While some are again seeking to blame Moscow for recent American failures (Vietnam, Angola, etc.), according to Yur'yev, Kissinger shuns this approach. "Many political and governmental figures in the West," he writes, "realize the absurdity of attempts to blame their own failures on the 'intrigues' of Soviet diplomats. For example, H. Kissinger pointed out

122

the following . . . in December 1975: 'Many of our failures and difficulties are in no way the result of détente or Soviet policy.'"[107]

The Nixon administration was, indeed, given high marks for its "sober" attitude towards the Soviet Union. The very essence of its "realism" consisted in its willingness to accept the USSR on its own terms, to treat Moscow as an equal, and to recognize the legitimacy of Soviet interests. Something more was perhaps involved. Soviet analysts seemed particularly attentive to Washington's acceptance of their country's special role in world affairs. Thus, V. P. Lukin, leading Sinologist at the institute, reported with no little pride that U.S. policy makers placed prime importance on "constructive Soviet-American relations" as the main precondition for dealing with other major world problems. "This makes them fully recognize," he argues, "the priority of Soviet-American relations over American-Chinese relations."[108] Washington's "recognition" of the "priority" of its relations with Moscow—especially over those with Peking—seems to have confirmed the long-standing Soviet claim to primacy in world affairs. The USSR, at least in Soviet eyes, has achieved special, not just equal, status.

In light of its "constructive and businesslike approach" to the Soviet Union, the Nixon administration won recognition, in Arbatov's phrase, as an "acceptable partner."[109] The perspicacity and judiciousness of its leadership was—and continues to be—applauded. Thus, in an article in the main theoretical journal of the Soviet Communist Party, *IMEMO* Director Nikolai Inozemtsev gives "due credit . . . to a number of eminent state leaders of the capitalist world" who have recognized the dangers of "continuing the cold war and the harsh confrontation with the socialist countries" and "agreed to definite compromises" with them "in the interests of maintaining peace."[110] For Soviet spokesmen this is clearly the cardinal issue. Whatever their specific attitude to particular issues, the "realism" of American policy makers, that is to say their willingness to accept the "legitimacy," "viability" and "full equality" of the USSR, is an absolute prerequisite to "normal" relations.

Given their acute sensitivity on this issue, the sharp reaction of the Soviet leaders to the Carter administration's human-rights campaign in the winter and spring of 1977 should not have been too surprising. The president's open support for Soviet political dissidents (including a personal letter to Andrei Sakharov) represented a direct challenge to the Soviet self-image. Despite White House disclaimers, the involvement of the United States government in Soviet internal politics was seen by the Kremlin leaders to be an intrusion on their domestic sovereignty. The president's initiative was also demeaning to their claim to equality. While such "meddling" might be appropriate to relations with a small power—as the Kremlin, say, attaches political conditions to its relations with Finland—the Soviet Union is not Finland! The basic attitude of the Carter White House to the USSR—whether it "relapses into thinking in cold war categories" or, more precisely, whether Soviet analysts perceive it to be doing so—will have a major impact on Moscow's image of the United States as an "acceptable partner."

5

POLICY EXPECTATIONS
AND IMPLICATIONS

What do Georgi Arbatov and his colleagues anticipate from the United States in the years ahead? Will détente prove durable? Will "normalization" of Soviet-American relations survive the departure of Richard Nixon and Henry Kissinger, the American policy makers most responsible for its inception? Will the Democratic administration of Jimmy Carter prove less "moderate" and "realistic" than its Republican predecessors? What of the longer term? Will "caution" and "restraint" endure if the balance of military power were to shift significantly back in the direction of American superiority? Will traditional "cold war myths and dogmas" remain durable and in time come to challenge the more "realistic" attitudes which have emerged in Washington? Will détente itself prove to be a self-limiting process?

Soviet judgements on these and other questions bearing on the future of America hinge on an analysis of both internal and external factors. As we are repeatedly told, U.S. behavior in the world is directly influenced by the changing international situation. Thus the "realism" to be found among current Washington policy makers is explained largely in terms of their response to an increasingly unfavorable international environment, one in which their major adversary has achieved nuclear parity with the United States. American policy in Vietnam, to take a recent case, was directly affected by Soviet strategic power. The American leaders were fully aware, writes Trofimenko, that uncontrolled military escalation could lead to a general war, which might even result in a nuclear confrontation. "It was precisely for this reason and not for any other that Washington exerted the harshest political control over the operations of the U.S. armed forces in Vietnam." Given their need to act "within the framework of what was 'permitted,'" he concludes, the American forces could not achieve military success.[1]

It is beyond the scope of this analysis to deal directly with the issue of external constraints. Our concern is with Soviet assessments of the impact of domestic factors—the "internal struggle" (economic, political, bureaucratic) for influence over official policy—on American behavior in the years ahead. Though our focus is essentially domestic, we do share Arbatov's view that "the intense political struggle in the United States" is "developing under the influence of both internal and external factors."[2] We shall return to this point shortly.

Two Tendencies—The Dialectics of American Politics

Soviet Americanists approach their analysis of this internal political struggle in terms of a theory whose antecedents go back to Lenin. As they frequently point out, Lenin saw the political leadership of Western countries as divided into "two tendencies," those inclined to intervene militarily against Soviet Russia and those holding pacifist views. Soviet diplomacy, he argued, should take this situation into account. As he told a delegation of Soviet officials in 1922:

> It is by no means a matter of indifference to us whether we are dealing with those representatives of the bourgeois camp who gravitate toward a military solution of the problem or with those representatives of the bourgeois camp who gravitate toward pacifism, be it of the shoddiest kind and, from the communist point of view, unable to withstand the slightest criticism.

While in a purely theoretical sense the differences between these groups are "abstract" and insignificant, Lenin argued, from the viewpoint of "practical action," they are "terribly, terribly important."[3]

What Lenin was saying, in effect, was that there were two trends in Western politics in terms of their attitude towards the Soviet regime—one favorably inclined, one not. There were, after all, some in the United States—like Senators La Follette and Borah—who had

126

opposed the U.S. intervention against Soviet Russia. Should such a moderate group come to power, this might be, as Lenin said, "terribly, terribly important."

Since the mid-1950s, Soviet scholars and officials have made this perspective the core of their analysis of Western politics. Departing from the Stalinist approach, which saw the men in power in the West as more or less homogeneously hostile, it became official Soviet doctrine during the Khrushchev era that two distinct and radically different tendencies were to be found within the capitalist ruling elite: one bellicose and aggressive, pursuing a policy of international crisis and conflict; the other moderately sober, supporting cautious policies, avoiding conflict and tension. During the Stalin period differences among Western politicians were characterized as being little more than a "distinct game" designed to lure Moscow into making diplomatic concessions to the "moderate" forces. "Don't be taken in by the differences they are staging," warned one source in 1951.[4] Under Khrushchev, the differences between the "two tendencies" were found to be real, a fact with significant policy implications.

The existence of "two tendencies," or schools of thought, among the American policy elite explains what are often described as the "duality" and zigzags of U.S. foreign policy. The "instability" of American attitudes towards the USSR before World War II, argued Ernst Genri, was a result of the conflict between President Roosevelt and a right-wing, anti-Soviet "grouping" in the State Department and elsewhere in official Washington. "Not everything in American policy followed the same course nor could all of its representatives be put in the same camp." Roosevelt and "his closest advisors," Genri declared, were "divided from the right-wing camp . . . by acute disagreements" over both foreign and domestic policy.[5] Embellishing on Lenin's "two tendencies" model, Arbatov has described the whole evolution of this country in terms of a conflict between "two social and political tendencies: democratic and reactionary." The struggle between these two currents—one a product of this country's revolutionary origins and the traditions of Jefferson, Lincoln and the American labor movement; the other "inherent in the very nature of capitalism"—explains, according to Arbatov, the "complex and at times contradictory course" taken by the United States.[6] Originally said to concern primarily

127

attitudes towards the USSR, this struggle between "two tendencies" has apparently become the key to explaining the dialectical course of all of American history.

This Soviet view of Washington as a battleground on which rival "tendencies" seek to shape policy assumes, if only implicitly, that the American political process is relatively open. Though they may differ considerably in terms of their power and influence, each "tendency" can and does participate. It is also assumed that U.S. foreign policy towards the USSR is not fixed or predetermined. It tends, rather, because of internal political struggles between rival factions, towards uncertainty (duality, instability, complexity, contradictoriness). Given the fluidity of the policy process, careful analysis of the "correlation of forces" between the bellicose-aggressive tendency and the moderately sober one—their relative power, resources, leadership—is of critical importance. Distinguishing among the various elements in American political life, declared Arbatov, is a matter of "immense political urgency." Though from a communist point of view differences between them may seem small, "they spell the difference between a thermonuclear war and a policy envisaging methods . . . that would not undermine the principle of peaceful coexistence."[7] Arbatov warns against oversimplifying. The distinction between these tendencies, he writes, should not be considered as complete. There are many intermediate forces, groups and trends which tend to make the political climate unstable and always subject to major reshuffles. As a result "one can always find in the actual program of one or another politician elements of both . . . policies." Though the two tendencies are clearly different, in any one political situation "it is rather a question of proportions."[8] But the basic question remains, i.e., which "tendency" dominates? *Kto-kogo?* (Who [prevails] over whom?)

How then have Soviet analysts evaluated the "correlation of forces" in American political life? As indicated earlier, until the mid-1970s the assessment was strikingly positive. Though their language was guarded and their judgements set forth in the framework of protective ideological formulations, the articles published in *SShA* concluded that the forces of "realism" and moderation were increasingly the dominant ones. The change in tone from earlier years was most dramatic. In 1969 Gromyko could write only about "the out-

128

croppings of a realistic policy,"[9] while in 1970 Arbatov warned that although moderate forces were becoming stronger, this did not settle anything, for the "vanquished" die-hards might yet seek to take revenge. Further, the moderates could not be trusted not to make concessions to the more extremist elements.[10] In 1972 Arbatov would conclude that the views of the more moderate elements "are still far from having become predominant within the U.S. ruling classes. The positions of the supporters of traditional policy . . . remain very strong."[11] In 1973 there was a distinct change in tone. Arbatov, writing in *Kommunist*, argued that a more realistic "frame of mind is becoming characteristic of a significant segment" of the American leadership.[12] In 1974 he would observe that "the strength and influence" of the enemies of détente "are no longer what they were,"[13] while in early 1975 a veteran analyst noted that, "Although the most reactionary circles of present-day imperialism have in no way laid down their arms, their counterattacks at times resemble rearguard skirmishes following a battle which they have lost."[14] Summing up the results of the first half of the seventies, the editors of *SShA* wrote in their first issue for 1975 that "on the whole positive trends have prevailed over negative ones."[15]

Such enthusiastic judgements, as we have seen, did not long survive. The events of 1975–76 inspired considerably less optimism. The forces of the right, it was repeatedly argued, had taken the offensive. Seeking to exploit the whole "complex of crises"—rapid inflation and high unemployment, the post-Watergate political crisis, the exacerbation of legislative-executive relations, "the unprecedented loss of confidence in governmental authority"—reactionary circles, according to Arbatov, went on the attack.[16] They became especially assertive during the election campaign, when "many politicians were prepared to make concessions for the sake of immediate advantages and the gaining of support from various 'power centers.'"[17] The offensive, apparently, was in some measure successful for, according to Arbatov (reporting the results of a public opinion poll taken at the end of the election campaign), a "shift of opinion" had occurred in the United States toward "increased distrust" of the USSR and growing support for expanding U.S. military power.[18] Matters are believed to have worsened under the Carter administration. As a result

129

of the increased activity of "militaristic right-wing forces" during the preceding eighteen months, Arbatov reported in August 1977, "The political atmosphere in the relations between the two countries has changed for the worse."[19]

Such shifts in evaluation reflect, of course, the ever-changing Soviet mood, i.e., whether the political climate in Soviet-American relations is seen at the moment of publication to be stormy or bright. A more sophisticated barometer of Soviet expectations can be found in their analyses of the internal character of the rival American political factions and, especially, the dynamics of their interrelationship.

The Opponents of Détente

The "conscious and active enemies of détente," (i.e., of the Soviet Union) are generally classified in terms of three basic groups:

(a) Those whose economic interests are seen to be "incompat-ible" with a relaxation of tension—most notably the top Pentagon officials and the corporations dependent on mil-itary contracts united together in the "military-industrial complex";

(b) special interest groups—"counter-revolutionary" emigré organizations, Zionist circles; and

(c) those whose professional careers have been associated with the cold war—government bureaucrats, social scientists (Soviet specialists) and journalists.

To allow for the errant troglodyte who does not fit easily into one of the above, mention is sometimes also made of "extreme right-wing elements" and "professional anti-communists and anti-Soviets of every stripe."[20]

This is the core of the "bellicose aggressive tendency," forces which, according to Trofimenko, "in one way or another—from considerations of profit, career, the preservation of professional bureaucratic and institutional privileges, because of primitive anti-communism—have a 'deep-rooted interest' in the cold war and the arms race."[21] Frightened by détente, these groups resist its implemen-tation. Added to this "open, outspoken opposition," however, "in the very thick of American political life, so to speak, there are still very noticeable vestiges and traditions of the cold war, which are still making themselves felt."[22] "Force of habit, harmful traditions and inertia stemming from the prolonged 'cold war,'" writes Arbatov, "are on the side of such forces and groups."[23]

What Soviet analysts are suggesting here is the importance of subjective factors, of states of mind which reflect not simply economic—or even organizational phenomena such as concern for bureaucratic privileges—but the impact of experience on the psychological outlook of political leaders. It is precisely here, according to Arbatov, that we find the "sources" of current "problems and difficulties" in Soviet-American relations. They stem from "the burden of mentality and emotions inherited from the cold war days" which, he writes, "all of us bear, to some extent or other."

> After all, it lasted for a quarter of a century. Moreover, the principles of the cold war are engagingly simple and easy to understand: there is a particular enemy that is the source of all evil; there is a clear-cut aim—to fight the enemy—might and main; and there are habitual and history-tested methods of such [a] fight.[24]

And the burden of this heritage weighs heavily. "Suspicion, guardedness, extreme caution, distrust of the other side's sincerity and other such traditions engendered by the conditions of the cold war," writes Trofimenko, "are very much alive and well established."[25]

The vitality and tenacity of such attitudes are sustained by the "enemies of détente." "Old dogmas" regarding, for example, the need to maintain American military supremacy and the "red menace" are vigorously exploited by such groups. "The same old warhorses of reaction and of the cold war—Reagan, Wallace, Meany, Buckley, Goldwater," wrote Arbatov in April 1976, gave voice during the election campaign to "the same old cock-and-bull stories about a 'communist conspiracy' and a 'Soviet menace.'"[26] Their campaign was not without its effect. The "intensive propaganda aimed at undermining public support for détente," he wrote in December, "will leave its mark for some time."[27] Still the captives of old myths regarding American omnipotence and American superiority, writes Trofimenko, many in the United States are receptive to the anti-détente, anti-Soviet arguments of the right-wing.[28]

"All taken together," writes Arbatov, "this is a serious force" which "will do everything to impede the process of détente."[29] Though scorned as representing "forces of the past" whose "influence is being eroded,"[30] the enemies of détente are seen to "create obvious additional difficulties" in Soviet-American relations "which are already difficult enough." Their activities, he asserts, have "become a constant and essential source of mistrust in the Soviet Union about U.S. intentions and policies."[31] Given the Carter administration's human-rights campaign—denounced by Arbatov as part of "a large-scale campaign of political pressure [against the USSR] in which the U.S. government plays an active role," and "massive interference" in Soviet internal affairs bordering on "subversive activity"[32]—doubts have undoubtedly arisen at the institute whether, as was argued earlier, the battle waged by the enemies of détente has indeed been lost.

The Forces of Moderation

The individuals and groups generally identified with the policy of détente have in recent years included the president, the Congress (especially the Senate), influential corporate interests, the Arms Control Community and American public opinion. This "sober-moderate" tendency, long regarded as weak and diffuse—confined to individual personalities (who, with rare exceptions, were politically isolated) and "progressive" segments of the public—has had the support of the most powerful political and economic forces in the country, and received broad-scale, if not always consistent popular approval.

The factors identified by Soviet analysts to explain the moderate views of these groups have been discussed previously in some detail. They include the surprisingly damaging economic consequences of a rapidly escalating military budget (the product of the war in Vietnam and strategic arms competition); "unprecedented" social and political "instability"; declining self-confidence and faith in "the American era"; waning American military superiority; the failure of "the Pentagon's military adventure" in Vietnam; growing concern regarding the stability of the strategic weapons competition; and the decline in "bellicose anti-communism." In the judgement of Soviet Americanists, then, "highly influential segments of the ruling circles of the United States" are persuaded that their class interests—that is to say, the interests of the American socio-economic and political system—are best served by a policy of "realism."

The consequences of recent experiences on the "frames of mind" of specific groups are seen to have been profound. The highest echelon of authority in the American political system—the office of the president—has shown special concern regarding the potential danger of a nuclear confrontation and has taken important initiatives to "normalize" Soviet-American political and economic relations and stabilize the strategic arms competition. Major corporate representatives—the traditional "ruling circles"—have asserted their belief that the limitation of the arms race is vital to restore the health and trade position of the American economy (Arbatov quotes Lundborg of Bank of America and Watson of IBM to this effect)[33] and that "peaceful coexistence is more in accord with their economic interests than the 'cold war,' "[34] (with frequent reference to Rockfeller, Kendall, Hammer, et al.).

Additionally, the American political elite is judged to be generally more cautious than in the past. The loss of American military supremacy and especially the failure of U.S. policy in Vietnam have raised questions in Washington regarding the efficacy of military force as an instrument of foreign policy. In some circles, particularly in the Congress, "no more Vietnams" has become a guiding principle. Hence their opposition to military aid to Angola. The post-Nixon White House, as we have seen, has not come quite so far. Its occupants remain considerably more restrained, however, than they were ten years ago.

Official Washington seems to have developed, in addition, a heightened sensitivity to the domestic repercussions of prolonged military involvement. American theorists and policy makers, writes Petrovsky, have long held to a "voluntaristic approach to the evaluation of foreign policy. . . . Distorting or clouding over the relationship between domestic and foreign policy . . . ," he writes, they "attributed primary and decisive importance to the will of the creators" of policy in Washington. Convinced that they were masters of their own destiny, U.S. policy makers acted as they pleased. Thus, in

133

practice, "voluntarism serves as a theoretical justification of the political adventurism inherent in many foreign-policy actions of the American government."[35]

In view of the experience of the last several years, this voluntaristic approach has been called into question. The domestic consequences—rampant inflation, recession, the massive anti-war movement, etc.—of American policy in Vietnam were a crucial reminder that foreign and domestic policy are indeed intertwined. Davydov thus writes:

> The domestic factor (state of the economy, level of social movements, and so on), which during the early postwar period hardly hindered the expansion of American activity in the international arena at all, has now increasingly begun to operate in the opposite direction. "The American people have tired of that international burden which they have had to bear now for twenty-five years," admits President Nixon.[36]

Concern regarding the "domestic factor" as well as the "correlation of forces" now affect the judgement of U.S. policy makers regarding "what is permitted."

The influence of domestic constraints is not judged to be only of transient importance. While the powerful anti-war movement of the late 1960s and early 1970s began to fade abruptly in 1973 with the signing of the Paris accords, the mood of the American people remains hostile to "militarism." Thus, according to a specialist in U.S. science policy, Americans in the late 1960s became increasingly sensitive to the social responsibilities of scientists, especially those dealing with military research. This phenomenon has taken "the most varied forms"—from the picketing by students of the Stanford Research Institute because of its Pentagon connections to the complaints by officials of centers engaged in military research that talented young people no longer wish to work for them. These developments, she writes, are "closely connected with the growth of anti-militarism" in the United States.[37] Even more important, however, has been the mood of the U.S. Congress, especially the Senate, where the "liberal wing" critical of Pentagon requests for new weapons systems has grown in size and effectiveness. The close votes on military appropriations bills demonstrated, according to Popova, the existence of a "stable opposition to militarism and anti-Sovietism" in the Senate. Furthermore, she writes, on the issue of the Vladivostok agreement-in-principle on the limitation of strategic arms, the "inveterate militarists" were "opposed by a vast camp of agreement supporters."[38]

The growth of anti-militarist sentiment in the Senate and elsewhere is seen to reflect something quite profound in American political life. As Arbatov has argued, the anti-war movement has now become "a serious political force." The appearance of weapons of mass destruction, he suggests, has both broadened and intensified the anti-war movement. Given the great dangers which war now threatens, the desire to prevent a thermonuclear catastrophe has "grown into a movement against predatory wars and militarism in general." In fact, he argues, this movement is acquiring "considerable revolutionary potential." The dread of war has become so intense that it "poses serious problems for bourgeois politicians, forcing many of them to think seriously about the prospect of a political course which is not only doomed to failure . . . but also fraught with profound domestic consequences."[39]

As the war in Vietnam demonstrated, "these tremendous forces of self-salvation,"[40] as Arbatov called them, should not be underestimated. Washington's Vietnam policy evoked enormous popular resentment, he wrote, because it was seen by the American people to be "a threat to their vital interests, a threat which was especially frightening in that it concerned a policy being carried out in the nuclear age."[41] Such perils, presumably, will not vanish short of effective nuclear disarmament. Given the dimness of this prospect, the underlying popular suspicion of "militarism" will undoubtedly remain— whatever the political mood of the movement.

While disappointed by recent events, Soviet analysts view post-Vietnam America, for all its shortcomings, as a healthier place politically than it was a decade ago. Despite the uncertainties of the Carter White House, important elements in the Congress and in the business community, scientists and other influential groups nonetheless continue to speak out forcefully in support of "realistic policies." "On the whole," reports Shimanovsky, "liberal activists, representing political, business and academic circles support the measures being taken by the

135

U.S. government designed to reduce the danger of nuclear war and to hold back the arms race" as well as "the development of Soviet-American cooperation."[42] Davydov reports détente "is supported by broad segments of the public and a considerable part of the business world." It is also endorsed, he points out, by those in American politics who "are particularly concerned about the new and complex problems never before encountered by the United States"—currency crisis, energy crisis, raw materials shortages, urban problems, etc. These people have come to understand, he argues, that not only is the resolution of these increasingly acute problems "much more important to the United States . . . than the continuation of useless confrontations . . . or the arms race" but itself "requires the normalization of the international situation and, in some cases, constructive cooperation with the socialist nations as well."[43]

The "sober-moderate" coalition therefore remains a potentially powerful force on the American political scene. Its members are not, to be sure, about to join forces in a "civilian-social complex" capable of acting as a "countervailing force" to the "military-industrial complex."[44] Nonetheless, the prevailing outlook—the "more humble" self-image, the awareness that America's traditional freedom of action has in some measure been eroded, the heightened concern regarding domestic problems, especially economic ones—reflects more restrained, more circumspect attitudes towards foreign policy than have been seen in Washington in many decades.

Furthermore, jingoism and super-patriotism are not the only emotions found "lurking deep" in the American consciousness. There are also the "progressive heritage and traditions" of its people, and "the traditions of democratic isolation and pacifism," which go back to the Spanish-American War.[45] Soviet analysts are also aware that Senator William Borah, "the ideologist of the pacifist wing" of the Senate, led the struggle against American intervention in the Soviet Union and subsequently urged American recognition and trade. As Popova notes, the seemingly futile activities of Senator Borah, who headed the Senate Foreign Relations Committee from 1924 to 1933, "prepared the way" for recognition in 1933.[46] Following "Lenin's instructions regarding the need to study divergent opinions in the bourgeois camp on the question of war and peace," which she quotes, Popova may well be aware that the likely next Chairman of the Foreign Relations Committee, Senator Frank Church, has a picture of Senator Borah hanging in his office.

The Dynamics of Détente

Recent concern about the resurgence of "militaristic right-wing forces" in the United States and the policy intentions of the Carter White House is unquestionably genuine. After the heady days of the Nixon-Kissinger administration, developments in Soviet-American relations since early 1975 have undoubtedly been disappointing and worrisome. Nonetheless, the outlook of Soviet Amerikanisty is not at all pessimistic. In fact, especially in the long run, they seem remarkably hopeful.

The explanation for this optimism lies in the distinctive Soviet view of détente. As seen in Moscow, especially by those hewing close to the Leninist "two-tendency" model of capitalist politics, the recent "normalization" in Soviet-American relations involves something more than just a relaxation of international relations. It is also understood to be part of a political process which itself feeds back on the United States—with positive results.

Current Soviet literature on détente assumes that there is a direct linkage between domestic and foreign politics, that, in the words of an article in *Pravda*, "the state of international relations has always influenced the development of internal processes."[47] The author suggests, more particularly, that the "state of international relations" affects the rival tendencies in American politics in strikingly different ways. He writes:

international tension means that imperialist reaction, citing an external "communist" threat, has an opportunity to give militarism a free reign, to suppress the workers' movement more openly and mercilessly, to institute a state of emergency in order to take reprisals against "subversive" elements, and to flout elementary democratic rights. . . . That is why the easing, and even better the removal, of tension in the world arena knocks out of the hands of reaction the main key to "turning the screws" and deceiving the working people. . . . Détente expands considerably the opportunities for the forces of . . . liberation to oppose imperialist pressure and use their growing political potential.[48]

137

While this argument was made principally to counter charges from the communist "Left" that détente with the U.S. was a sell-out—by arguing that this policy was not only beneficial to Soviet interests but also served to weaken capitalism—Soviet analysts seem persuaded that détente has a beneficial impact on the alignment of forces in the West. This view is strongly held by analysts at the USA Institute. As Deputy Director Zhurkin has observed, "In countries of the West, 'cold war' and the worsening of international tension is always connected with the activization of the rightist forces."[49] Conversely, in periods of détente such groups are in a much more difficult position. "The process of détente," he writes, "enchains the aggressive forces to a considerable degree, makes it more difficult for them to take cruel interventionist decisions . . . forces them ever more frequently to maneuver and retreat."[50]

The cold war, as Soviet analysts invariably point out, was of enormous benefit to the political right in the United States. The great power and influence of the "military-industrial complex" (MIC), wrote Trofimenko, cannot be understood in terms of the proportion of firms belonging to it—only 1 percent of the total registered in the country—or even as a function of the funds it received from the federal budget. (During the wars in Korea and Vietnam, he noted, it controlled no more than 14 percent of the total U.S. GNP.) "The root of the MIC's colossal influence . . . lay elsewhere." It is to be found, argues Trofimenko, in the external environment.

> The U.S. ruling circles' obsession with the global nature of the "cold war" automatically gave priority to foreign political problems over domestic ones, and . . . an orientation toward military means of solving them. . . . Under these conditions, the MIC indeed proved to be not only the main inspiration and main ideologist of foreign political decisions, but also the indispensable supplier of those "metal parts" with the aid of which "positions of strength" were to be created and armed interventions carried out.[51]

Under conditions of cold war, therefore, where foreign policy received priority over the domestic sphere and military force is seen to be a major instrument of policy, the "military-industrial complex" came to occupy "a privileged, if not dominating, position."[52]

Spawned and nurtured in an atmosphere of tension, the "militarists" fared poorly as the environment changed. At the start of the 1970s, wrote Trofimenko, as the United States "turned toward realism, détente and a constructive dialog with the USSR," a "positive trend" began to develop which greatly "narrowed the militarists' opportunity to dictate their will to society."[53] As the political climate became more benign, their role and place in American society was increasingly called into question. Worried lest détente affect their profits, privileges and prestige, that it deprive them of "their freedom of maneuver and their certainty about the future,"[54] they are active in the campaign to maintain international tension and oppose efforts to curb the arms race. Nonetheless, the impact of détente has been devastating. As Davydov has pointed out, "it is unlikely that the Lockheed scandal would have come to light during the cold war."[55]

Others among the opponents of détente face parallel difficulties. "It is natural to assume," wrote N. A. Olenov, "that détente . . . must entail a restriction of the subversive operations of the American intelligence agencies on the world scene."[56] Such indeed, Soviet analysts argue, is now taking place. The CIA, notes Linnik, is under sharp attack at home and abroad. The intensity of public criticism of its illegal activities, he points out, is a direct function of détente. He writes: "the general changes in the international climate played . . . a definite role. With the departure from the cold war policy, criticism of the CIA ceased to be considered a seditious matter."[57] Furthermore, argues Linnik, the public now recognizes that in the new political environment the CIA "is becoming an anachronism." Though perhaps justifiable previously, during a period of international relax-ation "the methods used by the agency abroad and within the coun-try are causing growing indignation and alarm within the United States."[58] A similar fate, as we noted earlier, is reported by Gromyko to have overtaken academic Sovietology.[59]

Thus, in a period of relaxation of international tension, the need for vigilance and strict discipline to defend against an "external enemy" seems less compelling. Finding less and less justification for their enormous budgets, clandestine subversion abroad and abuses and violations of the law at home, writes Yur'yev, American taxpayers, through their representatives in Congress, are raising serious questions about "the privileged position" of such groups as the Pentagon, corporations manufacturing weapons, the CIA and the FBI, and about the legality of their activities.[60]

As détente progresses, the danger to their position grows; their resistance, as a result, becomes increasingly acute. Thus, writing in *Izvestia*, Arbatov observed:

> It is natural that with each new step along the path of improving Soviet-American relations, their opposition becomes fiercer, particularly when matters start moving toward changes and decisions which not only do not please these circles but which also pose a direct threat to their profits, interests and influence.[61]

The greater the success, the more real the fear, the more intense the opposition. This explains, according to Soviet sources, the "offensive" by the "militarist right-wing forces" in 1975–76, their "fanning of a war psychosis," their propaganda about a "Soviet menace." It is nothing less, according to Yur'yev, than an effort "to further the selfish interests of groups in the capitalist nations which are hoping to undermine international détente, to return the world to the time of the cold war and to give the arms race a new impetus."[62]

In the judgement of Soviet analysts, therefore, the policy of détente is in itself a powerful political force. The active pursuit of "normalization" of relations between the United States and the Soviet Union, and the relaxation of international tension, undermines the political processes and structures generated by the cold war and those who benefitted from them. Paradoxically, the official most responsible for creating the new political environment may be its main casualty. As Arbatov writes: "I have serious doubts whether the U.S. could have afforded Watergate . . . during the cold war."[63] Such, indeed, may well be the ultimate irony of Richard Nixon's tragic political career.

The pursuit of détente, furthermore, tends to encourage those in the United States who support the policy of improved relations with the Soviet Union. One of the consequences of expanded East-West trade, notes Oleshuk,

> is the strengthening of the immediate interests of influential U.S. business circles in the improvement of Soviet-American relations. . . . In turn, these representatives of the U.S. business world who, according to politi-

cal scientist[!] Marshall Shulman, have become "persistent adherents of peaceful coexistence," are actively influencing sentiment in the United States in favor of deepening and expanding relations with the Soviet Union.[64]

Increased trade strengthens the "immediate interests" of David Rockefeller, Armand Hammer et al. in the political "normalization" of Soviet-American relations. Active Soviet support for the policy of détente, therefore, not only weakens the political position of their critics but also helps bolster support for more "realistic" forces in the United States.

What policy implications, if any, do Soviet Amerikanisty derive from their assessments? One conclusion—which both fits their basic analysis and serves to protect their political position (of which more in a moment)—relates to the Soviet military posture. To the extent that the moderation which characterizes American policy makers today is interpreted to be a function of the "objective fact" of Soviet nuclear capabilities, maintenance of strategic parity with the United States is an essential prerequisite for the continuation of détente. Writing in 1972, Arbatov noted that "the change in the correlation of forces is not some abstract formula, but a perceptible reality, which compels the imperialist powers to adjust." Preservation of this new balance of power is thus crucial. As he observes: "One cannot doubt that any change in the correlation of forces in favor of imperialism would have led not to a relaxation but an increase in tension, whipping up the aggressive aspirations of reactionary circles."[65]

Though Arbatov frequently quoted Kissinger to the effect that "power no longer automatically translates into influence," he clearly believes that military strength remains essential to protect against "imperialism's predatory instincts." Only in conditions of nuclear parity, he argues, will American policy makers be compelled "to adapt to reality" and curb their instinctive resort to military force. Writing in 1973, the institute director carried his argument a step further. "Power in and of itself," he observed,

does not guarantee peace, let alone détente. The growth of power at one pole can ultimately—and this has happened quite often in the past—lead to attempts to build up power at the other pole; in other words, it may lead to unrestrained military competition entailing armed clashes.[66]

141

What Arbatov is suggesting is that the "correlation of forces"—important though it is, does not itself ensure stable or peaceful relations. Despite a balance of military power, should the political intentions of one side appear menacing, détente between them is in jeopardy.

The psychological climate is, therefore, seen to be a vital part of the political equation. And, while acutely aware of the many problems involved and the unevenness of the process, Soviet Americanists seem persuaded that the dynamics of détente work to their advantage. The active pursuit of "normalization" of Soviet-American relations helps undermine "cold war myths" in the United States. It also weakens the "bellicose" forces hostile to the Soviet Union and strengthens those of a less belligerent disposition. As Trofimenko observed:

> The foreign policy of one side which is favorably disposed and friendly toward the other strengthens in this latter side an atmosphere of public support for a similar policy in return which creates an additional stimulus for them to move toward each other along the path of peace.[67]

In other words, détente feeds back on the United States, promoting the fortunes and influence of the "realistic," "sober" elements in the American political elite, with whom political agreements and economic relations are feasible.

This strategem, which stresses the need to support "moderate" elements in the American political leadership, is very much in the Leninist tradition. As Lenin told the Soviet delegation to the 1922 Genoa Conference: "To do everything possible and perhaps even impossible to bolster the pacifist wing of the bourgeoisie and to increase, however slightly, its chances for victory at the polls—this is primary."[68] In line with this injunction, efforts were apparently made during the Khrushchev era to "bunch Soviet actions" during the pre-election periods in the U.S. political cycle in the hope of promoting the "liberal" tendency in American domestic and foreign policy.*

---

* Khrushchev explained Soviet policy during the Cuban missile crisis as designed, in part, to undercut the position of "lunatic" politicians in Washington. As he told the December 1962 session of the Supreme Soviet:

Among the U.S. ruling circles are politicians who are rightly called "lunatic." . . . Is it not clear that if we had taken an uncompromising stand we would only have

However, as Griffiths points out, the sharp increases in the U.S. military budget during the Kennedy administration and escalation in Vietnam under President Johnson "may . . . have cast doubt on the reliability of the electoral mechanism and the capacity to encourage reformist trends in American political behavior."[69]

Soviet confidence in their ability to forecast the behavior of the "two tendencies" in U.S. politics was undoubtedly further undermined by more recent experiences. Neither faction has been predictable. As Arbatov likes to point out, "President Nixon was not the best friend of the Soviet Union or of communists—he had a perfect anti-communist, anti-Soviet record in the fifties and sixties—but under his presidency changes began."[70] Liberals, for their part, are more often than not afflicted by "chronic anti-communism."[71] Furthermore, though they had been strong supporters in the 1950s and 1960s of the campaign to control the arms race, liberals have proved to be lacking in steadfastness. After the first steps were taken towards détente, wrote Trofimenko,

> there occurred what might be described as a "disintegration" of interests of the various political groups in the United States. "All right, now that we have détente, what else do we need?," proclaimed numerous representatives of the American political elite. The danger of war has been eliminated, they argue, and so now it should again be possible to pursue their private, petty group interests and even demagogically to criticize those who persist in following the former line.[72]

The liberal supporters of détente, therefore, are "contradictory and inconsistent," tend toward "oscillation," and, at times (as in their support of the Jackson Amendment), "act in unison with militant anti-Soviets."[73]

Despite the obstacles and uncertainties involved, Soviet analysts seem convinced that a détente posture remains in the long-term best interests of their country. They appear especially sensitive, in this regard, about their own responsibility for controlling the political

---

helped the "lunatic" camp to utilize the situation in order to strike at Cuba and unleash a world war? . . . Among the ruling circles of the United States there are also persons who appraise the situation more soberly.

Pravda, 13 December 1962; in CDSP 14, no. 51 (16 January 1963), p. 6.

atmosphere. They recognize, for example, that the image of the USSR held in the United States—whether it is seen to be menacing or benign—is directly affected by Soviet behavior. Just as Lenin warned Soviet diplomats in 1922 to refrain from presenting "frightening" communist views and argued against the use of "terrible words" such as "inevitable violent revolution," "bloody struggle." and "the inevitability of new world wars,"[74] so, today, Soviet writers urge caution in order to avoid giving credence to the "myth of a 'Soviet threat.' " Thus, referring to the "new tricks" of the "military-industrial complex," Arbatov and his son warned that the strategic doctrines set forth by Defense Secretary Schlesinger may have been "aimed at provoking the other side [i.e., the Soviet Union] to take military measures that could be used by the Pentagon as a pretext for hatching new arms programs."[75] The Arbatovs were apparently apprehensive that the "militarists" might manipulate Soviet behaivor to suit their own purposes. To avoid falling victim to such snares, the Kremlin should take care and not overreact to "pinpricks" and "provocations."

The institute director urges circumspection; he clearly seems convinced that détente is worth taking pains to preserve. He and his colleagues have pointed out that on virtually all issues—from SALT and Soviet-American trade to supplying arms to Angola or the countries of the Persian Gulf[76]—there exist "two tendencies" within American policy-making circles. They believe that the outcome of the struggle between these groups and the policies which emerge on these issues are more likely to be positive, from the Soviet point of view, in a non-threatening international environment than in a period of tension. More specifically they have argued that the policies supported by "moderate" forces (in the White House itself, in the Congress, and in the defense and foreign-policy bureaucracies, major business corporations and banks), will have greater resonance in an era of détente than during a renewed cold war.

They undoubtedly argue that détente has, moreover, given Soviet officials direct entrée to the American policy process itself. In 1974, to take a notable but not unusual case, a parade of representatives from the Soviet Embassy actively lobbied on Capitol Hill against the Jackson Amendment. (Daniel Yergin described this as a "spectacle . . . suggestive almost more of a platoon of out-of-town shoe manufacturers worried about tariff protection than of emissaries from America's most deadly rival."[77]) Though their efforts were without success, Soviet access to Congress was—and remains—a major benefit of détente. During the cold war, needless to say, Soviet diplomats enjoyed no such privileges.

Soviet interest in the "alignment of forces" in Washington and their concern to influence, to the extent that this is possible, the course of the policy debate, is heightened by the fact that, as numerous analysts have reported, the turn toward "realism" on the part of the United States, is not yet "irreversible." Thus, writing in August 1977, it was Arbatov's impression that "the problem of continuity in U.S. policy has still not been decided, that something resembling a struggle is still underway around it and that forces which would like to 'correct' détente and see it 'differently'—giving more advantages to the United States—have been activated."[78] In such circumstances, reversion to a cold war posture by Moscow would be especially dangerous. Not only could the "forces of the past" be revivified and perhaps even regain their previous positions of dominance, but such a turn of events might well redound to the benefit of Peking. As Soviet analysts point out, the Chinese leaders are themselves alert to internal divisions in Washington and, according to a ranking Soviet Sinologist, seek to use "new tendencies in the domestic political life of the United States . . . to their own advantage." Lukin writes that "Peking is obviously trying . . . to stimulate and accentuate the anti-Soviet attitudes of the most reactionary circles in the United States, to strive to spread these attitudes to broader segments of the American ruling class and, in this way, to disrupt the course toward international détente.[79] China's ability to speculate on anti-Soviet currents in American political life would be enhanced, it is feared, were Soviet-American relations to take a serious turn for the worse.

What these arguments seem to suggest, therefore, is that the USA Institute has itself become a spokesman for détente. Soviet Americanists appear convinced that a policy of international relaxation presents Moscow with opportunities which a more aggressive political line would preclude. Not only does such an approach help achieve a number of other policy objectives—increased trade with the West, reduction of the pace and burden of the arms race, a more stable

145

international environment in which greater attention to domestic problems is feasible—but, as we have seen, it has a generally positive impact on American politics and policies. Thus while a hard line, in given circumstances, may offer certain benefits, institute spokesmen in Soviet policy circles are likely to urge caution. Any premature or imprudent action which might jeopardize Soviet-American relations would, in their view, risk the loss of significant advantages. Given the logic of their assessments, the Amerikanisty are most likely to be found among the Kremlin's counselors of restraint.

6

CONCLUSIONS

The conclusions one draws from reading the publications of the USA Institute reflect in considerable measure one's starting point. Approaching these materials from the perspective of a Western political and intellectual environment, some observers are struck by the distortion and misunderstanding which they find. Hans Morgenthau, the eminent political scientist, was "shocked" by Anatoly Gromyko's study of the Kennedy administration, by the "quality of caricature" which, in his view, permeates the book.[1]

There is considerable merit in this charge. The picture of the United States presented by Gromyko and other Americanists often does resemble a caricature. While capturing many of its essential features, they seriously distort them by exaggeration and suppression for their own polemical purpose. Moreover, while some analysts are quite well informed, the need to fit all the detailed information concerning this country—from the Byzantine world of Washington politics to the federal government's energy policies—into an all-embracing Marxist-Leninist framework imposes a rigidity and uniformity on American public life which can only be regarded as, at best, simple-minded.

Moscow's glaring indifference to the institutions and values of Western politics gives further credence to Morgenthau's harsh comments. As we noted in Chapter II, Soviet analysts cannot seem to understand the meaning of such basic ideas as political pluralism,

147

limited government and personal freedom. Such centrally-important issues in contemporary American politics as the constitutional principles involved in the Watergate affair, the adversary role of the communications media, and President Carter's human-rights policies are thus incomprehensible to them.[2]

Nonetheless, Morgenthau and other critical Western observers miss a crucial point. Though Soviet analysts read the *Washington Post* and carefully study congressional hearings and debates, they live in a Soviet political universe. That is to say, they succeed (or fail) according to the rules of the game which prevail in Moscow—not American universities or even political Washington. Unless this central fact is kept in mind, their written accounts cannot be fully understood or appreciated.

For reasons I have elaborated more fully elsewhere,[3] the internal dynamics of the Soviet political system place a high premium on doctrinal orthodoxy and continuity. Relying heavily on ideology as the justification for their political authority, the Soviet Party leadership insists that the canons of Marxism-Leninism be rigidly adhered to. They continue to stress such hallowed Leninist principles as "the leading role of the Party," in the conviction that tampering with these beliefs (or, as the Czechs and Slovaks did in 1968, revising them substantially) "would endanger the philosophical and psychological underpinnings of Soviet political power."[4]

A cardinal principle of Leninist doctrine, as we noted earlier, is the assumption concerning the "predatory essence of imperialism." As former Soviet Defense Minister Marshal Grechko wrote, Lenin instructed that "the first commandment of our policy and the first lesson . . . which all workers and peasants must learn is to be on their guard and to remember that we are surrounded by people, classes and governments which openly express the greatest hatred of us."[5] This view remains the current orthodoxy. In his report to the 24th Party Congress in 1971, in which he set forth the Soviet Union's "peace program," General Secretary Brezhnev felt compelled when referring to "the foreign policy of imperialism" to note "the immutability of its reactionary and aggressive nature." And two quite sophisticated Soviet analysts feel obliged to quote Brezhnev.[6]

The centrality of this dogma in contemporary Soviet political doctrine has a profound effect on the activities of the USA Institute.

Institute Director Georgi Arbatov, himself a high ranking Party official (he is currently a candidate member of the CPSU's Central Committee) fully identifies himself with this Leninist belief, of course. So, furthermore, must his colleagues. Given their sensitive position—to travel abroad and to read "bourgeois" political materials, Party clearance is required—Soviet Americanists must be especially careful to remain certified as ideologically reliable. Furthermore, they are constantly subject, as are all others who take up the pen in the USSR, to criticism and attack by militant elements in the Party (or by political enemies) for any hint of ideological "softness."

How, then, can the leadership of the United States, the "prime strike force" of predatory imperialism, be viewed in anything less than hostile terms? How can international relaxation and normalization of relations with an inherently aggressive enemy be rationalized? Arbatov offers the following explanation:

> If many of the imperialist powers are becoming acceptable partners . . . this does not at all indicate that the class nature of their policies has changed—this has not happened and *could not have happened*. But the world in which the imperialists have to live and act has changed. It is to these changes, to the objective reality of the present situation, that they have to adapt. [Italics added.][7]

Bound by obligations of doctrine and Party authority to an image of an "immutably hostile" United States, the "realistic" behavior of its leadership must be understood as a product of necessity rather than virtue. The possibility of good will on the part of the United States simply cannot be countenanced. As Arbatov has argued, "in analyzing imperialist policy, its assessment as 'friendly' or 'hostile' cannot be used as a point of departure. This policy will always be intrinsically anti-socialist."[8]

Thus, even though they are recognized as less antagonistic toward the Soviet Union than most of their predecessors, the moderation of the contemporary political elite in Washington is seen to be a function of changes in the "correlation of forces." Nothing less is possible. As Arbatov points out, a truly "class approach," i.e., one consistent with Party principles,

> demands a clear understanding of the fact that no matter how far the process of the adaptation of imperialism to the situation goes, this does not change the nature of imperialism or the oppressive essence of this system.

149

This distinguishes the Marxist-Leninist approach from the reformist and revisionist approach, which essentially preaches the accommodation of the workers' movement to present-day imperialism and a reconciliation with it.[9]

To suggest that the "class nature" of U.S. foreign policy has changed, that a close relationship between the two countries is now or ever could be possible, is to open oneself up to charges of "reformism and revisionism," i.e., ideological heresy. Détente cannot be taken to mean or even to allow for the possibility of a genuine reconciliation between the two systems. As a guardian of Party orthodoxy wrote, "Communists would cease to be communists if they did this."[10]

Within the ideological constraints of the Soviet system, it seems, normalized relations with the United States are inconceivable unless the USSR can be seen to be as strong or stronger than its capitalist adversary. Otherwise advocates of normalization would appear as capitulationists. To reduce their vulnerability to such criticism, Soviet analysts stress that it was Washington—not Moscow—that was forced to adapt its policies to changing international circumstances. (This argument also helps allay the unspoken apprehension that détente derives in fact from Soviet weakness.)[11] They also seek to emphasize the offensive implications of détente. The policy of normalization is characterized as a continuation of the "class struggle." Insofar as arms control agreements, summit-level negotiations, expanded trade and scientific exchanges help reinforce political moderates and isolate "reactionary" forces in the United States, détente can be viewed as part of the "struggle for socialism."

Basing their arguments on the primacy of "objective factors," therefore, helps justify the policy of détente in the face of potential opposition at home and abroad. By emphasizing the importance of "the objective state of affairs" in the world, improved Soviet-American relations are seen to have "nothing in common with Peking's slanderous fabrications regarding 'collusion between the two super-powers.'"[12] It also helps protect against the charge made by domestic critics that, given its imperialist nature, détente with the United States can only be a temporary "episode." The change in U.S. policy, argue Soviet Americanists, was not a fortuitous phenomenon based on short-term considerations, but a recognition of international realities. Thus, wrote Berezhkov in 1973, the American commitment to détente was a "question not simply of the good will of the present administration but also of objective conditions."[13]

The perceptions of the United States to be found in the pages of *SShA* must be understood in this context. Whether from ideological conviction or political necessity, or a mixture of both, Soviet analysts are obliged to keep within the confines of the "class approach," i.e., to the view that détente is a product not of the well-meaning desires of the American "ruling elite" but of objective necessity. Whatever the specific issue—the limitation of strategic weapons, trade relations with the USSR, budgetary priorities—the policy of the United States government is never attributed to decent instincts or a commitment to the public good, but to narrowly-defined class interests which generally (though not always) are seen to be at odds with the real interests of the American people. To take a crude example, the federal government's social policies (social security, public welfare, education, health care, etc.) are characterized by one Americanist as nothing more than "an instrument for preserving the existing social class structure and social injustice," a policy, in short, of "social maneuvering."[14] Politics and ideology clearly give a hard cast to Soviet appraisals of American capitalism.

Given the intellectual-political constraints imposed by the "class approach," the Amerikanisty have often been quite imaginative. Theirs is not, despite the accusations of some, a simplistic conceptual scheme in which "politics is a mere function of economics, the political leaders do the bidding of the monopolies and foreign policy is bound to be imperialistic."[15] While lip service is frequently given to such crude dogmas, often this is no more than ritual deference. Furthermore, as Soviet analysts fully appreciate, in the sphere of doctrine much depends on interpretation. His Soviet training serves Orlov well when he observes that the United States Constitution "often allows arbitrary interpretations." As a result, he writes, it has been "converted into a weapon in the struggle between individual groups which adapt it to their own political interests."[16] A better description of the role of Party doctrine in Soviet political life would be hard to find.

Though confining, ideology has not proven to be all-inhibiting. The analyses of Soviet Americanists have been strikingly differentiated. The contributors to *SShA* vary, considerably, in both knowledge and judgement. Nonetheless, the overall pattern reveals much less dogmatism than one unfamiliar with Soviet intellectual traditions might discern. The vulgar Marxism of the Stalin era, with its crude economic determinism, has given way to considerably more perceptive assessments.

One index of their growing sophistication is the increased willingness of Soviet analysts to recognize that they do not always have the answers. For all their efforts to understand American political behavior, there are still considerable areas of uncertainty. Even looked at through the prism of "scientific Marxism," much in American life, they have found, is perplexing and ambiguous, even at times paradoxical.

A recent case which generated much confusion in Soviet ranks was the endorsement by the Congress of the Jackson Amendment (see above p. 50). Despite the fact that the Nixon administration was strongly opposed to Senator Jackson's proposal, a position reaffirmed by President Ford, and though "leading business circles" vigorously endorsed the administration's policy, Senator Jackson managed to secure passage of his amendment. Vitaly Kobysh, *Izvestia* correspondent in the United States, revealed his confusion openly. Noting that Secretary Kissinger and President Ford both endorsed "détente" as "state policy," he exclaimed that it was

> strange, if not wholly unnatural, that a political course supported . . . by powerful sectors of big business and the government can be opposed by forces of any significance. I would say that many people . . . do not understand what is happening. To many, this aspect of the present situation in the country appears to be a daub of surrealist colors.[17]

Savel'yev's explanation—that congressional passage of the Jackson Amendment was due in considerable measure to the fact that "influential business circles . . . did not exert as much pressure on Congress as they could have, limiting themselves to an essentially well-disposed neutral attitude toward the USSR"[18]—reflects Moscow's tendency to overestimate the role of the business sector in U.S. policy making. Soviet analysts are, apparently, still unaccustomed to the idea that the American "ruling circles"—Wall Street in tandem with the White House—cannot always work their will. One source, however, came close to the mark. In an interview with an Italian journalist,

Soviet editor Daniel Kraminov noted that though "as many as 240 big U.S. companies proved to be against the Jackson Amendment," this in itself was not sufficient. "Unfortunately in this instance the industrialists have the money but not the power or the opportunity to influence the masses and major decisions."[19] The policy-making process in Washington, Soviet observers are discovering, is significantly more complex than they initially assumed.

Soviet tolerance of ambiguity seems to have grown considerably as a result of their greater familiarity with the American political scene. Institute analysts have observed, for example, that even when confronted by the same facts, Americans often come to very different conclusions. Thus, notes Kokoshin, although all international-relations theorists in the United States recognize that Washington has had to abandon its voluntaristic approach and take the "real state of affairs in the world" into greater consideration, "this understanding leads different authors to different conclusions." Thus some stress the heightened importance of military force and military-political considerations in the years ahead, while others see this variant as "too dangerous" and urge further relaxation of tensions.[20] Arbatov argues similarly: recent policy failures have led some in the United States to reexamine traditional cold-war policies, while others seek a way out of the "blind alley of the policy of force" by perfecting the American military machine and developing new strategic doctrines.[21] Recent internal difficulties have also provoked different responses. Some have argued, as we saw in Chapter One, that Washington must give greater attention and resources to help solve American economic and social problems, i.e., that the government should reorder "national priorities" in favor of domestic policy goals. Others, notes Yur'yev, reached precisely the opposite conclusion, that is to say they seek to deal with internal problems by focusing even greater attention on external dangers. Thus, he writes, "exaggeration of the 'Soviet menace' serves the desire of certain circles in the United States to divert the attention of the American public away from the domestic problems which are still unresolved."[22]

This dualism found in American thinking reflects, of course, Soviet reliance on their "two-tendencies" analysis — and helps explain the ambiguity they see in American policy. As Arbatov suggests, both "sober" and "militaristic" responses to recent foreign misadventures "are interwoven in the official policy of the United States, determining its contradictoriness and inconsistency."[23] This approach also suggests that, despite their stress on the "correlation of forces," Soviet Americanists recognize that objective factors are not wholly determining. The much-heralded "change in the correlation of forces in the world in favor of socialism" may encourage a "realistic" response on the part of U.S. policy makers—or it may not. Objective factors are only preconditions. Subjective factors—the attitudes, perceptions and experiences of those who shape policy—play a crucial role.[24] And here the two-tendencies analysis is not very helpful. Too much is unpredictable. As Arbatov has noted, even moderate American leaders have been known to pursue dangerous policies. He writes for example, that "mankind was brought closest to a thermonuclear war during the 1962 Caribbean crisis," that is, during the administration of a "sober" president. Moreover, he observes, "that crisis was not provoked by President Kennedy and his advisors deliberately steering towards a world war." Rather, it was the result of the "entire logic of imperialist policy." Thus, in his view, "even regardless of the subjective intentions of individual Western leaders," crises and tension may occur.[25]

Thus, in place of the simplistic economic determinism of the Stalin period, Soviet analysts today find "contradictoriness and inconsistency" in U.S. policy. Their uncertainty is a direct result of the fact that, as we have seen, official governmental policies are now recognized to be the product of a medley of influences—political, bureaucratic, historical, even psychological—as well as the once-dominant "class interests" of the "ruling circles."

This sensitivity to historical and psychological factors seems especially prominent among those analysts dealing with Soviet-American strategic relations. Trofimenko, as noted earlier, views deterrence as a psychological problem, taking place in people's minds (quoting Kissinger),[26] and sees the key problem in current Soviet-American relations to be a function of the "suspicion, guardedness, extreme caution, distrust of the other side's sincerity" and other such psychological propensities engendered by a prolonged period of mutual confrontation.[27] In Trofimenko's judgement, détente involves, in considerable part, a "process of psychological reorientation."[28]

Moreover, although the United States is identified as a capitalist society, it is no longer regarded as having the same fixed qualities or believed to pursue certain predetermined policies attributed by the orthodox guardians of doctrine to "state-monopoly capitalism." The politics and policies of American capitalism are now by and large treated separately from its economic system; the American political system is seen to be a policy-making apparatus independent of its economic substructure.[29] As we have discussed in some detail, individual political leaders may have a very considerable policy role, sometimes pursuing programs in the face of bitter opposition on the part of the "ruling class." Indeed, the "ruling class" itself is now seen to be divided, with a relatively small—though still powerful—component which still retains a stake in an aggressive foreign policy. The bulk of the "ruling class" is believed to have an increasing interest in a relaxed international climate. Moreover, the organizational interests of officials in the executive branch of government are seen to have been a significant influence on state policy. The Congress, public opinion (the anti-war movement, the Jewish vote, anti-militarism), special interest groups ("think tanks," "counterrevolutionary emigrés, Sovietologists) all have a political role. The orientation of the American political leadership is no longer imbued with "class hatred" and, in critical areas, it shares parallel interests with the Soviet Union.

There are even occasional hints that, although the United States is still seen to be the main culprit responsible for international tension, its attitudes are in some measure understandable. Trofimenko notes that "colossal distrust built up on *both* sides during the cold war." Furthermore, he takes the position that even when both the Soviet Union and the United States are equally committed to searching for agreement on a particular issue, "misunderstandings arise through different intepretations of the agreed provisions as a result of the differences in the interests and philosophies of the sides."[30] Bovin takes a similar position. He writes that "decades of enmity and confrontation created in the West *as well as in the East* tenacious stereotyped views of the other side—views obtained primarily through the prism of suspicion." While recent "headway" in political relations has "begun to alter the psychological climate," he notes, "there still remains a heavy ballast of distrust which continues to inhibit the actions of the sides," i.e., *both* sides.[31] Oleshuk carries this one step farther and suggests that the Soviet Union may bear some of the responsibility for past tensions. "The period of the 'cold war,'" he writes, "abounded in examples of how certain forces carried on ideological subversion which led to alienation or even hostility between nations." Those Americans who associate the continuing ideological competition between the USSR and the United States with such subversion, he confesses, "naturally object to it with the best of motives."[32] The "certain forces" which prompted such suspicions among Americans could only be the Soviet secret police.

Arbatov goes further still. In his major work, *Ideologicheskaya bor'ba v sovremennykh mezhdunarodnykh otnosheniyakh* [*The Ideological Struggle and Contemporary International Relations*] (1970), the Institute's director condemns the baneful influence of Soviet writers, claiming to be Marxist, who "rejected modern genetics, the theory of relativity, cybernetics and some other major discoveries" and who produced "vulgaristic works" in the social sciences. The authors of these works, who "masked their own dogmatism, laziness of thought or simply lack of knowledge with lofty ideological considerations, with 'concern' for the purity of Marxist-Leninist theory," he suggests, seriously damaged the reputation of Soviet science and nourished anti-communist sentiments in the West. The "upswing of creative Marxism," the "extensive efforts carried out in the recent period to overcome stagnation, dogmatism and subjectivism," all helped to bring about "a marked change in world public opinion, in its attitude toward communism."[33] In Arbatov's view, then, anti-communism in the West was, in some measure, a response to Soviet intellectual obscurantism! A unique confession, to say the least.

Much indeed is new in Soviet perceptions of the United States (and, to some extent, even of themselves). Interests, attitudes, expectations, influences—the underlying "motive forces" of American foreign policy—are recognized to be more differentiated than originally assumed.

What all this seems to suggest, therefore, is that U.S. policy makers do not conform to doctrinal expectations, i.e., they are not genetically programmed to act solely in response to the inescapable economic laws of capitalism. Soviet Americanists recognize that Washington policy makers often act in terms not of what they must do as bourgeois capitalists or want to do but, rather, of what they think they *can* do (or sometimes, as Trofimenko suggests, in terms of "what is permitted"). Within these limitations they are often flexible and adaptive, capable of moving in more than one direction.

These analyses also imply that in the view of Soviet Americanists the United States is a declining threat to the basic security interests of the USSR. While the fundamental character of U.S. foreign policy—its capitalist nature—has not been altered, serious modifications have begun to occur in its behavior and even its political outlook. As we noted earlier, anti-communism and anti-Sovietism, though not completely eviscerated, are no longer the vital force they once were in the minds of America's "ruling circles." Further, the legitimacy of the USSR is accepted, with scarcely any mention of the once ominous danger of "capitalist restoration." And the status of the Soviet Union as a major world power is hardly subject to challenge.

Most reassuring, in this regard, is the increased Soviet awareness that White House policy is, in some measure, open to influence. Not only does Soviet military power exert constraint on Washington's "aggressive imperialist ambitions"—a fact understood even by Stalin—but Soviet analysts now assume, as we have seen, that Soviet diplomacy itself can affect the political balance in the United States and influence the perceptions of its leaders. And former SShA board member V. S. Zagladin reminds his readers of the

> conclusion reached by the CPSU Central Committee to the effect that it would be erroneous to consider the development of imperialism only as a result of the effects of its own internal laws. . . . It means that the possibilities of the socialist world actively to influence imperialist policy are growing. This also means that socialism has a growing responsibility for the utilization of these possibilities.[34]

Whatever the intentions of the United States, it would seem, Soviet diplomacy has numerous "possibilities" through which it can parry or soften initiatives from Washington.

What does all this add up to? We have seen that, in contrast even to the Khrushchev period, recent efforts to develop greater expertise have led to a considerable broadening of views on the United States. Greater objectivity and sophistication has resulted in a more benign, less threatening appraisal of America's policies and purposes. What bearing, it might be asked, does this development have on Soviet behavior? Does a more realistic outlook encourage more temperate Soviet policies toward this country?

The answer to this question is somewhat problematic. It can be argued that increased sophistication does not necessarily lead to greater Soviet moderation. Better informed and more judicious analyses of American foreign policy may have various results. "With greater knowledge," Merle Fainsod observed several years ago, ". . . also comes greater uncertainty."[35] In a number of instances, as we have seen, this has precisely been the case. Even so dogmatically self-assured a figure as Anatoly Gromyko has found American political life to be so "varied and multiform" that, "now and then it is difficult to make out the real situation of things in the chaotic conglomeration of facts."[36] Having come to see ambiguity and contradictoriness in American policy, having learned of the variety of forces at work and views held, the problem for Soviet analysts of interpreting U.S. behavior is in many ways more complex now than in earlier days, when less subtle views held sway. Thus, far from encouraging Soviet policy makers to take a conciliatory posture, greater knowledge may have aggravated the problem of making any decision at all.

A moderate policy stance may, furthermore, result not from more realistic perceptions but precisely the reverse, from misperceptions. Theoretically an exaggerated regard for another nation's military capabilities, its economic power and efficiency, the unity and commitment, i.e., the "political will," of its ruling elites, may encourage interest in political accommodation at a time when an assertive policy might prove fruitful. Misperception may, of course, also lead to a more aggressive posture than the facts warrant—as in the 1930s when a mixture of ignorance and prejudice led the Nazi leadership in Berlin to discount the possibility of American intervention in World War II. Hitler's contempt for a "mongrelized" America, his disdain for democratic forms and processes, led him to create an image of America as weaker and less dangerous than the real one—a misperception with fatal consequences for its holder.

158

Clearly the accuracy—or inaccuracy—of a leadership's perceptions does not by itself produce any particular policy outlook. Moreover, the Kremlin—like the White House—must weigh a variety of other considerations, both international and domestic. A more realistic "image of the adversary" is therefore but one of many factors which bear upon policy choices.

Nonetheless, the evidence seems persuasive that a correlation exists between improved perceptions on the one hand and attitudes towards the United States on the other. Allowing that in particular circumstances individual analysts might feel hostile towards the United States, our analysis leads us to concur with the "general rule" set forth by Griffiths: "the more perceptive an individual's stated view of the adversary, the less hostile his apparent feelings toward it, the more he was inclined to urge policies of conflict limitation and agreement."[37] This conclusion seems warranted for at least two reasons. First, as the Stalin period amply demonstrated, acceptance of a simplistic, crudely deterministic Marxist-Leninist world view has distinctly hostile policy implications. Living on the same planet with a United States perceived to be undifferentiatedly aggressive, expansionist and anti-Soviet places a premium on suspicion, mistrust, and deception, diplomatic qualities necessary to ensure national survival. Sharing a less theological, increasingly pragmatic and objective world outlook, Soviet analysts today endorse a more hopeful view of capitalist foreign policy than did their Stalinist predecessors, and are as a result more optimistic about the prospects for coexistence and accommodation.

Second, along with their improved perceptions, Soviet Americanists seem to have developed a particularly acute appreciation of the advantages which a relaxed international atmosphere holds for Soviet diplomacy. They have argued, as we saw in the previous chapter, that in a non-threatening international environment the United States would have little reason or pretext to pursue a "hard" line internationally and thereby possibly endanger Soviet security interests. A conciliatory posture would also promote the interests and policies of the more tractable, less belligerent elements in Washington. Thus though Arbatov derides the view that America's acceptance of détente is in any sense the result of "some sudden captivation by the idea of good will toward the Soviet Union,"[38] he clearly favors continuation of such a policy as best suited to Soviet interests.

What is the significance of this phenomenon? How important are these more temperate views expressed by Soviet Amerikanisty? How, if at all, do they influence Soviet policy? Does the existence of such moderate perspectives have any policy implications for the United States? While outsiders can only guess at the answers to these elusive questions, a number of points suggest themselves.

It must be recognized, first of all, that discussions of the United States set forth by Soviet analysts are not simply the findings of scholarly investigation. Given the intensely politicized nature of intellectual activity in the USSR, the research findings presented by Soviet Americanists should not be viewed primarily in terms of a search for some objective reality. They are more properly seen as arguments in an ongoing political debate. As Griffiths has persuasively argued, political analyses published in the Soviet Union are never "value free" research efforts aimed at finding the truth, but always positions intimately related to matters of policy. They are designed more to win debates and bolster policy preferences than to set forth individual perceptions.[39]

Thus the "moderate" views regarding the United States expressed by Soviet Americanists are being printed in SShA for policy-related reasons, viz., to justify and gain support for a conciliatory posture towards the United States. Given the anti-American prejudices of the Stalinist tradition, such justification was essential. After all, if fruitful contacts are even to be considered, "realistic" leaders had to be found in Washington with whom negotiations could honorably be contemplated. For détente policy to be creditable, especially at home, the image of the United States as a "predatory imperialist power" had to be modified. Capitalist America somehow had to appear to present no dangers to Soviet security and to share common interests with the USSR in a number of areas.

Soviet Americanists are, therefore, the scholar-publicists of détente. Created originally to help Soviet policy makers gain a better understanding of the "complex and contradictory nature" of the United States, the USA Institute also serves as the handmaiden of policy, justifying and legitimizing the Kremlin's current political line. This is true in a more direct sense. The work of the institute, like that of many other academic organizations in the Soviet Union, is directly intertwined with policy making. As one well-informed source has observed, "The research institutes of the USSR Academy of Sciences act practically as research departments of various bureaucracies. In a sense, those which deal with foreign policy matters function as do departments of fundamental research in any intelligence service."[40] The USA Institute should therefore also be considered a research adjunct of the Soviet foreign-policy apparatus.

Moscow's Amerikanisty are also the salesmen of détente. In addition to performing the functions of policy-oriented research and policy rationalization, they have the responsibility of helping to promote improved relations with the United States. Whether on Capitol Hill or in joint symposia with the Stanford Research Institute in Moscow, Mr. Arbatov and his colleagues are striving to win the attention—and, to the extent possible, the respect—of influential Americans, to help encourage a greater understanding of Soviet views on such issues as arms control and trade relations, and in general to help develop a personal commitment on the part of their American contacts to the continuing importance of "normalized" Soviet-American relations.

Given these functions, it is logical that the Americanists should have developed a vested interest in détente. They have, as Robert Legvold points out, an "intellectual stake in détente."

> They are the ones who have explained the forces compelling the Western powers to abandon aggressive foreign policies or "positions of strength" strategies and to embrace the Soviet formula of peaceful coexistence. And they are the ones who have calculated the promise and the durability of this new era.[41]

They also have a personal stake in this policy. After all, the very existence and influence of the institute depend on a continuation of something approximating "normal" relations between the two superpowers. Should the international situation seriously deteriorate, the raison d'être of the institute might well be called into question. A return to the dark days of the cold war would eliminate the need for carefully refined, subtle analyses of American politics and society. As

Arbatov has noted, the principles of the cold war are "engagingly simple": there is a "particular enemy," there is a "clear-cut aim"—to fight him might and main, and there are well-established methods of doing so (see p. 131). Traditional state and Party security organs—the Ministry of Defense, the Committee on State Security (KGB), the Central Committee's Institute of Marxism-Leninism, its Higher Party School and its Department of Propaganda—are all seasoned hands in dealing with such contingencies.

Given such a turn of events, the funds and access to the corridors of power, privileges and perquisites (trips to the United States, opportunities to purchase Western consumer goods) currently available to Soviet Americanists would vanish. The conservative ideologues waiting in the wings would reassert themselves much as they did when the cold war began in 1947–48. Arbatov and his co-workers, despite efforts to cloak their comments in appropriate ideological garb, would be denounced (as was Varga) as "soft on capitalism."

The point to be made is that the USA Institute has developed an institutional interest in—and become a lobby for—the policy of détente. It favors détente because the improvement in Soviet-American relations has conferred upon its members considerable rewards, contributes to their professional status and promotes their political influence. The institute benefits from détente; its members therefore endorse it and advocate its continuation. Like members of other interest groups, the Amerikanisty tend "to perceive the interests of Soviet society as a whole through their own prism and to distort and adjust the national interest accordingly."[42] That is to say, institute officials tend to give strong support to détente policies and are inclined to cast their assessments of the United States in a generally positive light.

This is not to suggest, however, that the Americanisty are cynically manipulating their analyses for the purpose of enhancing their status and institutional privileges. Insofar as can be judged from the published record, the views expressed by institute analysts seem to be authentic and sincerely held. Arbatov, for example, has for many years taken moderate positions on a variety of issues. He was an active exponent of Khrushchev's peaceful coexistence policies and defended negotiations with "realistic" capitalist leaders; he strongly endorsed

Khrushchev's campaign to improve the per capita consumption of the Soviet consumer.[43] He has, as we have seen, been critical of "left sectarianism," "dogmatism," and "vulgar Marxism" in Soviet political and intellectual life. Rather than being compelled by the exigencies of self-interest to tailor his views, Arbatov was undoubtedly chosen to head the institute because he was personally committed to a pragmatic and open approach to Soviet-American relations.

Thus whether out of interest or conviction—or, more probably, a combination of the two—Soviet Amerikanisty endorse a comparatively realistic assessment of the United States. Their relatively pragmatic analysis tends to weaken the hold of traditional ideological imagery, and at the same time to reduce apprehension regarding the intentions of American policy makers. How seriously, it may be asked, are such views taken in the Politburo? Judging by external evidence—Arbatov's elevation to the highest organs in the Soviet Communist Party, his election to the Supreme Soviet in 1974 and to full membership in the Academy of Sciences in 1975, his participation in the official delegation accompanying Party Secretary Brezhnev on his visit to the United States in 1973, his prominent role in publicizing current policies in the Soviet media—the USA Institute does seem to have access to the top echelons of power. There is also considerable unofficial testimony—volunteered, especially, by institute officials—that the analyses of senior Amerikanisty are read "at the highest levels."

Without exaggerating their political influence or the degree of objectivity they have attained—their achievements, on both counts, are undoubtedly less than they claim—it seems fair to conclude that Soviet Americanists tend toward the "soft" or moderate view. That is to say, in the continuous Soviet political dialogue on foreign policy, Arbatov and his colleagues—because of professional preoccupations and organizational interests—tend to emphasize the positive aspects of détente and of political trends in the United States. It is their mission, their intellectual commitment and their interest to do so.

What this analysis seems to suggest, therefore, is that, whatever its original motivation, the policy of détente has fed back upon the USSR. We can assume that pragmatic considerations of national interest—the worsening of the Sino-Soviet conflict, deteriorating relations with Eastern Europe (leading in 1968 to the invasion of Czechoslovakia), a sharpening of the arms race—took precedence in both time and importance in the Politburo's decision in the late 1960s to improve relations with the United States. Nevertheless, that decision, once taken, nurtured the growth of a reasonably moderate trend within the Soviet political elite.

In Moscow, as in Washington, it would seem, tension and cold war bolsters the position of Party militants and ideological fundamentalists. A relaxed international climate strengthens the more moderate and more pragmatic elements. While the political mechanisms encouraging moderate trends are similar in both countries, their internal dynamics are, of course, vastly different. Soviet political culture—its anti-capitalist ideology, traditional Russian suspicion of foreigners, the conservatism of the current Soviet leadership—is biased in favor of a basically militant outlook. Nevertheless, one may well argue that two distinct tendencies can be found in Soviet leadership circles: one aggressive, militaristic, mistrustful of the United States, hostile to détente; the other sober, moderate, concerned less about the danger of war than the benefits to be gained in specific areas from mutual collaboration.

This analysis suggests the following by way of policy implications: the United States should seek to conduct itself, as former Deputy Defense Secretary Roswell L. Gilpatrick wrote several years back, "so as to strengthen the dove faction rather than the hawk faction in the political leadership group."[44] To the extent feasible, a conscious effort should be made to act so as not to undermine whatever authority the moderate groups in Moscow may have acquired. Put somewhat differently, we should attempt—taking a feather from Arbatov's cap—to see the détente relationship dynamically, i.e., as a political force in and of itself, which can be used to bolster the influence of the more moderate tendencies in the Soviet leadership, to increase the authority of the more "realistic," less militant elements, and at the same time to weaken the position of the more conservative, ideologically orthodox groups.

The policy orientation of the moderate group toward the United States is, of course, basically different from that of their traditionalist colleagues. They view U.S. foreign policy today as less belligerent, less anti-Soviet, less prone to taking unnecessary military risks, and generally less threatening than at any time in the past. These elements do not see this country as threatening basic Soviet security interests. But they do not regard us as weak, passive or isolationist. The vast military resources of the United States are known and respected, as are our economic capabilities, especially in the area of "scientific-technical revolution." While America's expansionist proclivities (as seen by Moscow) have waned, our international interests and commitments remain considerable and our willingness to use force where necessary to protect them is recognized. There seems little evidence of a loss of will on the part of high-level American officials or, for that matter, that domestic concerns are paralyzing their ability to act. The image, then, is of a still powerful but more restrained, more circumspect, less menacing United States, a nation with which one can do business, but one not to be regarded lightly. The prevalence of such attitudes in the Kremlin would be far more conducive to political accommodation and mutual agreement in Soviet-American relations than would more militant, anti-American views. They should, where possible, be encouraged.

There are some, it should be noted, who reach rather different conclusions. They suggest that, based on the findings of Soviet researchers, Moscow is beginning to see this country as increasingly impotent. One group fears, for example, that Soviet analysts "perceive an antimilitaristic trend" in the United States.

> The ending of conscription, a new budget appraisal system in the Congress, the problem of high unemployment and inflation, the effects of the anti-war movement, resentment of the military-industrial complex, opposition to foreign aid programs, and a general disillusionment in the public mind regarding the integrity and effectiveness of "big government" are among the factors the Soviets see as eroding the U.S. will to continue the active role the United States has played in the international arena. . . . America's political will to compete and take risks has in the Soviet view taken a major setback from the strength it had in the 1960s.[45]

In other words, internal economic and political crises "have contributed to a weakening of the U.S. national will, among both the leadership and society."[46] Soviet awareness of this situation, apparently, makes this especially ominous.

Should the Kremlin come to perceive an internally deteriorating America, one lacking credibility abroad and political will at home, this might well be serious cause for concern. Such a development could, of course, have a significant impact on Soviet policy calculations, on the Kremlin's assessment of the risks and opportunities associated with various policy options available to them. This is not, however, an accurate reading of the evidence. As we have shown at some length, Soviet analysts have not portrayed the United States as in any real sense debilitated. Though deeply troubled by the increasing disenchantment and war-weariness of the American public and the intense, interlocking social and economic crises of the last decade, U.S. "ruling circles" have not been described as politically enfeebled or paralyzed by internal conflict. On the contrary, U.S. political leaders have generally been held in high regard by analysts at the USA Institute. They have been characterized, as we saw earlier, as adaptive, resourceful, flexible defenders of their national (class) interests.

Internationally, furthermore, American policy has been seen as forceful, not withdrawn. Though more "sober" than during the 1960s, Washington policy makers were not, as they might have been, affected by a post-Vietnam isolationist syndrome (a view strongly argued by Zhurkin). Moreover, despite their sensitivity regarding "the internal contradictions of capitalism," Soviet analysts have avoided suggesting that recent economic problems would result in a ruinous depression. In fact, as Robert Legvold has pointed out, Moscow's Amerikanisty were among "the least distracted by the revolutionary implications of capitalism's 'deepening general crisis.'"[47] Thus, to the extent that the Kremlin's image of America has been shaped by the research studies undertaken at the USA Institute, its overall assessment of U.S. "political will" has not been seriously diminished.

The partisans of this more cautionary outlook do, however, have a point. Soviet policy choices are affected by their estimates of the intentions and capabilities of the United States. In this regard, the Kremlin leaders keep a careful eye on the strategic military balance. Should the military position of the United States seem to have been significantly weakened, the men in the Politburo might be emboldened to undertake a more adventurous policy course. A deterioration of the American military position would also imperil the political position of the Soviet moderates. By reducing American military power, the risks of militancy would decline and their main argument against the "hawks" in the Soviet political elite would be undermined.* The advantages of détente might then seem rather insignificant (certainly slow and long-term) in contrast to immediate opportunities for gain from a more aggressive posture. As a prior condition to what we earlier called "the strategy of reassurance," the United States must therefore strive to maintain a strategic military capability sufficiently impressive to stay the "hawks" in Moscow and provide credence to the arguments of the "doves."

Put more broadly, in order to bolster the position of the moderate trend within the Soviet political leadership, the United States should—as a matter of deliberate policy—seek to act in such a way as to reinforce the position of those who share it. At the same time we should consciously strive to avoid giving credence to the arguments of those opposed. We should, to take another and rather different example, make due allowance for Soviet sensitivites regarding the issue of equality of status. From the tone and intensity of their arguments, Soviet sources to this day remain extraordinarily touchy about being dealt with as an inferior power. Their complaints about being regarded as illegitimate, about the desire of the West to "restore capitalism" in their country, about the Western policy of seeking to harm their interests, about being treated as a pariah, as being economically second-rate and militarily incompetent, all of this is taken to imply second-class status.

Given their acute sensitivity on this issue, a conscious effort should be made—*to the degree this is not inconsistent with overall American interests*—to avoid policies which indicate that the Soviet Union is being dealt with by the United States on anything less than a fully equal basis. While the United States should clearly not abandon its diplomatic advantages in the Middle East solely out of concern for Moscow's chronic difficulties in the area, the White House should be aware that its human-rights policy is, inevitably, seen in the Kremlin

---

*I am grateful to Vernon Aspaturian for reminding me of this important point.

as an affront to Soviet domestic sovereignty and international prestige.* In other words, it remains important to behave in a way that avoids giving unnecessary umbrage. Talk of capitalist "class hatred" and imperialism's "utopian strategy of social revenge" still echo in the Soviet corridors of power. We should not contribute to its credibility.

Another step in this direction, one geared in particular to ensure the continuation of a moderate orientation in the Soviet leadership after the departure of Brezhnev, would be to seek to reinforce the sentiment that the Soviet Union will benefit from a continuation of détente. In this regard, special attention should be focused on what increasingly have been called questions of a "pan-human" or "global" scale. *IMEMO* Director Nikolai Inozemtsev, in particular, has been stressing the existence of common problems confronting all nations of whatever social system, problems deriving, as he describes it *"from contradictions in the development of the human race as a whole."* Among these, he focuses on two: the prevention of a new world war, which is "the prime task of all mankind, on it depends 'the preservation of human society,' " and environmental questions—depletion of resources, pollution of the environment, population growth— "problems of the greatest import from the point of view of future prospects."[48]

Concentrating on "spheres of common interest"—concern regarding which is clearly growing—will tend to demonstrate that the cold war policy of seeking to harm the other side has indeed been jettisoned. The Apollo-Soyuz mission had precisely this effect.[49] And to the extent that problems of ensuring adequate energy supplies or controlling water pollution are, like strategic weapons limitation, questions of both a technical and political nature, the sophistication and political sensitivities which have emerged in the Soviet arms control community may also develop elsewhere during the long-term discussions and negotiations on these vexing and difficult issues.

* In pointing up some of the difficulties which the Carter administration's aggressive stance on human rights has generated, I am not, it should be noted, condoning Soviet practices. No honest observer of Soviet affairs can possibly remain insensitive to the regime's callous and often brutal disregard of the rights and liberties of its citizens. While detesting such practices, I nevertheless question the tactical wisdom of the administration's policy of open and direct confrontation on this highly sensitive issue.

The Soviet view, as espoused by moderate elements, has been that "the emergence of progressively new problems on a global scale" requires "joint efforts by all states," that "peaceful competition not only does not rule out but on the contrary presupposes the wide-scale development of mutually advantageous cooperation among states."[50] The focus here is on problems of a "pan-human" scale, in which all sides have interests—interests defined by membership in the human race rather than class. This approach—common concern, similarity of interest rather than class conflict and struggle—should be endorsed.

Much as Soviet Americanists view détente as a dynamic process by which "sober" elements can be bolstered, Washington policy makers should attempt to do likewise. While maintaining a strong military posture—which, somewhat paradoxically, is vital to the argument of Soviet moderates—the United States should strive to use détente to further diminish the Soviet fear of American hostility and neutralize Soviet leadership opinion which inclines toward a policy of confrontation and antagonism. The Kremlin leaders might then, over time, come to accept the view that "realism" in Soviet-American relations, while in our interest, also serves theirs. Then, it may be hoped, this more moderate orientation will eventually prevail.

NOTES

All of the books and articles cited below are given in condensed form; for full data see Works Cited. A few frequently cited sources and journals are given in abbreviation throughout:

SShA   *SShA: ekonomika, politika, ideologiya*
MEMO   *Mirovaya ekonomika i mezhdunarodnye otnosheniya*
CDSP   *Current Digest of the Soviet Press*
FBIS   *Foreign Broadcast Information Service, Daily Reports*, vol. 3, *The Soviet Union*

An English-language translation of *SShA* has been made available to the public by the U.S. government for the period January 1970 through December 1975 and again since April 1977. (*USA: Economics, Politics, Ideology*. Arlington, Virginia: U.S. Joint Publications Research Service.) Responsibility for the translations appearing here is the author's.

Introduction

1. Barghoorn, *The Soviet Image*, p. 277.

2. See especially Robert C. Tucker, "The Dialectics of Coexistence," *The Soviet Political Mind* (New York: Praeger, 1963), pp. 201–22; Zimmerman, *Soviet Perspectives*; and Griffiths, "Image, Politics and Learning."

3. Adomeit, *Soviet Risk-Taking*, p. 19.

4. See, for example, Shulman, "SALT," pp. 101–21.

5. Urban, "A Conversation," p. 61.

6. Ra'anan, *The Changing American-Soviet Strategic Balance*, pp. 11–12.

7. Ibid, p. 12.

8. Under the editorship of Valentin M. Berezhkov, the current circulation of *SShA* is 34,000, having begun in 1970 with 22,000. While it is closely connected with the *USA Institute*, Berezhkov told me that he seeks to keep it

somewhat independent. Thus not only is it housed separately but about half the members of its editorial board are non-institute Amerikanisty either from other research establishments, such as the Institute for World Economy and International Relations, or from the International Department of the Central Committee of the Soviet Communist Party. Among the latter, V. V. Zagladin, deputy chief of the International Department, served on *SShA*'s Editorial Board until August 1973. The current ranking Party official on the journal is N. V. Mostovets, identified by Berezhkov as chief of the International Department's North American section. K. N. Brutents, also from the International Department, serves on the editorial board. Thus while not simply the house organ of the *USA Institute*—it is described on its masthead as a "Scholarly and Public Affairs Journal"—*SShA* is a carefully monitored and officially sanctioned source of information and analysis on current developments in the United States.

9. The main sources reviewed have been the writings of the institute's Director Georgi Arbatov; Deputy Director Vitaly V. Zhurkin; Genrykh A. Trofimenko, chief of the institute's U.S. Foreign Policy Department; Yuri A. Shvedkov, chief of section on U.S. Foreign Policy Machinery and Doctrines; Igor A. Geyevsky, chief of section on U.S. Mass Social Movements; Anatoly A. Gromyko, former chief of section on U.S. Foreign Policy Doctrine; as well as articles by numerous other analysts. Many of the members of this group have spent considerable time in the United States. I have on several occasions interviewed most of the abovementioned authors, most recently on a research trip to Moscow in May 1974.

10. *Izvestiya*, 30 October 1973, p. 4.

Chapter 1

1. Hollander, *Soviet and American Society*, p. 25.

2. It also reflects their abiding concern regarding the chronic economic backwardness of their own country. Despite fifty years of diligent efforts, Soviet industry and agriculture—much like those in a developing country—still require outside economic assistance. They must view American aid, as Nathan Leites suggests, with a deep sense of "shame" and "subdued despair" ("The New Economic Togetherness," pp. 257, 263).

3. Friedberg, "The U.S. in the U.S.S.R.," p. 530.

4. Ibid., p. 539.

5. Quoted in *Soviet Policy-Making*, ed. Peter H. Juviler and Henry W. Morton (New York: Praeger, 1967), p. 17.

6. For a discussion of the deep psychological resentments attached to Moscow's "catching up with America" slogan, see Schwartz, *The Foreign Policy of the USSR*, pp. 84–89.

7. Quoted in *Current Soviet Policies —II: The Documentary Record of the 20th Communist Party Congress and its Aftermath*, ed. Leo Gruliow (New York: Praeger, 1957), pp. 30–31.

8. Chossudovsky, "Genoa Revisited," p. 574.

9. Inozemtsev, "Sovremennye SShA," pp. 6–7.

10. Ibid, p. 8.

11. Dalin, "Sovremennyi krizis," p. 19.

12. Bobrakov, "Amerikanskaya ekonomika," p. 58.

13. Bobrakov, "O poslaniyakh," p. 61.

14. Dalin, "Sovremennyi krizis," p. 20.

15. Quoted in David Lascelles, "Soviet Expert Predicts Economic Growth in the West," *Financial Times* (London), 3 November 1976, p. 4; in *FBIS*, 5 November 1976, p. E2.

16. Zorin, "Vnutrennie problemy," p. 13.

17. Shapiro, "SShA," p. 16.

18. Kudrov, "Nekotorye voprosy," pp. 15–29.

19. Arbatov, G. A., "Vneshnyaya politika—I," p. 6.

20. Ibid., pp. 3–4.

21. Arbatov, G. A., "Vneshnyaya politika—II," p. 6. He notes: "the country possessing scientific and technical superiority could scarcely count on successfully utilizing it in order to place others in a position of firm and long-term dependence . . . remember the history of radar, aircraft engines, nuclear power and missiles[!]" The fact that Gagarin was first in space but Armstrong first on the moon still galls.

22. Ibid., p. 7.

23. Arbatov, G. A., ed., *SShA: Nauchno-tekhnicheskaya revoliutsiya*, pp. 25, 26.

24. The tone of Arbatov's language—either compete with the United States or walk in its shadow—is reminiscent of that of Stalin, who warned in 1934 of Russia's need to catch up with the advanced industrial nations. "Either we do it," he said, "or we shall be crushed" (J. Stalin, *Problems of Leninism* [Moscow: Foreign Languages Publishing House, 1954], p. 592).

25. Arbatov, G. A., "Vneshnyaya politika—II," p. 6.

26. Arbatov, G. A., ed., *SShA: Nauchno-tekhnicheskaya revoliutsiya*, p. 122.

27. Shapiro, "SShA," p. 28.

28. Kudrov, "Glavnye," pp. 36–40. See also Gromeka, "SShA," pp. 38–41 and Arbatov, G. A., ed., *SShA: Nauchno-tekhnicheskaya revoliutsiya*, pp. 76–80.

29. Rachkov, "The Monopolies," p. A7.
30. Inozemtsev, "The Nature of Contradictions," p. 19.
31. Dalin, "Sovremennyi krizis," p. 20.
32. Bobrakov, "Gosudarstvenno," p. 52.
33. Pechatnov, "Demokraty," p. 58.
34. Bogdanov, "Antiinflatsionnaya politika," p. 13. Bogdanov, undoubtedly, was not only referring to American economists. Soviet writers during the mid-1960s were themselves rather enthusiastic regarding the accomplishments of "state-monopoly regulation." See V. M. Shamberg, "Amerikanskie zametki" [American Notes], MEMO, no. 9 (September 1966), pp. 121–24.
35. Dalin, "Sovremennyi krizis," p. 19.
36. Bobrakov, "Amerikanskaya ekonomika," p. 61.
37. "Ekonomicheskoe polozhenie—I," p. 127.
38. Bobrakov, "Gosudarstvenno," p. 58.
39. Bobrakov, "Ekonomicheskie problemy," p. 32.
40. "Ekonomicheskoe polozhenie—II," p. 59. This issue of SShA contains an interview with Arjay Miller of the Stanford School of Business Administration, in which he is cited as having declared that "National planning is essential."
41. "Ekonomicheskoe polozhhenie—I," p. 127. Anikin even suggests that certain branches of the economy—namely the railroads—might "revert to the state."
42. Boffa, "How it is Possible to Cooperate," p. B3.
43. Inozemtsev, "Peculiarities of Contemporary Imperialism," p. 2, and his "On Contemporary Imperialism," p. 20.
44. Geyevsky, "Sotsial'nyi mir," pp. 30–31, 26.
45. Geyevsky, "Raznolikaya amerika," p. 54.
46. Gromyko, Diplomatiya p. 396.
47. See, for example, the article on "Militarism" in the Bol'shaya Sovetskaya Entsiklopediya, 2d ed. (Moscow, 1954), vol. 27, p. 481.
48. Trofimenko, review of B. D. Pyadyshev, p. 84.
49. Tsagolov, "Voenno-promyshlennyi kompleks," p. 24.
50. Kuusinen, ed., Fundamentals of Marxism-Leninism, p. 331.
51. Tsagolov, "Voenno-promyshlennyi kompleks," pp. 27–28.
52. Gromyko, 1036 dnei, pp. 87–88.
53. Gromyko, Diplomatiya, pp. 395–96.
54. Arbatov, G. A., "Sovetsko-amerikanskye otnosheniya v 70-e gody," p. 30.

55. Arbatov, G. A., "Vneshnyaya politika—I." p. 9.

56. Arbatov, G. A., "O sovetsko-amerikanskikh otnosheniyakh," pp. 109–10.

57. Arbatov, G. A., "Shag," p. 57.

58. Arbatov, G. A., "Administratsiya Niksona," p. 10.

59. Trofimenko, "Militarizm," p. 71.

60. Geyevsky, "Obostrenie," p. 5.

61. Trofimenko, "Militarizm," p. 71.

62. Shvedkov, "'Doktrina Niksona,'" p. 32.

63. Arbatov, G. A., "Strength-Policy Stalemates," p. 19.

64. Arbatov, G. A., "Administratsiya Niksona," p. 11.

65. Svyatov and Sergeyev, "Politika," p. 74.

66. Arbatov, G. A., ed., *SShA: Nauchno-tekhnicheskaya revoliutsiya*, p. 21.

67. Mileikovsky, "Tsennoe issledovanie," p. 94.

68. Arbatov, G. A., "Administratsiya Niksona," p. 11.

69. See, for example, V. Nazarevsky, "U.S. Aggressor's Troubles at Home," *International Affairs*, no. 8 (1966), pp. 46–48.

70. Arbatov, G. A., "Administratsiya Niksona," p. 11.

71. See, for example, Turkatenko, "Korporatsii SShA," p. 36, where it is suggested that "the factor of military might . . . is moving into the background," as a means to protect the interests of the multinational corporations. "Full emphasis is now being given to the 'primacy of economics.'"

72. Arbatov, G. A., ed., *SShA: Nauchno-tekhnicheskaya revoliutsiya*, p. 68.

73. Kruglov, "Amerikanskie monopolii," pp. 69–70.

74. Arbatov, G. A., "Sovetsko-amerikanskie otnosheniya v 70-e gody," p. 33.

75. Zorin, "Vnutrennie problemy," p. 5. A veteran journalist, then a leading member of the institute staff, Zorin had visited the United States in the early 1960s. When I met him in Moscow in 1967 he was proudly wearing a PT-109 tie clip given to him by Robert Kennedy. Though now active as a TV commentator and no longer at the institute, Zorin remains a member of *SShA*'s editorial board.

76. Oleshchuk, review of *Moral and Military Aspects*, p. 67.

77. Arbatov, G. A., "American Imperialism," pp. 1–2.

78. Geyevsky, "Obostrenie," p. 6.

79. Zorin, "Vnutrennie problemy," p. 10.

80. Arbatov, G. A., and Zhurkin, "Podkhod k peregovoram," p. 44.

81. Trofimenko, "From Confrontation to Coexistence," p. 38.
82. Geyevsky, "Obostrenie," p. 6.
83. Ibid., pp. 7–8.
84. Dolgopolova, "Voennye raskhody," p. 114.
85. Svyatov and Sergeyev, "Politika i prioritety," pp. 94–95.
86. Arbatov, G. A., "O sovetsko-amerikanskikh otnosheniyakh," p. 107.
87. Ibid., p. 107.
88. Ibid., pp. 107–8.
89. Zhurkin, "Politika imperializma," pp. 24–25.
90. "O dolgosruchnykh tselyakh," p. 127.
91. Berezhkov, "Yedinstvennaya al'ternativa," p. 3.
92. Geyevsky, "Bor'ba chernykh," p. 25.
93. Shvedkov, "Doktrina Niksona,'" p. 33.
94. Geyevsky, "Sotsial'nyi mir," pp. 30–31.
95. See Mileikovsky, "Krizisnye protsessy," Parts I and II.
96. "Nauchnaya konferentsiya," p. 33.
97. Boffa, "How it is Possible to Cooperate," p. B1.
98. Zorin, "Vnutrennie problemy," p. 9.
99. Mostovets, "Novaya vekha," p. 17. Mostovets was paraphrasing a speech by Gus Hall, general secretary of the Communist Party of the USA to its 21st Congress in June 1975.
100. Quoted in Legvold, "Four Policy Perspectives," p. 71.
101. Ponomarev, "Speech to All-Army Conference," p. R3.

Chapter 2

1. Kuusinen, ed., Fundamentals of Marxism-Leninism, p. 327.
2. Ibid., p. 326.
3. Lenin on the United States, p. 401.
4. This view is fully described in Barghoorn, The Soviet Image, and Griffiths, "Image, Politics and Learning," esp. pp. 123–40. For a discussion of this harsh image of America in the context of Stalin's foreign policy doctrines, see Paul Marantz, "Prelude to Détente," pp. 505–9.
5. See especially Griffiths, "Image, Politics and Learning," passim.
6. Gromyko, 1036 dnei, p. 93.
7. Gromyko, Diplomatiya, pp. 234–43.
8. Bessmenykh, "Diplomaticheskii apparat," p. 104.
9. Shvedkov, "Glavnye tsentry," p. 78.
10. Yermolenko, "O 'reideologizatsii,' " pp. 24, 25.

11. Arbatov, G. A., ed., *SShA: Nauchno-tekhnicheskaya revoliutsiya*, p. 38.

12. Khlebny, "Kapitalizm SShA," pp. 22–23.

13. Yakovin, "Okean," p. 80.

14. Turkatenko, "Korporatsii SShA.," p. 30.

15. Petrovsky, "Anatomy of Presidential Power," p. 129.

16. Menshikov, *Ekonomicheskaya politika*, pp. 114–15.

17. Borisov, review of Gromyko's *1036 dnei*, p. 184.

18. Yakovlev, *Prestupivshie gran'*, p. 6.

19. Griffiths, "Image, Politics and Learning," pp. 330–31.

20. Ibid., p. 86.

21. Quoted in Nordahl, "Stalinist Ideology," p. 241. For a thoughtful analysis of the controversy over Varga's unorthodox views, see Marantz, "Soviet Foreign Policy Factionalism Under Stalin?"

22. *Washington Post*, 27 October 1973.

23. Arbatov, G. A., *Ideologicheskaya bor'ba*, p. 259.

24. Inozemtsev, "Sovremennye SShA," p. 12.

25. "Text of Gromyko speech at UN General Assembly," *Pravda*, 26 September 1973, p. 4; *FBIS*, 27 September 1973, p. A5.

26. Shvedkov, "Strategiya," pp. 22–23, 37.

27. Gromyko, *1036 dnei*, p. 158.

28. Ibid., p. 224.

29. Shvedkov, "Strategiya," p. 23.

30. Gromyko, *Diplomatiya*, pp. 229–30.

31. Zhurkin, "SShA," p. 22.

32. Shvedkov, "Novaya kniga," p. 96.

33. Gromyko, *Diplomatiya*, p. 231.

34. Genri, "Protiv," pp. 21–22.

35. Yakovlev, "SSSR-SShA," p. 13.

36. Gromyko, *1036 dnei*, p. 82.

37. Gromyko, *Diplomatiya*, p. 230.

38. Trofimenko, "From Confrontation to Coexistence," p. 36.

39. Gromyko, "Menyayushchiesya nastroeniya," p. 74.

40. Tomashevsky, "Na puti," pp. 5–6.

41. "Vstrechi v verkhakh," p. 3.

42. Yakovlev, "SSSR-SShA," p. 17.

43. Shvedkov, "Glavnye tsentry," p. 46.

44. See Yakovlev's *Prestupivshie gran'*.

45. Gusev, "Moscow, on Sakharov."

46. Shulman, "On Learning to Live with Authoritarian Regimes," p. 330.

47. Shvetsov, "Rol' kongressa," p. 259.

48. Portnyagin, "Kritika planov," pp. 75–76.

49. Anichkina, "Bor'ba v kongresse," pp. 78–79.

50. Shvetsov, "Rol' kongressa," p. 278.

51. Ibid., p. 269.

52. Konovalov and Savel'yev, "Aktsiya," p. 97.

53. Belonogov, "Ispolnitel'noe soglashenie," p. 19.

54. Shershnev, "Soblyudat' usloviya ravnopraviya," p. 69.

55. Anichkina, "Bor'ba v kongresse," p. 80.

56. Solomatina, "Predely," p. 91.

57. New York Times, 30 September 1976.

58. Mosely, "The Soviet Citizen," p. 454.

59. Smith, The Russians, pp. 245–60.

60. Zorin, "200-letie," pp. 25–26. See also Petrovsky, "Anatomy of Presidential Power," p. 129.

61. Chetverikov, Kto i kak delaet politiku SShA, p. 20; and Yanchuk, "Mekhanizm," p. 78.

62. Shvetsov, "Rol' kongressa," p. 278, and Konovalov and Savel'yev, "Aktsiya," p. 94.

63. Popova, "Senat," p. 23.

64. Zolotukhin, "Na puti," pp. 21–22.

65. Malakhin, "Rezhim," p. 112.

66. Lebedev, "Snova problema," p. 30.

67. Ibid., p. 30.

68. Shimanovsky, "Liberaly," p. 43.

69. Ibid., p. 44.

70. Ibid., pp. 44–45.

71. Ibid., p. 44.

72. Ibid., pp. 41–42.

73. Anichkina, "Bor'ba v kongresse," pp. 79–80.

74. Popova, "Senat," pp. 23–24.

75. Ibid., p. 22.

76. Shvetsov, "Rol' kongressa," p. 276.

77. Ibid., p. 278.

78. Dolgopolova, "Voennye raskhody," p. 114.

79. Mosin, "Krizis," p. 23.

80. Ibid., pp. 15–26.

81. Linnik, "Rassleduetsya 'delo Tsru,'" p. 73.

82. Kislov and Osipova, "Obsuzhdenie," p. 72.

83. Pakhomov, "Trezvyi podkhod," pp. 66, 67, 69.

84. Savel'yev, "Vneshnyaya politika," p. 87.

85. Seregin, "Bor'ba," p. 87.

86. Semeyko, "Springs and Levers," p. B3.

87. Lebedev, "Snova problema," p. 33.

88. Savel'yev, "Sotsial'no-politicheskii sostav," p. 113.

89. Savel'yev, "Vneshnyaya politika," passim.

90. Savel'yev, "Sotsial'no-politicheskii sostav," p. 113. The author here is quoting F. Lundberg's *The Rich and the Super-Rich* (Russian edition, Moscow: 1971).

91. Shimanovsky, "Liberaly," p. 49.

92. See Portnyagin, "Kritika planov," passim; Popova, "Senat," passim; and Linnik and Savel'yev, "Ukhod Uil'yama Ful'braita," pp. 122–26 (which should be compared with Robert Kaiser's "Soviets: Zionists Beat Fulbright," *Washington Post*, 8 June 1974). See also Linnik and Savel'yev, "Dzhon Sparkmen," pp. 124–27, and Savel'yev, "Sluzhebnyi apparat," pp. 122–27. There has also been considerable improvement in the treatment of Congress in the popular press. In October 1975, for example, a *Pravda* article focused on the considerable diversity of views to be found in the Congress. This fact was explained by noting that the position of a particular legislator is determined by "interrelated factors," including "his business ties and the special features of his electoral district" (G. Vasilyev and T. Kolesnichenko, "The View from Capital Hill," *Pravda*, 17 October 1975, p. 4; *FBIS*, 24 October 1975, p. B12). This description is not very different from those found in conventional Western analyses.

93. Savel'yev, "Vneshnyaya politika," p. 87.

Chapter 3

1. Shvedkov, "Strategiya," p. 35.

2. Chetverikov, "'Organizatsionnye problemy,'" pp. 32–33.

3. Ibid., p. 29.

4. Ibid., p. 29.

5. Gromyko, "1036 dnei," p. 142.

6. Ibid., p. 89.

7. Ibid., pp. 264–65.

8. Arbatov, G. A., "Soviet-American Relations," p. 4.

9. Chetverikov, "'Organizatsionnye problemy,'" pp. 31–32.

10. Shvedkov, "Strategiya," pp. 20–21.

11. Chetverikov, "'Organizatsionnye problemy,'" p. 31.

12. Shvedkov, "Strategiya," pp. 23–24.

13. Chetverikov, "'Organizatsionnye problemy,'" p. 34.

14. Ibid., p. 31. For a sympathetic account of the "bitter intra-bureaucratic struggle" provoked by the reform—in which all agencies concerned with foreign policy sought "to defend their own purely departmental interests and prerogatives," see Shvedkov and Lesnoy, "Upravlencheskie zaboty," p. 36.

15. Chetverikov, "'Organizatsionnye problemy,'" p. 31.

16. Bobrakov and Novikov, "Ekonomicheskie rychagi," p. 184.

17. Shvedkov, "Glavnye tsentry," p. 81.

18. Bobrakov and Novikov, "Ekonomicheskie rychagi," p. 209.

19. Bessmenykh, "Diplomaticheskii apparat," pp. 115–18. See also Olenev, "Razvedyvatel'noe soobshchestvo," p. 183.

20. Bessmenykh, "Diplomaticheskii apparat," pp. 93–94, 105–6.

21. Arbatov, G. A., "Administratsiya Niksona," p. 12.

22. Arbatov, G. A., "Perspektivy razryadki," p. 30. While Acheson refers to an argument within the "State Department itself . . . between the Planning Staff [with whom he sided] and Soviet experts" (*Present at the Creation* [New York: W. W. Norton and Co., 1959], pp. 375–76), Arbatov writes that "the policy planners and then Secretary of State Acheson opposed the academic Sovietologists [*vystupili protiv uchenykh-sovetologov*]." Is Arbatov simply a hasty reader or does he assume that there is no meaningful difference between the two?

23. Bessmenykh, "Diplomaticheskii apparat," pp. 89, 98.

24. Ibid., p. 102.

25. Chetverikov, "'Organizatsionnye problemy,'" p. 34.

26. Shvedkov, "Strategiya," p. 34.

27. Kulagin, "Voennyi kompleks," pp. 133–34. See also Osipov, "A Complex of Opponents of Détente," p. A9.

28. Kulagin, "Voennyi kompleks," p. 135.

29. Chetverikov, "'Organizatsionnye problemy,'" p. 33.

30. Ibid., p. 33.

31. Kulagin, "Voennyi kompleks," p. 139.

32. Ibid., p. 154.

33. Ibid., p. 144.

34. Tsagolov, "Voenno-promyshlennyi kompleks," p. 26.

35. Zabliuk, "Lobbizm," p. 114.

36. Trofimenko, "Militarizm," p. 66.

37. Oleshuk, "O teorii," p. 9.

38. Arbatov, G. A., "Perspektivy razryadki," p. 26.

39. Kulagin, "Voenny kompleks," pp. 135–36.

40. Ibid., p. 148.

41. Arbatov, G. A., ed., SShA: Nauchno-tekhnicheskaya revoliutsiya, pp. 63–65.

42. Zhurkin, "Vzglyad iznutri VPK," p. 80. The author here is reviewing Elmo R. Zumwalt's On Watch, a Memoir (New York: Quadrangle/The New York Times Book Co., 1976). Zumwalt also refers to "intrabranch" struggles, notes Zhurkin. "For example, within the Navy, a fight is going on between three main 'alliances, . . . fliers, submarines and surface sailors.'"

43. G. A. Trofimenko, "Sovetsko-amerikanskie soglasheniya," pp. 8–9.

44. Arbatov, G. A., ed., SShA: Nauchno-tekhnicheskaya revoliutsiya, p. 47.

45. Mil'shteyn and Semeyko, "Problema nedopystimosti," p. 11.

46. Arbatov, A. G., and Arbatov, G. A., "The Schlesinger Approach," p. 19.

47. Chetverikov, "'Organizatsionnye problemy,'" p. 33.

48. Ibid., p. 32.

49. Semeyko, "Voenno-promyshlennyi kompleks," p. 29.

50. Tsagolov, "Voenno-promyshlennyi kompleks," p. 26.

51. Konovalov, "O programme," p. 69.

52. Mil'shteyn and Semeyko, "Problema nedopystimosti," p. 4.

53. Osipov, "A Complex of Opponents of Détente," p. A9.

54. Shvedkov, "Novaya kniga," p. 94.

55. Browder, The Origins of Soviet-American Diplomacy, p. 18.

56. Gromyko, "Menyayushchiesya nastroeniya," p. 69.

57. Ibid.

58. Berezin, "Ispol'zovanie," p. 291.

59. Ibid., pp. 291–92.

60. Lukin, "'Posle V'etnama,'" pp. 99–100.

61. Trofimenko, "Sovetsko-amerikanskie soglasheniya," p. 11.

62. Potashov, "Ogranichenie vooruzhenii," p. 73. Trofimenko et al. note the "undoubted strengthening of the position of scientists, political activists and broad layers of society in general speaking out against the arms race." Arbatov, G. A., ed., SShA: Nauchno-tekhnicheskaya revoliutsiya, p. 72.

63. See, for example, Trofimenko, "Po povodu knigi Gerberta Iorka," pp. 104–6. Installments from York's book, *Race to Oblivion*, were published (in Russian translation), in the March-August 1971 issues of *SShA*. Most of his discussion of the Soviet role in the arms race was not included.

64. Mil'shteyn, "Progress," pp. 7–8.

65. Gromyko, "Menyayushchiesya nastroeniya," p. 73. (Italics added.)

66. Ibid.

67. Ibid., pp. 71–73.

68. Soll, *The Role of Social Science Research Institutes*, pp. 93–95.

69. Arbatov, G. A., "Sovietology or Kremlinology?," p. 208.

70. Gromyko, "Menyayushchiesya nastroeniya," p. 69.

71. Arbatov, G. A., "United States Foreign Policy," p. 4.

72. Aleksandr Krivitsky, "How Crabs are Caught in San Francisco," *Literaturnaya gazeta*, 14 August 1974, p. 14; *FBIS*, 22 August 1974, p. B11.

73. Arbatov, G. A., "Novye rubezhi," p. 4.

74. Oleshuk, "O teorii," pp. 5, 8.

75. Yuli Yakhontov, "The International Week," *Pravda*, 17 October 1976, p. 4; *FBIS*, 19 October 1976, p. A2.

76. Gromyko, "Menyayushehiesya nastroeniya," pp. 71, 74.

77. Ivanyan, "Obshchestvennoe mnenie," p. 17.

78. Trofimenko, "Militarizm," p. 70.

79. Geyevsky, "Raznolikaya Amerika," p. 51.

80. Linnik, "Zakryto li 'delo TsRU'?," p. 73.

81. Dolgopolova, "Voennye raskhody," p. 114.

82. Zhurkin, "Rol' obshechestvennykh sil," p. 92.

83. Turkatenko, "Korotkoe puteshestvie," pp. 66–67.

84. Quoted in Arbatov, G. A., *Ideologicheskaya bor'ba*, p. 58.

85. Ivanyan, "Obshchestvennoe mnenie," p. 17.

86. Trofimenko, "Politicheskii realizm," p. 7.

87. Ibid.

88. Trofimenko, "Militarizm," p. 71.

89. " 'Doktrina Niksona,' " pp. 45–46.

90. Shvedkov, " 'Doktrina Niksona,' " pp. 28–29.

91. Quoted in Schwartz, "The 1964 Presidential Elections," p. 663.

92. Linnik and Saval'yev, "Ukhod Uil'yama Ful'braita," passim.

93. Kremenyuk, "Prezidentskie vybory," pp. 73, 71, 75–77.

94. Primakov, "Pruzhiny," p. 11.

95. Ibid., pp. 10–11.

96. Kislov, "Antisovetskie proiski," pp. 53–54.

97. Pakhomov, "Trezvyi podkhod," p. 68.

98. Zhurkin, "Rol' obshehestvennykh sil," p. 89.

99. Ibid., p. 92.

100. Ibid., pp. 91–93.

101. Ibid., p. 94.

102. Ibid., pp. 94–95.

103. Ibid., pp. 91, 95,

104. Kremenyuk, "Yeshchë odna popytka," p. 91.

105. Ibid., p. 91. See also M. M. Petrovskaya, review of John E. Mueller's *War, Presidents and Public Opinion* (New York: Wiley, 1973), *SShA*, no. 6 (June 1975), p. 101.

106. Yur'yev, "Chto stoit za mifom," p. 67. See also Turkatenko, "Vzaimosvyaz' problem," p. 62.

107. Trofimenko, "Vneshnyaya politika," p. 17.

108. Arbatov, G. A., "The Dangers of a New Cold War," p. 33.

109. Popov, A. A., "Razryadka," pp. 57–58.

110. Berezhkov, "Politicheskaya obstanovka," pp. 8–10. On "blue collar" support for Goldwater in 1964, see Schwartz, "The 1964 Presidential Elections," p. 667.

111. Popov, N. P., "Predvybornaya kampaniya," p. 57.

112. Petrovsky, "Anatomy of Presidential Power," p. 129.

113. Arbatov, G. A., "Sovetsko-amerikanskie otnosheniya segodnya" (1976), p. 4.

114. Trofimenko, "Vneshnyaya politika," p. 20.

115. See, for example, Popova, N. P., "Predvybornaya kompaniya," p. 59. The veteran *Izvestia* correspondent Stanislav Kondrashov refers to the "political naiveté and lack of information" of the average American (*Izvestia*, 14 October 1976; in *FBIS*, 19 October 1976, p. B2), while *Literaturnaya Gazeta* (20 October 1976) notes his "political ignorance" (*FBIS*, 27 October 1976, p. B7).

116. Hollander, *Soviet and American Society*, p. 26.

117. Ivanyan, "Obshchestvennoe mnenie," p. 17.

118. Ibid., pp. 25–26.

119. Vasil'yev and Parkhitko, "Vozdeistvie," pp. 231–32.

120. Petrusenko, "'Svoboda pechati,'" p. 44.

121. Ibid., pp. 44, 45, 46.

122. Vasil'yev and Parkhitko, "Vozdeistvie," pp. 252–53.

123. Izakov, "Doklad Pentagona," p. 13.

124. Trofimenko, "Militarizm," p. 71.
125. Shvedkov, "'Doktrina Niksona,'" p. 35, and "Strategiya," pp. 38–39.
126. Petrusenko, "O makrekerskom techenii," p. 60.
127. Ibid., pp. 60, 61.
128. Vladimirov, "Pered vyborami," p. 42.
129. Kremenyuk, "Mrak v kontse tunnelya," p. 96.
130. *Radio Moscow* in English to North America 2230 GMT, 22 October 1976; in *FBIS*, 29 October 1976, pp. B4–5.
131. Turkatenko, "Vzaimosvyaz' problem," p. 63.

Chapter 4

1. Gromyko and Kokoshin, "U.S. Foreign Policy Strategy," p. B5; and Gromyko and Shvedkov, *USSR-USA Relations Today*, p. 31.
2. Mil'shteyn and Semeyko, "Problema nedopystimosti," p. 3.
3. Shvedkov, "'Doktrina Niksona,'" p. 29.
4. Trofimenko, "SSSR-SShA," p. 6.
5. Gromyko, *Diplomatiya*, pp. 153–55.
6. Zhurkin, "'Doktrina Niksona,'" p. 87.
7. Trofimenko, "SSSR-SShA," p. 8.
8. Trofimenko, "'Novye rubezhi,'" pp. 63–64. On this same point also see Trofimenko, "From Confrontation to Coexistence," pp. 36–37.
9. Zhurkin, "'Doktrina Niksona,'" p. 86.
10. Ibid., p. 87.
11. Trofimenko, "Voenno-strategicheskie aspekty," p. 56.
12. Arbatov, G. A., "Predislovie," p. 3.
13. Zhurkin, *SShA i mezhdunarodno-politicheskie krizisy*, p. 261.
14. Zhkurin, "Politika imperializma," p. 19.
15. Zhurkin, "'Doktrina Niksona,'" p. 98.
16. Zhurkin, "Politika imperializma," p. 19.
17. "O nekotorykh novykh tendentsiyakh," p. 123.
18. Arbatov, G. A., "Administratsiya Niksona," pp. 3–4.
19. Ibid., p. 14.
20. "'Doktrina Niksona,'" p. 21.
21. Zhurkin, "'Doktrina Niksona,'" p. 90.
22. Zhurkin, "SShA," pp. 23–24.
23. Zhurkin, *SShA i mezhdunarodno-politicheskie krizisy*, p. 157.
24. Zhurkin, "SShA," p. 24.
25. Ibid., p. 24.

26. Ibid., p. 22.
27. Zhurkin, "'Doktrina Niksona,'" p. 91.
28. Shvedkov and Lesnoy, "Upravlencheskie zaboty," p. 37.
29. Arbatov, G. A., "Administratsiya Niksona," p. 15.
30. Zhurkin, "SShA," p. 23.
31. Zhurkin, *SShA i mezhdunarodno-politicheskie krizisy*, p. 160.
32. Ibid., p. 160.
33. Zhurkin, "SShA," p. 23.
34. Zhurkin, "'Doktrina Niksona,'" p. 95.
35. Zhurkin, "SShA," p. 24.
36. Ibid., p. 25. (Italics added.)
37. Zhurkin, *SShA i mezhdunarodno-politicheskie krizisy*, p. 165.
38. Ibid., pp. 25–26.
39. "'Doktrina Niksona,'" p. 42.
40. Jacques Duclos, "October and Modern Times," *Pravda*, 7 November 1973, p. 5; *FBIS*, 9 November 1973, p. P6.
41. Zhurkin, "'Doktrina Niksona,'" p. 96.
42. Ibid., p. 97.
43. Zhurkin, *SShA i mezhdunarodno-politicheskie krizisy*, p. 167.
44. Arbatov, G. A., "Amerikanskaya vneshnyaya politika," p. 28.
45. Mil'shteyn and Semeyko, "Problema nedopystimosti," pp. 3–4.
46. Zhurkin, *SShA i mezhdunarodno-politicheskie krizisy*, p. 166.
47. Lukin, "O nekotorykh aspektakh," pp. 42–43.
48. Pakhomov, "Trezvyi podkhod," pp. 66, 69.
49. Zhurkin, *SShA i mezhdunarodno-politicheskie krizisy*, p. 7. The manuscript was set in type on 22 August 1974 and sent to the printer on 14 January 1975.
50. Ibid., pp. 17–18.
51. Ibid., p. 282.
52. Ibid., pp. 286–89. G. I. Svyatov, military analyst at the institute, pointed out that U.S. military forces had declined from 3.5 million in 1968 to between 2.2–2.5 million in the mid-70s and that the percentage of U.S. Gross National Product devoted to defense had declined from 9.5 percent (1968) to 5.8 percent (1976). Further, in terms of "constant prices," i.e., taking account of inflation, the U.S. defense budget decreased by "approximately 30 percent" ("O stroitel'stve," pp. 115, 117).
53. Trofimenko, "Na sterzhnevom napravlenii," pp. 6–7.
54. Ibid., p. 7. (An editorial in *SShA* refers to this agreement as "one of the

most important documents in the history of international relations" ("Novyi bol'shoi shag vperëd" ["A New Great Step Forward"], no. 8 [August 1973], p. 3).

55. Valerianov, "SSSR-SShA," p. 5.
56. Arbatov, G. A., "On Soviet-American Relations," p. 3.
57. Trofimenko, "Vneshnyaya politika," pp. 18, 26.
58. Corbi, "Two Russias," pp. A1, 2.
59. Ibid., p. A1.
60. "'Doktrina Niksona,'" p. 42.
61. Zhurkin, "SShA," p. 21.
62. See, especially, Chetverikov, "'Organizatsionnye problemy.'"
63. Trofimenko, "The Most Urgent Problem," p. B7.
64. Trofimenko, "Voprosy," pp. 9–10.
65. Trofimenko, "SSSR-SShA," p. 7.
66. Petrovsky, "V poiskakh," p. 317.
67. Quoted by Kokoshin, "SShA," p. 64.
68. Chetverikov, "'Organizatsionnye problemy,'" p. 29.
69. Quoted in Svyatov, "Bol'shaya strategiya," p. 98.
70. Krivozhika, "Ponyatie 'natsional'nyi interes,'" p. 124.
71. Trofimenko, "Traditsiya realizma," pp. 27–28.
72. Kokoshin, "SShA," p. 64.
73. Trofimenko, "Traditsiya realizma," p. 28.
74. Kokoshin, "Ot nauki v politiku," p. 90.
75. Trofimenko, "Voenno-strategicheskie aspekty," pp. 64–65.
76. Ibid., p. 65.
77. Ibid., p. 64.
78. Turkatenko, "Iskat' resheniya," p. 6.
79. Trofimenko, "Voenno-strategicheskie aspekty," pp. 65–66.
80. Trofimenko, "Vneshnyaya politika," p. 25.
81. Ibid.
82. Arbatov, G. A., "On Soviet-American Relations," p. 5.
83. "O dolgosruchnykh tselyakh," p. 124.
84. Ibid., pp. 124–25.
85. Trofimenko, "Vneshnyaya politika," pp. 15–16.
86. Ibid., p. 19.
87. Ibid. Another source reports that "some groups . . . find it difficult to dispense with the strategy of military superiority" and "are trying to establish

the scientific foundations in the development of military technology which will guarantee the scientific superiority of the United States in this field for many years ahead." Mosin, "Prezidentskoe poslanie," p. 68.

88. See Schwartz, *The Foreign Policy of the USSR*, pp. 71–92.

89. Arbatov, G. A., "Perspektivy razryadki," p. 30.

90. "Nauchnaya konferentsiya," p. 37.

91. Davydov, "'Doktrina Niksona,'" p. 12.

92. Arbatov, G. A., "Sovetsko-amerikanskie otnosheniya v 70-e gody," p. 31.

93. Ibid., p. 32.

94. Trofimenko, "Nekotorye aspekty," p. 24.

95. Trofimenko, "Voprosy ukrepleniya mira," p. 16.

96. Arbatov, G. A., "O sovetsko-amerikanskikh otnosheniyakh," p. 106.

97. Ibid.

98. Davydov, "SShA i Soveshchanie po bezopasnosti," p. 4.

99. Ibid., p. 6.

100. Ibid.

101. Arbatov, G. A., "'Politicheskii god,'" p. 5.

102. Trofimenko, "Voprosy ukrepleniya mira," p. 17.

103. Arbatov, G. A., "O sovetsko-amerikanskikh otnosheniyakh," p. 102.

104. Kudrin, "An Important Step," pp. 10–11.

105. Gromyko, *1036 dnei*, pp. 264, 266.

106. Kokoshin, "Ot nauki v politiku," p. 90.

107. Yur'yev, "Chto stoit za mifom," p. 66.

108. Lukin, "O nekotorykh aspektakh," p. 46. Participants in a symposium at the institute made much the same point when they concluded that "Priority in the present foreign-policy strategy of the United States is indisputably given to Soviet-American relations, which is explained by military-political considerations, the prospects for commercial cooperation between the two countries and also an understanding of fact of global involvement of the two powers" ("O dolgosruchnykh tselyakh," p. 124).

109. Arbatov, G. A., "O sovetsko-amerikanskikh otnosheniyakh," p. 105.

110. Inozemtsev, "Unity of Theory and Practice," p. A1.

Chapter 5

1. Trofimenko, "Uroki V'etnama," p. 77.

2. Arbatov, G. A., "Amerikanskaya vneshnyaya politika," p. 34.

3. Cited by Gromyko, "'Krizisnaya diplomatiya,'" p. 216.

4. Quoted in Griffiths, "Image, Politics and Learning," p. 59, n. 100.

5. Genri, "Protiv iskazhenii," p. 22.

6. Arbatov, G. A., "Vstupitel'noe slovo," pp. 13–14.

7. Arbatov, G. A., *Ideologicheskaya bor'ba*, pp. 250–51. He condemns unnamed "left-sectarian elements" who regard "imperialism as some deliberately abstract, almost mystical force" and "ignore all its inner shadings and contradictions" (p. 248). These distinctions must be borne in mind, he writes, "so that we do not . . . artificially increase the number of our enemies" (p. 132).

8. Ibid., p. 255.

9. Gromyko, *Diplomatiya*, p. 397.

10. Arbatov, G. A., *Ideologicheskaya bor'ba*, p. 253.

11. Arbatov, G. A., " 'Politicheskii god,' " p. 13.

12. Arbatov, G. A., "O sovetsko-amerikanskikh otnosheniyakh," p. 106.

13. Arbatov, G. A., "Novye rubezhi," p. 4.

14. Tomashevsky, "Na puti," p. 10.

15. "God 1975," p. 4.

16. Arbatov, G. A., "On Soviet-American Relations," p. 2.

17. Ibid., p. 3.

18. Arbatov, G. A., "Sovetsko-amerikanskie otnosheniya segodnya" (1976), p. 4.

19. Arbatov, G. A., "Sovetsko-amerikanskie otnosheniya segodnya" (1977), p. 4.

20. Arbatov, G. A., "Novye rubezhi," p. 4.

21. Trofimenko, "SSSR-SShA," p. 14.

22. Arbatov, G. A., "O sovetsko-amerikanskikh otnosheniyakh," p. 112.

23. Arbatov, G. A., "Sobytie," p. 11.

24. Arbatov, G. A., "The Dangers of a New Cold War," p. 33.

25. Trofimenko, "SSSR-SShA," p. 14.

26. Arbatov, G. A., "On Soviet-American Relations," p. 2.

27. Arbatov, G. A., "Sovetsko-amerikanskie otnosheniya segodyna" (1976), p. 4.

28. Trofimenko, "Vneshnyaya politika," p. 17.

29. Arbatov, G. A., "Soviet-American Relations at a New Stage," p. 4.

30. Arbatov, G. A., "The Dangers of a New Cold War," p. 34.

31. Ibid.

32. Ibid., p. 40; "A New U.S.-Soviet Era?," p. 11; idem, "Sovetsko-amerikanskie otnosheniya segodnya" (1977), p. 4.

33. Arbatov, G. A., "O sovetsko-amerikanskikh otnosheniyakh," p. 106; idem, "Soviet-American Relations at a New Stage," p. 3.

34. Sheydina, "Nauchno-tekhnicheskie svyazy," p. 19.

35. Petrovsky, "V poiskakh," p. 323.

36. Davydov, "'Doktrina Niksona,'" p. 16.

37. Sheydina, "V Alabame," p. 55.

38. Popova, "Senat," pp. 22–23.

39. Arbatov, G. A., "Vneshnyaya politika—I," pp. 8–9. The "revolutionary potential" of nuclear war is explained by the fact that "such a war affects the interests of the masses in no less a degree than poverty, social injustice and national oppression, which have served up to now as the chief motives of revolutionary actions." For a more elaborate statement of this argument, see his *Ideologicheskaya bor'ba*, pp. 81–83.

40. Arbatov, G. A., ed., *SShA: Nauchno-tekhnicheskaya revoliutsiya*, p. 13.

41. Ibid., p. 13.

42. Shimanovsky, "Liberaly," p. 45.

43. Davydov, "SShA: god posle Khel'sinki," p. 24.

44. When this notion was first mentioned, Trofimenko gave it short shrift. He wrote that "it is hardly possible to create such a state force sanctioned by the system itself which could effectively oppose the forces of militarism" ("Militarizm," p. 72).

45. Parkhomenko, "Teorii," p. 95.

46. Popova, "1920–1922," p. 62.

47. Shakhnazarov, "Peaceful Coexistence and Social Progress," p. A2.

48. Ibid., pp. A2–3. Similar arguments were made in the early 1960s by the advocates of Khrushchev's peaceful coexistence policy. See, especially, F. Burlatsky, "Concrete Analysis is a Major Requirement of Leninism," *Pravda*, 25 July 1963, pp. 2–3; and N. Inozemtsev, "Peaceful Coexistence and the World Revolutionary Process," *Pravda*, 28 July 1963, pp. 4–5., in *CDSP* 15, no. 30 (21 August 1963), pp. 7–9.

49. Zhurkin, "'Rol' obshchestvennykh sil," p. 89.

50. Ibid., pp. 100–101.

51. Trofimenko, "VPK," p. 103.

52. Trofimenko, "Why the Pentagon is Against Détente," p. B3.

53. Ibid., p. B3.

54. Davydov, "SShA: god posle Khel'sinki," p. 18.

55. Ibid., p. 18.

56. Olenov, "Razvedyvatel'noe soobshchesto," p. 186.

57. Linnik, "Zakryto li 'delo TsRU'?," p. 74.

58. Linnik, "Rassleduetsya 'delo TsRU,'" p. 76.

59. Gromyko, "Menyayushchiesya nastroeniya," p. 74.

60. Yur'yev, "Chto stoit za mifom," pp. 53–54.

61. Arbatov, G. A., "Novye rubezhi," p. 4.

62. Yur'yev, "Chto stoit za mifom," p. 55.

63. Arbatov, G. A., "A New U.S.-Soviet Era?," p. 15.

64. Oleshuk, "O teorii," p. 8.

65. Arbatov, G. A., "Sobytie," p. 9.

66. Arbatov, G. A., "Soviet-American Relations at a New Stage," p. 2.

67. Trofimenko, "SSSR-SShA," pp. 15–16.

68. Quoted in Marantz, "Prelude to Détente," p. 519.

69. Griffiths, "Image, Politics and Learning," pp. 457–58.

70. Arbatov, G. A., "A New U.S.-Soviet Era?," p. 15.

71. Shimanovsky, "Liberaly," p. 45.

72. Trofimenko, "Voprosy," p. 18.

73. Shimanovsky, "Liberaly," pp. 46, 47.

74. Quoted in Griffiths, "Image, Politics and Learning," p. 333.

75. Arbatov, A. G. and Arbatov, G. A., "The Schlesinger Approach," p. 20.

76. One Soviet author has observed that "there currently exist two tendencies in the United States regarding the mass supplying of weapons to the countries of the Persian Gulf. The partisans of one tendency believe that, in order to achieve its objectives, the United States should encourage the arms race in that region. The second school of thought is characterized by attempts to find such forms and directions for American policy which would correspond possibly to a greater degree to the spirit of the times" (Anatol'yev, "Amerikanskoe oruzhie," p. 105).

77. Yergin, "Politics and Soviet-American Trade," p. 520.

78. Arbatov, G. A., "Sovetsko-amerikanskie otnosheniya segodnya" (1977), p. 4.

79. Lukin, "O nekotorykh aspektakh," pp. 44, 45.

Chapter 6

1. Morgenthau, "Epilogue," p. 229.

2. Many observers have noted that the Russians are acutely insensitive to democratic values. For example, the Russian historian Andrei Amalrik wrote in his book *Will the Soviet Union Survive Until 1984?* that

To the majority of people the very word "freedom" is synonymous with "disorder" or the opportunity to indulge with impunity in some kind of antisocial or dangerous activity. As for respecting the rights of an individual as such, the idea simply arouses bewilderment. One can respect strength, authority, even intellect or education, but it is preposterous to the popular mind that the human personality should represent any kind of value. (Quoted in Smith, *The Russians*, p. 256.)

3. Schwartz, *The Foreign Policy of the USSR*, pp. 137–50.

4. Ibid., p. 143.

5. Grechko, "The Great Victory and its Historical Sources," p. R7.

6. Davydov and Lukin, "Idologicheskie aspekty," p. 46.

7. Arbatov, G. A., "O sovetsko-amerikanskykh otnosheniyakh," p. 105.

8. Arbatov, G. A., *Ideologicheskaya bor'ba*, p. 269.

9. Arbatov, G. A., "American Imperialism and New World Realities," p. 8.

10. Stepanov, "Peaceful Coexistence· is Not Class Peace," pp. A1–2. Stepanov is a member of the editorial board of *Kommunist*, the Party's main theoretical journal.

11. The appearance of weakness, Nathan Leites points out, is disturbing for psychological reasons as well. See his *Kremlin Moods* (Santa Monica, Calif.: The Rand Corporation, 1964). The basic Soviet line on this issue was set forth by Brezhnev in 1969 when, in a speech to the International Meeting of Communist and Workers Parties, he declared:

The growth of socialism's might, the abolition of colonial regimes and pressure by the working class movement influences the inner processes and policies of imperialism with ever greater force. Many important features of modern imperialism can be explained by the fact that it is compelled to adapt itself to new conditions. (Quoted in Arbatov, G. A., *Ideologiches-kaya bor'ba, p. 254.*)

12. Georgiyev and Kolosov, "Sovetsko-amerikanskie otnosheniya," p. 18.

13. Berezhkov, "Sovetsko-amerikanskie otnosheniya," p. 12.

14. Kassirova, "Sotsial'no manevrirovanie," p. 94. While admitting that "dozens of billions of dollars are allocated by the bourgeois government" for welfare programs, such "concessions" are seen to have been won by the "persistent class struggle of the workers" and by the "revolutionizing effect" of the socialist countries on the American workers, both of which have "forced the bourgeoisie to be more tractable." Furthermore, sizeable though it has been, "this kind of 'aid' cripples people morally and physically." Moreover, such programs are seen to be mere "palliatives" with the aid of which the ruling class is trying to buy off a "large-scale anti-monopolistic movement" (p. 95).

15. Morgenthau, "Epilogue," p. 230.

16. Orlov, "Prezident," p. 98.

17. Radio Moscow, International Service in Russian, 0730 GMT, 13 April 1975; *FBIS*, 14 April 1975, p. A6. (Kobysh presents a similar interpretation in *Kommunist*, no. 8 [May 1975], p. 111.)

18. Savel'yev, "Vneshnyaya politika," p. 85.

19. Corbi, "Has the Post-Brezhnev Period Begun?," p. B4.

20. Kokoshin, "SShA," p. 64.

21. "O nekotorykh novykh tendentsiyakh," p. 127.

22. Yur'yev, "Chto stoit za mifom," p. 67.

23. "O nekotorykh novykh tendentsiyakh," p. 127.

24. In a review of John Gaddis, *The United States and the Cold War, 1941–1947,* V. S. Anichkina observed the following:

> Gaddis' research is sufficiently convincing to lead the reader to the conclusion that during the war years and immediately after the war there existed objective preconditions for the broad development of Soviet-American relations. However, writes the author, "subjective factors"—the views of some people, the ignorance and inexperience of others, the fear and hatred of still others, etc., together with what Senator Fulbright later described as "the arrogance of power"—have for a long time hindered and reversed the positive development of Soviet-American relations ("Byla al'ternativa," p. 58).

25. Arbatov, G. A., *Ideologicheskaya bor'ba,* pp. 301–2.

26. See above, p. 112.

27. See above, p. 131.

28. Trofimenko, "SSSR-SShA," p. 14.

29. As recently as 1970 this separation of politics from economics was still in dispute. See Griffiths, "Image, Politics and Learning," p. 122.

30. Trofimenko, "SSSR-SShA," pp. 9, 14.

31. Bovin, "Détente," pp. 4–5 (italics added).

32. Oleshuk, "O teorii," p. 11.

33. Arbatov, G. A., *Ideologicheskaya bor'ba,* pp. 149–50, 162.

34. Zagladin, V., "The Revolutionary Process and the International Policy of the CPSU," *Kommunist,* no. 13 (September 1972), p. 22; quoted in Soll, *The Role of Social Science Research Institutes,* p. 11.

35. Fainsod, "Through Soviet Eyes," p. 60.

36. Gromyko, *1036 dnei,* p. 277.

37. Griffiths, "Image, Politics and Learning," p. 473.

38. Arbatov, G. A., "Sovetsko-amerikanskie otnosheniya segodnya" (1976), p. 4.

39. Griffiths, "Image, Politics and Learning," pp. 228–29.

40. Eran, "Soviet Foreign Policy," p. 89.

41. Legvold, "Four Policy Perspectives," p. 73.

42. Aspaturian, "Internal Politics and Foreign Policy," p. 255.

43. See Schwartz, *The Foreign Policy of the USSR*, p. 153, fn 47. Arbatov also contributed to the compendium *The Fundamentals of Marxism-Leninism*, which was attacked by the Chinese as "reformist."

44. Gilpatrick, "We Should Encourage the Doves in the Kremlin," p. 9.

45. Carpenter, "Soviet Perceptions of the United States," pp. 21–22.

46. Ibid., p. 126.

47. Legvold, "Four Policy Perspectives," p. 73.

48. Inozemtsev, "The Nature of Contradictions Today," pp. 18–19 (italics in the original).

49. See, for example, Khozin, "EPAS," p. 39.

50. Tomashevsky, "Na puti," pp. 11, 12. See also Arbatov, G. A., ed., *SShA: Nauchno-tekhnicheskaya revoliutsiya*, pp. 35, 39–40, 149–50, 208–29.

WORKS CITED

Non-Soviet Sources

Adomeit, Hannes. *Soviet Risk-Taking Behavior: From Confrontation to Coexistence.* Adelphi Papers, no. 101. London: International Institute for Strategic Studies, Autumn 1973.

Aspaturian, Vernon V. "Internal Politics and Foreign Policy in the Soviet System." In *Approaches to Comparative and International Politics*, edited by R. Barry Farrell, pp. 212–87. Evanston, Ill.: Northwestern University Press, 1966.

Barghoorn, Frederick A. *The Soviet Image of the United States.* New York: Harcourt Brace and Co., 1950.

Boffa, Giuseppe. "How It Is Possible to Cooperate." Interview with Georgi Arbatov. *L'Unita*, 10 May 1974, p. 3; *FBIS*, 29 May 1974, pp. B1–4.

Browder, Robert Paul. *The Origins of Soviet-American Diplomacy.* Princeton: Princeton University Press, 1953.

Carpenter, William, et al. "Soviet Perceptions of the United States." Mimeographed Study prepared for the Department of the Army. Arlington, Va.: Stanford Research Institute, Strategic Studies Center, November 1975.

Corbi, Gianni. "Has the Post-Brezhnev Period Begun?" *L'Espresso*, 26 January 1975; translated in *FBIS*, 10 February 1975, pp. B3–5.

————. "Two Russias." *L'Espresso*, 2 February 1975, pp. 30–31; translated in *FBIS*, 14 February 1975, pp. A1–2.

Eran, Oded. "Soviet Foreign Policy—Random Institutional Observations." *International Journal* 12, nos. 1–2 (23) (June 1973):82–94.

Fainsod, Merle. "Through Soviet Eyes." *Problems of Communism* 19, no. 6 (November–December 1970): 59–64.

Freidberg, Maurice. "The U.S. in the U.S.S.R.: American Literature Through the Filter of Recent Soviet Publishing and Criticism." *Critical Enquiry* 2, no. 3 (Spring 1976):519–83.

Gilpatrick, Roswell L. "We Should Encourage the Doves in the Kremlin." *New York Times Magazine*, 30 July 1967.

Griffiths, Franklyn J. C. "Image, Politics and Learning in Soviet Behavior Towards the United States." Ph.D. Dissertation, Columbia University, 1972.

Hollander, Paul. *Soviet and American Society.* New York: Oxford University Press, 1973.

Legvold, Robert H. "Four Policy Perspectives: The Soviet Union and Western Europe." Mimeographed. Washington, D.C.: Department of State, 1976.

Leites, Nathan. "The New Economic Togetherness: American and Soviet Reactions." *Studies in Comparative Communism* 7, no. 3 (Autumn 1974): 246–85.

Marantz, Paul. "Prelude to Détente: Doctrinal Change Under Khrushchev." *International Studies Quarterly* 19, no. 4 (December 1975):501–27.

———. "Soviet Foreign Policy Factionalism under Stalin?: A Case Study of the Inevitability of War Controversy." *Soviet Union*, vol. 3, part 1 (1976):91–107.

Morgenthau, Hans J. "Epilogue" to Anatoly A. Gromyko's, *Through Russian Eyes: President Kennedy's 1036 Days*, pp. 229–31. Washington, D.C.: International Library, Inc., 1973.

Mosely, Philip E. "The Soviet Citizen Views the World." *Review of Politics* 26, no. 4 (October 1964):451–72.

Nordhal, Richard. "Stalinist Ideology: The Case of the Stalinist Interpretation of Monopoly Capitalist Politics." *Soviet Studies* 26, no. 2 (April 1974):239–59.

Ra'anan, Uri. *The Changing American-Soviet Strategic Balance: Some Political Implications.* Memorandum Prepared at the Request of the Subcommittee on National Security and International Operations, Committee on Government Operations, United States Senate, 92d Congress, 2d session. Washington, D.C.: Government Printing Office, 1972.

Schwartz, Morton. *The Foreign Policy of the USSR: Domestic Factors.* Encino, Calif.: Dickenson Publishing Co., 1975.

———. "The 1964 Presidential Elections—Through Soviet Eyes." *Western Political Quarterly* 19, no. 4 (December 1966):663–71.

Shulman, Marshall D. "On Learning to Live With Authoritarian Regimes." *Foreign Affairs* 55, no. 2 (January 1977):325–38.

———. "SALT and the Soviet Union." In *SALT, The Moscow Agreements and Beyond*, edited by Mason Willrich and John B. Rhinelander, pp. 101–21. New York: The Free Press, 1974.

Smith, Hedrick. *The Russians*. New York: Quadrangle/The New York Times Book Co., 1976.

Soll, Richard S., et al. *The Role of Social Science Research Institutes in the Formulation and Implementation of Soviet Foreign Policy.* Mimeographed technical note prepared for the Department of Defense Advanced Research Projects Agency. Arlington, Va.: Stanford Research Institute, Strategic Studies Center, March 1976.

Urban, George. "A Conversation with Robert F. Byrnes, Cultural Exchange and its Prospects—II." *Survey* 20, no. 4 (93) (Autumn 1974): 41–66.

Yergin, Daniel. "Politics and Soviet-American Trade: The Three Questions." *Foreign Affairs* 55, no. 3 (April 1977):517–38.

Zimmerman, William. *Soviet Perspectives on International Relations, 1956–1967.* Princeton, N.J.: Princeton University Press, 1969.

Soviet Sources

Anatol'yev, G. P. "Amerikanskoe oruzhie v raione Persidskogo zaliva" ["American Arms in the Persian Gulf"]. *SShA*, no. 6 (June 1976): 103–5.

Anichkina, V. S. "Bor'ba v kongresse po voprosu sovetsko-amerikanskikh otnosheniyakh" ["Struggle in Congress on Soviet-American Relations"]. *SShA*, no. 6 (June 1974):78–81.

——— . "Byla al'ternativa 'kholodnoi voine' " ["There Was an Alternative to the 'Cold War' "]. *SShA*, no. 10 (October 1973):55–58.

Arbatov, A. G., and Arbatov, G. A. "The Schlesinger Approach—Its Form and Content." *New Times*, no. 30 (July 1975):18–20.

Arbatov, G. A. "Administratsiya Niksona u serediny distantsii ["The Nixon Administration at the Half-way Mark"]. *SShA*, no. 8 (August 1970):3–16.

——— . "American Imperialism and New World Realities." *Pravda*, 4 May 1971, pp. 4–5; translated in *CDSP* 23, no. 18 (1 June 1971):1–3,8.

——— . "Amerikanskaya vneshnyaya politika na poroge 70-kh godov" ["American Foreign Policy on the Threshold of the 1970s"]. *SShA*, no. 1 (January 1970):21–34.

——— . "The Dangers of a New Cold War." *Bulletin of the Atomic Scientists* 33, no. 3 (March 1977):33–40.

——— . *Ideologicheskaya bor'ba v sovremennykh mezhdunarodynkh otnosheniyakh* [The War of Ideas in Contemporary International Relations]. Moscow: Politizdat, 1970. English language edition published by Progress Publishers (Moscow: 1973).

——— . "A New U.S.-Soviet Era?" *Atlas* 24, no. 7 (July 1977):11–15.

————. "Novye rubezhi sovetsko-amerikanskikh otnoshenii" ["New Frontiers of Soviet-American Relations"]. *Izvestiya*, 13 July 1974, pp. 3–4.

————. "O sovetsko-amerikanskikh otnosheniyakh" ["On Soviet-American Relations"]. *Kommunist*, no. 3 (February, 1973), pp. 101–13.

————. "On Soviet-American Relations." *Pravda*, 2 April 1976; translated in *CDSP* 28, no. 13 (28 April 1976):1–5.

————. "Perspektivy razryadki sovetsko-amerikanskikh otnoshenii" ["Outlook for Soviet-American Détente"]. *SShA*, no. 2 (February 1972):26–31.

————. "'Politicheskii god' i problema politicheskikh prioritetov" ["The 'Political Year' and the Problem of Political Priorities"]. *SShA*, no. 6 (June 1972):3–15.

————. "Predislovie" ["Forward"]. In *"Doktrina Niksona" [The "Nixon Doctrine"]*, edited by Yu. P. Davydov, V. V. Zhurkin, and V. S. Rudnev, pp. 3–7. Moscow: Izd. "Nauka," 1972.

————. "Shag, otvechayushchii interesam mira" ["A Step in the Interests of Peace"]. *SShA*, no. 11 (November 1971):55–57.

————. "Sobytie vazhnogo mezhdunarodnogo znacheniya" ["An Event of Important International Significance"]. *SShA*, no. 8 (August 1972): 3–12.

————. "Sovetsko-amerikanskie otnosheniya segodnya" ["Soviet-American Relations Today"]. *Pravda*, 11 December 1976, pp. 4–5.

————. "Sovetsko-amerikanskie otnosheniya segodnya" ["Soviet-American Relations Today"]. *Pravda*, 3 August 1977, pp. 4–5.

————. "Sovetsko-amerikanskie otnosheniya v 70-e gody" ["Soviet-American Relations in the 1970s"]. *SShA*, no. 5 (May 1974):26–40.

————. "Soviet-American Relations at a New Stage." *Pravda*, 22 July 1973; translated in *CDSP* 25, no. 29 (15 August 1973):1–5.

————. "Sovietology or Kremlinology?" *Survival* 12, no. 6 (June 1970): 208–9.

————. "Strength-Policy Stalemates." *World Marxist Review* 17, no. 2 (February 1974):18–21.

————. "United States Foreign Policy and Prospects for Soviet-American Relations." In *A Nation Observed: Perspectives on America's World Role*, edited by Donald Lesh, pp. 2–17. Washington, D.C.: Potomac Associates, 1974.

————. "Vneshnyaya politika SShA i nauchno-tekhnicheskaya revoliutsiya" ["U.S. Foreign Policy and the Scientific-Technical Revolution"]. Parts I and II. *SShA*, nos. 10 and 11 (October and November 1973):3–11, and 3–16.

————. "Vstupitel'noe slovo" ["Introductory Remarks"]. Scholarly Conference on "Two Hundred Years of the American Revolution, History and the

Present" held by the Scientific Council on the Economic and Ideological Problems of the United States, USSR Academy of Sciences. *SShA*, no. 7 (July 1976):13–15.

Arbatov, G. A., ed. *SShA: Nauchno-tekhnicheskaya revoliutsiya i tendentsii vneshnei politiki* [USA: The Scientific-Technical Revolution and Trends in Foreign Policy]. Moscow: Izd. "Mezhdunarodnye otnasheniya," 1974.

Arbatov, G. A., and Zhurkin, V. V. "Podkhod k peregovoram" ["The Approach to Negotiations"]. In *Doktrina Niksona* [*The "Nixon Doctrine"*], edited by Yu P. Davydov, V. V. Zhurkin and V. S. Rudnev, pp. 40–53. Moscow: Izd. "Nauka," 1972.

Belonogov, A. M. "Ispolnitel'noe soglashenie kak forma mezhdunarodnykh obyazatel'stv SShA" ["Executive Agreements as a Form of U.S. International Committments"]. *SShA*, no. 6 (June 1973):8–19.

Berezhkov, V. M. "Politicheskaya obstanovka posle vyborov" ["The Political Scene After the Elections"]. *SShA*, no. 1 (January 1973):3–17.

———. "Sovetsko-amerikanskie otnosheniya i sovremennyi mir" ["Soviet-American Relations and the Contemporary World"]. *SShA*, no. 9 (September 1975):3–15.

———. "Yedinstvennaya al'ternativa" ["The Only Alternative"]. *SShA*, no. 9 (September 1974):3–6.

Berezin, L. B. "Ispol'zovanie nauchnykh resursov" ["The Use of Scientific Resources"]. In *SShA: Vneshnepoliticheskii mekhanizm* [*USA: The Foreign-Policy Mechanism*], edited by Yu. A. Shvedkov, pp. 280–97. Moscow: Izd. "Nauka," 1972.

Bessmenykh, A. A. "Diplomaticheskii apparat" ["The Diplomatic Apparatus"]. In *SShA: Vneshnepoliticheskii mekhanizm* [*USA: The Foreign-Policy Mechanism*], edited by Yu. A. Shvedkov, pp. 82–132. Moscow: Izd. "Nauka," 1972.

Bobrakov, Yu. I. "Amerikanskaya ekonomika v god vyborov" ["The American Economy in an Election Year"]. *SShA*, no. 11 (November 1976):58–63.

———. "Ekonomicheskie problemy SShA" ["Economic Problems of the United States"]. *SShA*, no. 7 (July 1976):30–32.

———. "Gosudarstvenno-monopolisticheskoe regulirovanie ekonomiki" ["State-Monopoly Regulation of the Economy"]. *SShA*, no. 10 (October 1971):49–58.

———. "O poslaniyakh prezidenta kongressu" ["The Presidential Messages to Congress"]. *SShA*, no. 4 (April 1975):60–68.

Bobrakov, Yu. I., and Novikov, V. T. "Ekonomicheskie rychagi" ["Economic Levers"]. In *SShA: Vneshnepoliticheskii mekhanizm* [*USA: The Foreign-Policy Mechanism*], edited by Yu. A. Shvedkov, pp. 187–210. Moscow: Izd. "Nauka," 1972.

Bogdanov, A. A. "Antiinflatsionnaya politika: poiski i protivorechiya" ["Anti-Inflation Policy: Explorations and Contradictions"]. *SShA*, no. 2 (February 1975):12–22.

Borisov, A. Yu. Review of Anat. A. Gromyko's *1036 dnei prezidenta kennedi* [*President Kennedy's 1036 Days*] (Moscow: Politizdat, 1968). *Voprosy istorii*, no. 6 (June 1969):183–86.

Bovin, Alexander. "Détente—The Purpose and How to Achieve It." *New Times*, no. 7 (February 1977):4–5.

Chetverikov, S. B. *Kto i kak delaet politiku SShA* [*Who Makes Policy in the United States—and How*]. Moscow: Izd. Mezhdunarodnye otnesheniya, 1974.

————. " 'Organizatsionnye problemy' vneshnei politiki" [" 'Organizational Problems' of Foreign Policy"]. *SShA*, no. 8 (August 1974):28–34.

Chossudovsky, Evgeny. "Genoa Revisited: Russia and Coexistence." *Foreign Affairs* 50, no. 3 (April 1972):554–77.

Dalin, S. A. "Sovremennyi mirovoi ekonomicheskii krizis i ekonomika SShA" ["The Current World Economic Crisis and the U.S. Economy"]. *SShA*, no. 8 (August 1975):5–21.

Davydov, Yu. P. " 'Doktrina Niksona'—krizis globalizma" ["The 'Nixon Doctrine'—Crisis of Globalism"]. In *"Doktrina Niksona" [The "Nixon Doctrine"*], edited by Yu. P. Davydov, V. V. Zhurkin and V. S. Rudnev, pp. 8–27. Moscow: Izd. "Nauka," 1972.

————. "SShA: god posle Khel'sinki" ["The United States: The Year After Helsinki"]. *SShA*, no. 8 (August 1976):14–25.

————. "SShA i Soveshchanie po bezopasnosti i sotrudnichestvu v Evrope" ["The United States and the Conference on Security and Cooperation in Europe"]. *SShA*, no. 10 (October 1975):3–13.

Davydov, Yu. P., and Lukin, V. P. "Ideologicheskie aspekty vneshnei politiki SShA" ["Ideological Aspects of U.S. Foreign Policy"]. *SShA*, no. 5 (May 1971):39–46.

" 'Doktrina Niksona': deklaratsii i real'nost' " ["The 'Nixon Doctrine': Declarations and Realities"]. Symposium at the USA Institute. *SShA*, no. 2 (February 1971):18–48.

Dolgopolova, N. A. "Voennye raskhody i obshchestvennost' " ["Military Spending and Public Opinion"]. *SShA*, no. 2 (February 1975):114–17.

"Ekonomicheskoe polozhenie Soyedinennykh Shtatov (nauchnaya konferentsiya)—I" ["The Economic Situation in the United States (Scientific Conference)—I"]. *SShA*, no. 9 (September 1974):120–27.

"Ekonomicheskoe polozhenie Soyedinennykh Shtatov (nauchnaya konferentsiya)—II" ["The Economic Situation in the United States (Scientific Conference)—II"]. *SShA*, no. 10 (October 1975):52–60.

Genri, Ernst. "Protiv iskazhenii istoricheskoi pravdy" ["Against Distortion of Historical Truth"]. *SShA*, no. 5 (May 1975):12–25.

Georgiyev, K. M. "Razryadka—formula i protsess" ["Détente—Formula and Process"]. *SShA*, no. 8 (August 1976):3–13.

Georgiyev, K. M., and Kolosov, M. O. "Sovetsko-amerikanskie otnosheniya na novom etape" ["New Phase of Soviet-American Relations"]. *SShA*, no. 3 (March 1973):8–20.

Geyevsky, I. A. "Bor'ba chernykh: neketorye teoreticheskie problemy" ["The Black Struggle: Certain Theoretical Problems"]. *SShA*, no. 4 (April 1971):15–25.

―――. "Obostrenie sotsial'nykh problem i pravitel'stvo Niksona" ["The Exacerbation of Social Problems and the Nixon Administration"]. *SShA*, no. 10 (October 1971):3–13.

―――. "Raznolikaya Amerika" ["Many-Faced America"]. *SShA*, no. 12 (December 1974):49–54.

―――. "Sotsial'nyi mir ili obostrenie protivorechii? ["Social Peace or Sharpened Conflict?"]. *SShA*, no. 10 (October 1975):23–35.

"God 1975" [The Year 1975]. *SShA*, no. 1 (January 1975):3–7.

Grechko, Marshal A. "The Great Victory and Its Historical Sources." *Problemy mira i sotsializma*, no. 3 (1975):3–10; translated in *FBIS*, 23 April 1975, pp. R5–17.

Gromeka, V. I. "SShA i Zapadnaya Evropa: 'tekhnologicheskii razryv'" ["The United States and Western Europe: The 'Technological Gap'"]. *SShA*, no. 7 (July 1970):29–43.

Gromyko, Anat. A. *Diplomatiya sovremennogo imperializma* [*Diplomacy of Contemporary Imperialism*]. Moscow: Izd. "Mezhdunarodyne otnosheniya," 1969.

―――. "'Krizisnaya diplomatiya' imperialisticheskikh derzhav" ["The 'Crisis Diplomacy' of the Imperialist Powers"]. In *Mezhdunarodnye Konflikty* [*International Conflicts*], edited by V. V. Zhurkin and E. M. Primakov, pp. 203–17. Moscow: Izd. Mezhdunarodnye otnosheniya, 1972.

―――. "Menyayushchiesya nastroeniya" ["Changing Moods"]. *SShA*, no. 4 (April 1973):63–75.

―――. *1036 dnei Prezidenta Kennedi* [*President Kennedy's 1036 Days*]. Moscow: Izd. politicheskoi literatury, 1968. Appeared in English as *Through Russian Eyes: President Kennedy's 1036 Days*. Translated by Philip A. Garon. Washington, D.C.: International Library, Inc., 1973.

Gromyko, Anat. A., and Kokoshin, A. "U.S. Foreign Policy Strategy in The Seventies." *Mezhdnunarodnaya zhizn'*, no. 9 (September 1973); translated in *FBIS*, 27 September 1973, pp. B3–11.

Gromyko, Anat. A., and Shvedkov, Yuri. *USSR-USA Relations Today.* Moscow: Novosti Press Agency Publishing House, 1973.

Gusev, Sergei. "Moscow on Sakharov." *New York Times,* 23 February 1977.

Inozemtsev, N. N. "On Contemporary Imperialism." *Pravda,* 18 July 1969, pp. 3–4; translated in *CDSP* 21, no. 29 (13 August 1969):20–21.

———. "The Nature of Contradictions Today." *World Marxist Review* 16, no. 9 (September 1973):16–19.

———. "Peculiarities of Contemporary Imperialism." *MEMO,* no. 5 (May 1970):7–8. Quoted in *The Soviet Union in World Affairs, A Documented Analysis, 1964–1972,* by W. W. Kulski, p. 2. Syracuse, N.Y.: Syracuse University Press, 1973.

———. "Sovremennye SShA i sovetskaya amerikanistika ["The Contemporary United States and Soviet American Studies"]. *SShA,* no. 1 (January 1970):6–14.

———. "Unity of Theory and Practice in the Leninist Peace Policy." *Kommunist,* no. 18 (December 1975):43–53; translated in *FBIS,* 9 January 1976, pp. A1–10.

Ivanyan, E. A. "Obshchestvennoe mnenie—ego rol' v politicheskoi zhizni" ["Public Opinion—Its Role in Political Life"]. *SShA,* no. 8 (August 1974):16–27.

Izakov, B. P. "Doklad Pentagona i 'krizis doveriya'" ["The Pentagon Papers and the 'Credibility Gap'"]. *SShA,* no. 9 (September 1971):3–13.

Kassirova, Ye. P. "Sotsial'noe manevrirovanie: ego tseli i rezul'taty" ["Social Maneuvering: Its Purposes and Results"]. *SShA,* no. 11 (November 1975):94–95.

Khlebnyi, Ye. S. "Kapitalizm SShA v seredine 70-kh godov" ["United States Capitalism in the Mid-70s"]. *SShA,* no. 4 (April 1976):14–24.

Khozin, G. S. "EPAS i perspektivy sotrudnichestva v kosmose" ["The Apollo-Soyuz Flight and Prospects for Cooperation in Space"]. *SShA,* no. 4 (April 1976):36–44.

Kislov, A. K. "Antisovetskie proiski amerikanskikh sionistov" ["Anti-Soviet Activities of American Zionists"]. *SShA,* no. 3 (March 1973):46–55.

Kislov, A. K., and Osipova, N. V. "Obsuzhdenie Sinaiskogo soglasheniya" ["Debate on the Sinai Agreement"]. *SShA,* no. 12 (December 1975): 71–77.

Kokoshin, A. A. "Ot nauki v politiku" ["From Science into Politics"]. Review of Stephen R. Graubard's *Kissinger: Portrait of a Mind* (New York: W. W. Norton and Co., Inc., 1973). *SShA,* no. 5 (May 1974):88–90.

———. "SShA i mezhdunarodnye otnosheniya v poslednei chetverti XX veka" ["The United States and World Affairs in the Final Quarter of the 20th Century"]. *SShA,* no. 2 (February 1976):56–66.

Konovalov, D. N. "O programme 'Traident'" ["The 'Trident' Program"]. *SShA*, no. 11 (November 1974):66–69.

Konovalov, D. N., and Saval'yev, V. A. "Aktsiya po ogranicheniyu voennykh polnomochii prezidenta" ["Action to Limit Presidential War Powers"]. *SShA*, no. 2 (February 1974):93–97.

Kremenyuk, V. A. "'Mrak v kontse tunnelya'" ["'Dark at the End of the Tunnel'"]. *SShA*, no. 7 (July 1973):96–97.

———. "Prezidentskie vybory i blizhnyi vostok" ["The Presidential Elections and the Middle East"]. *SShA*, no. 1 (January 1973):71–77.

———. "Yeshchë odna popytka pereosmysleniya vneshnei politiki" ["One More Attempt to Reappraise Foreign Policy"]. Review of Paul Seabury's *The United States in World Affairs* (New York: McGraw-Hill, 1973). *SShA*, no. 4 (April 1975):89–92.

Krivozhika, V. I. "Ponyatie 'natsional'nyi interes' v amerikanskikh vneshnepoliticheskikh issledovaniyakh" ["The Concept of the 'National Interest' in American Foreign Policy Research"]. *SShA*, no. 11 (November 1974):121–26.

Kruglov, Ye. G. "Amerikanskie monopolii i voina vo Vetname" ["American Monopolies and the War in Vietnam"]. *SShA*, no. 10 (October 1970): 69–73.

Kudrin, M. "An Important Step Toward Strengthening Peace." *International Affairs*, no. 10 (October 1973):10–14.

Kudrov, V. M. "Glavnye kapitalisticheskie strany: sopostavitel'nyi ekonomicheskii analiz" ["The Main Capitalist Countries: A Comparative Economic Analysis"]. *SShA*, no. 6 (June 1972):26–40.

———. "Nekotorye voprosy ekonomicheskogo sorevnovaniya SSSR i SShA" ["Some Questions on the Economic Competition Between the USSR and the USA"]. *SShA*, no. 9 (September 1975):15–29.

Kulagin, V. M. "Voennyi kompleks" ["The Military Complex"]. In *SShA: Vneshnepoliticheskii mekhanizm* [*USA: The Foreign-Policy Mechanism*], edited by Yu. A. Shvedkov, pp. 133–155. Moscow: Izd. "Nauka," 1972.

Kuusinen, Otto, ed. *Fundamentals of Marxism-Leninism*. Moscow: Foreign Languages Publishing House, 1961(?).

Lebedev, V. I. "Snova problema 'razdelennogo pravleniya'" ["'Divided Government' Again"]. *SShA*, no. 2 (February 1973):24–34.

Lenin, V. I. *Lenin on the United States*. New York: International Publishers, 1970.

Linnik, V. A. "Rassleduetsya 'delo TsRU'" ["The 'CIA Case' is Under Investigation"]. *SShA*, no. 10 (October 1975):71–76.

———. "Zakryto li 'delo TsRU'?" ["Is the 'CIA Case' Closed?"]. *SShA*, no. 5 (May 1976):71–76.

Linnik, V.A., and Savel'yev, V.A. "Dzhon Sparkmen" ["John Sparkman"]. *SShA*, no. 5 (May 1975):124–27.

————. "Ukhod Uil'yama Ful'braita" ["The Departure of William Fulbright"]. *SShA*, no. 2 (February 1975):122–26.

Lukin, V. P. "O nekotorykh aspektakh amerikanskogo podkhoda k Azii" ["Some Aspects of the American Approach to Asia"]. *SShA*, no. 5 (May 1976):36–49.

————. " 'Posle V'etnama': amerikanskaya politika v Azii" [" 'After Vietnam': American Policy in Asia"]. Review of R. Clough's *East Asia and U.S. Security* (Washington, D.C.: The Brookings Institution, 1975). *SShA*, no. 7 (July 1976):99–103.

Malakhin, P. M. "Rezhim naibol'shego blagopriyatstvovaniya vo vneshnetorgovoi politike SShA" ["Most-Favored Nation Treatment in U.S. Foreign Trade Policy"]. *SShA*, no. 10 (October 1974):107–12.

Menshikov, S. M. *Ekonomicheskaya politika pravitel'stva Kennedi, 1961–63* [*The Economic Policy of the Kennedy Administration, 1961–63*]. Moscow: Izd. "Mysl," 1964.

Mileikovskii, A. G. "Krizisnye protsessy v 'obshchestve protebleniya' " ["Crisis Processes in the 'Consumer Society' "]. Parts I and II. *SShA*, nos. 4 and 5 (April and May 1974):3–14, and 52–65.

————. "Tsennoe issledovanie monopolisticheskogo kapitalizma SShA" ["A Valuable Study of U.S. Monopoly Capitalism"]. Review of I. I. Beglov's *SShA: Sobstvennost' i vlast'* ["The United States: Property and Power"] (Moscow: "Nauka," 1971). *SShA*, no. 3 (March 1972):92–97.

Mil'shteyn, M. A. "Progress na glavnom napravlnii" ["Progress Along the Main Salient"]. *SShA*, no. 2 (February 1975):3–11.

Mil'shteyn, M. A., and Semeyko, L. S. "Problema nedopystimosti yadernogo konflikta" ["The Problem of the Inadmissability of a Nuclear Conflict"]. *SShA*, no. 11 (November 1974):3–12.

Mosin, I. N. "Krizis amerikanskykh programm 'pomoshchi' " ["The Crisis of American 'Aid' Programs"]. *SShA*, no. 7 (July 1975):15–26.

————. "Prezidentskoe poslanie po nauke i tekhnike" ["The Presidential Message on Science and Technology"]. *SShA*, no. 5 (May 1976):65–70.

Mostovets, N. V. "Novaya vekha v zhizni Kompartii SShA" ["New Landmarks in the Life of the CPUSA"]. *SShA*, no. 3 (March 1977):12–23.

"Nauchnaya konferentsiya v Institute SShA Akademii nauk SSSR" ["Scholarly Conference at the USA Institute, USSR Academy of Sciences"]. *SShA*, no. 12 (December 1972):22–42.

"O dolgosruchnykh tselyakh SShA na mezhdunarodnoi arene (k itogam nauchnoi diskussii)" ["U.S. Long-Term Goals in the International Arena

(Conclusions of a Scholarly Discussion)"]. *SShA*, no. 9 (September 1975): 121–27.

"O nekotorykh novykh tendentsiyakh v razvitii amerikanskikh voenno-strategicheskikh kontseptsii" ["Some New Trends in the Development of American Military-Strategic Concepts"]. *SShA*, no. 4 (April 1976): 122–27.

Olenov, N. A. "Razvedyvatel'noe soobshchestvo" ["The Intelligence Community"]. In *SShA: Vneshnepoliticheskii mekhanizm* [*USA: The Foreign-Policy Mechanism*], edited by Yu. A. Shvedkov, pp. 156–86. Moscow: Izd. "Nauka," 1972.

Oleshuk, Yu. F. "O teorii 'ogranichennoi razryadki'" ["On the Theory of 'Limited Détente'"]. *SShA*, no. 4 (April 1975):3–12.

———. Review of *Moral and Military Aspects of the War in Southeast Asia*. Hearings before the Committee on Foreign Relations, United States Senate, 91st Congress, 2d Session, May 1970 (Washington, D.C.: Government Printing Office, 1970). *SShA*, no. 12 (December 1970):66–67.

Orlov, V. N. "Prezident i kongress" ["The President and Congress"]. *SShA*, no. 11 (November 1974):96–100.

Osipov, V. "A Complex of Opponents of Détente." *Izvestia*, 15 February 1975, p. 4; translated in *FBIS*, 24 February 1975, pp. A8–9.

Pakhomov, N. I. "Trezvyi podkhod" ["A Sound Approach"]. *SShA*, no. 4 (April 1976):66–69.

Parkhomenko, V. K. "Teorii ekspansionizma i demokraticheskaya traditsiya" ["Theories of Expansionism and the Democratic Tradition"]. *SShA*, no. 9 (September 1974):94–95.

Pechatnov, V. O. "Demokraty: vozvrat k proshlomu?" ["Democrats: Back to the Past?"]. *SShA*, no. 4 (April 1973):52–62.

Petrovsky, V. "Anatomy of Presidential Power." Review of E. A. Ivanyan's *Belyi dom: prezidenti i politika* [*The White House: Presidents and Politics*] (Moscow: Politizdat, 1975). *International Affairs*, no. 6 (June 1976), pp. 128–30.

———. "V poiskakh teoreticheskoi osnovy" ["In Search of a Theoretical Foundation"]. In *SShA: Vneshnepoliticheskii mekhanizm* [*USA: Foreign-Policy Mechanism*], edited by Yu. A. Shvedkov, pp. 298–335. Moscow: Izd. "Nauka," 1972.

Petrusenko, V. V. "'Svoboda pechati': legendi i real'nost'" ["'Freedom of the Press': Legends and Reality"]. *SShA*, no. 3 (March 1971):40–48.

———. "O makrekerskom techenii v amerikanscoi zhurnalistike" ["The Muckraking Trend in American Journalism"]. *SShA*, no. 12 (December 1972):60–68.

Ponomarev, B. N. Abridged version of speech to All-Army Conference of Ideological Workers. *Krasnaya zvezda* [*Red Star*], 29 January 1975, p. 3; translated in *FBIS*, 31 January 1975, pp. R1–6.

Popov, A. A. "Razryadka i amerikanskie profsoyuzy" ["Détente and the American Labor Unions"]. *SShA*, no. 1 (January 1976):55–61.

Popov, N. P. "Predvybornaya kampaniya i obshchestvennoe mnenie" ["The Election Campaign and Public Opinion"]. *SShA*, no. 9 (September 1976):55–62.

Popova, Ye. I. "1920–1922: amerikantsii i Sovetskaya Rossiya" ["1920–1922: Americans and Soviet Russia"]. *SShA*, no. 11 (November 1970):56–62.

―――. "Senat i ogranichenie stratigeskikh vooruzhenii" ["The Senate and Strategic Arms Limitation"]. *SShA*, no. 4 (April 1975):13–24.

Portnyagin, A. D. "Kritika planov Pentagona v zone Indiiskogo okeana" ["Criticism of Pentagon Plans in the Indian Ocean"]. *SShA*, no. 3 (March 1975):74–76.

Potashov, V. V. "Ogranichenie vooruzhenii — realizm yadernogo veka" ["Arms Limitation — Realism of the Nuclear Age"]. Review of Frank Barnaby's *Nuclear Disarmament or Nuclear War?* (Stockholm: International Peace Research Institute, 1975) and *Arms Control*, edited by Herbert York (San Francisco: W. H. Freeman and Co., 1973). *SShA*, no. 4 (April 1976):72–75.

Primakov, Ye. M. "Pruzhiny blizhnevostochnoi politiki SShA" ["The Mainsprings of U.S. Middle East Policy"]. *SShA*, no. 11 (November 1976): 3–15.

Rachkov, B. "The Monopolies and the 'Raw Materials Crisis.'" *Ekonomicheskaya gazeta*, no. 4 (20 January 1975) p. 22; translated in *FBIS*, 4 February 1975, pp. A5–9.

Savel'yev, V. A. "Sluzhebnyi apparat kongressa" ["The Congressional Staff"]. *SShA*, no. 3 (March 1976):122–27.

―――. "Sotsial'no-politicheskii sostav kongressa 93-go sozyva" ["The Social-Political Composition of the 93d Congress"]. *SShA*, no. 10 (October 1973):112–15.

―――. "Vneshnyaya politika i kongress" ["Foreign Policy and the Congress"]. *SShA*, no. 12 (December 1976):80–87.

Semeyko, L. S. "Springs and Levers of the Military-Industrial Complex." *Krasnaya zvezda* [*Red Star*], 7 August 1976; translated in *FBIS*, 12 August 1976, pp. B1–3.

―――. "Voenno-promyshlennyi kompleks, ego vliyanie" ["The Military-Industrial Complex and Its Influence"]. *SShA*, no. 7 (July 1976):28–30.

Seregin, N. S. "Bor'ba vokrug trebovanii o narashchivanii voennykh raskhodov" ["Debate on Increased Military Spending"]. *SShA*, no. 1 (January 1976):84–87.

Shakhnazarov, G. "Peaceful Coexistence and Social Progress." *Pravda*, 27 December 1975, pp. 4–5; translated in *FBIS*, 3 December 1975, pp. A1–7.

Shapiro, A. I. "SShA v spektre protivorechii obshchego krizisa kapitalizma" ["The United States in the Spectrum of Contradictions of the General Crisis of Capitalism"]. *SShA*, no. 1 (January 1976):11–30.

Shershnev, Ye. S. "Soblyudat' usloviya ravnopraviya" ["Observe the Principles of Equality"]. *SShA*, no. 2 (February 1975):67–69.

Sheydina, I. L. "Nauchno-tekhnicheskie svyazy s amerikanskimi firmami" ["Scientific-Technical Ties with American Firms"]. *SShA*, no. 12 (December 1974):18–27.

———. "V Alabame yest' vse . . ." ["Alabama Has Everything . . ."]. *SShA*, no. 11 (November 1976):50–57.

Shimanovsky, V. V. "Liberaly i razryadka napryazhennosti" ["Liberals and Détente"]. *SShA*, no. 1 (January 1976):41–50.

Shvedkov, Yu. A. "'Doktrina Niksona' i vnutripoliticheskaya obstanovka v SShA" ["The 'Nixon Doctrine' and Domestic Political Conditions in the United States"]. In *Doktrina Niksona* [*The "Nixon Doctrine"*], edited by Yu. P. Davydov, V. V. Zhurkin and V. S. Rudnev, pp. 28–39. Moscow: Izd. "Nauka," 1972.

———. "Glavnye tsentry upravleniya" ["The Main Centers of Administration"]. In *SShA: Vneshnepoliticheskii mekhanizm* [*USA: The Foreign-Policy Mechanism*], edited by Yu. A. Shvedkov, pp. 41–81. Moscow: Izd. "Nauka," 1972.

———. "Novaya kniga o Genri Kissindzhere" ["New Book on Henry Kissinger"]. Review of Marvin and Bernard Kalb's *Kissinger* (Boston: Little, Brown and Co., 1974). *SShA*, no. 11 (November 1975):95–96.

———. "Strategiya, upravlenie i vnutripoliticheskii protsess" ["Strategy, Management and the Foreign-Policy Process"]. In *SShA: Vneshnepoliticheskii mekhanizm* [*USA: The Foreign-Policy Mechanism*], edited by Yu. A. Shvedkov, pp. 15–40. Moscow: Izd. "Nauka," 1972.

Shvedkov, Yu. A., and Lesnoy, P. T. "Upravlencheskie zaboty Vashingtona" ["Washington's Administrative Concerns"]. *SShA*, no. 11 (November 1970):31–40.

Shvetsov, Y. A. "Rol' kongressa" ["The Role of Congress"]. In *SShA: Vneshnepoliticheskii mekhanizm* [*USA: The Foreign-Policy Mechanism*], edited by Yu. A. Shvedkov, pp. 254–79. Moscow: Izd. "Nauka," 1972.

Solomatina, V. M. "Predely vneshnepoliticheskikh polnomochii kongressa" ["Limits of the Foreign-Policy Powers of the Congress"]. *SShA*, no. 3 (March 1972):87–91.

Stepanov, V. "Peaceful Coexistence is Not Class Peace." *Sovetskaya Kirgiziya*, [*Soviet Kirghizia*] 13 December 1974, p. 2; translated in *FBIS*, 31 December 1974, pp. A1–3.

Svyatov, G. I. "Bol'shaya strategiya" ["Grand Strategy"]. Review of John M. Collins' *Grand Strategy, Principles and Practices* (Annapolis, Md.: U.S. Naval Institute Press, 1973). *SShA*, no. 8 (August 1975):96–100.

————. "O stroitel'stve vooruzhennykh sil SShA v 70-e gody" ["On the Development of the U.S. Armed Forces in the '70s"]. *SShA*, no. 12 (December 1975):115–22.

Svyatov, G. I., and Sergeev, G. S. "Politika i prioritety federal'nogo byudzheta" ["Politics and the Priorities of the Federal Budget"]. *SShA*, no. 5 (May 1976):92–96.

————. "Prioretety i al'ternativy federal'nogo biudzheta SShA" ["Priorities and Alternatives in the U.S. Federal Budget"]. *SShA*, no. 10 (October 1974):73–76.

Tomashevsky, D. "Na puti k korennoi perestroike mezhdunarodnykh otnoshenii" ["Towards a Radical Reconstruction of International Relations"]. *MEMO*, no. 1 (January 1975):3–13.

Trofimenko, G. "From Confrontation to Coexistence." *International Affairs*, no. 10 (October 1975):33–41.

————. "Militarizm i vnutripoliticheskaya bor'ba" ["Militarism and the Domestic Political Struggle"]. *SShA*, no. 1 (January 1972):65–72.

————. "Na sterzhnevom napravlenii" ["On a Pivotal Course"]. *MEMO*, no. 2 (February 1975):3–11.

————. "Nekotorye aspekty voenno-politicheskoi strategii SShA" ["Some Aspects of U.S. Military and Political Strategy"]. *SShA*, no. 10 (October 1970):14–27.

————. "'Novye rubezhi.' Mify i deistvitel'nost" ["'New Frontiers.' Myths and Reality"]. *SShA*, no. 12 (December 1970):62–65.

————. "Po povodu knigi Gerberta Iorka" ["On Herbert York's Book"] Commentary on *Race to Oblivion* (New York: Simon and Schuster, 1970). *SShA*, no. 8 (August 1971):104–6.

————. "Politicheskii realizm i strategiya 'realisticheskogo sderzhivaniya'" ["Political Realism and the Strategy of 'Realistic Containment'"]. *SShA*, no. 12 (December 1971):3–15.

————. Review of B. D. Pyadyshev's *Voenno-promyshlennyi kompleks SShA* [*The U.S. Military-Industrial Complex*] (Moscow: Voenizdat, 1974). *SShA*, no. 12 (December 1974):84–85.

————. "SSSR-SShA: mirnoe sosushchestvovanie kak norma vzaimootnoshenii ["USSR-USA: Peaceful Coexistence as a Norm of Mutual Relations"]. *SShA*, no. 2 (February 1974):3–17.

——. "Sovetsko-amerikanskie soglasheniya ob ogranichenii strategicheskikh vooruzhenii" ["Soviet-American Agreements on the Limitation of Strategic Arms"]. SShA, no. 9 (September 1972):3–16.

——. "The Most Urgent Problem. The Moscow Summit and International Security." Izvestiya, 6 August 1974, p. 4; translated in FBIS, 8 November 1974, pp. B7–10.

——. "Traditsiya realizma i bor'ba vokrug razryadki" ["The Tradition of Realism and the Struggle Over Détente"]. SShA, no. 7 (July 1976):26–28.

——. "Uroki V'etnama" ["The Lessons of Vietnam"]. SShA, no. 6 (June 1976):76–80.

——. "VPK: novoe issledovanie" ["The Military-Industrial Complex: New Research"]. Review of V. M. Mil'shteyn's Voenno-promyshlennyi kompleks i vneshnyaya politika SShA [The Military-Industrial Complex and U.S. Foreign Policy] (Moscow: Mezhdnarodnye otnosheniya, 1975). SShA, no. 8 (August 1975):103–4.

——. "Vneshnyaya politika SShA v 70-e gody: deklaratsii i praktika" ["U.S. Foreign Policy in the 1970s: Words and Deeds"]. SShA, no. 12 (December 1976):14–28.

——. "Voenno-strategicheskie aspekty 'doktriny Niksona'" ["Military-Strategic Aspects of the 'Nixon Doctrine'"]. In "Doktrina Niksona" [The "Nixon Doctrine"], edited by Yu. P. Davydov, V. V. Zhurkin and V. S. Rudnev, pp. 54–80. Moscow: Izd. "Nauka," 1972.

——. "Voprosy ukrepleniya mira i bezopasnosti v sovetsko-amerikanskykh otnosheniyakh" ["Problems of Strengthening Peace and Security in Soviet-American Relations"]. SShA, no. 9 (September 1974):7–18.

——. "Why the Pentagon is Against Détente." Sovetskaya Estoniya [Soviet Estonia], 27 July 1975, p. 3; translated in FBIS, 4 August 1975, pp. B2–3.

Tsagolov, G. N. "Voenno-promyshlennyi kompleks: nekotorye obshchie aspekty" ["The Military-Industrial Complex: Some General Aspects"]. SShA, no. 11 (November 1970):21–30.

Turkatenko, N. D. "Iskat' resheniya na puti razryadki" ["Seeking Solutions on the Path to Détente"]. SShA, no. 10 (October 1974):3–7.

——. "Korotkoe puteshestvie po dlinnym dorogam" ["A Brief Journey Over Long Roads"]. SShA, no. 8 (August 1975):61–72.

——. "Korporatsii SShA v usloviyakh razryadki" ["U.S. Corporations in the Context of Détente"]. SShA, no. 6 (June 1974):30–43.

——. "Vzaimsvyaz' problem" [Interrelated Problems"]. SShA, no. 8 (August 1976):54–64.

Valerianov, M. V. "SSSR-SShA: itogi, trudnosti, perspektivy" ["USSR-USA: Results, Difficulties and Prospects"]. SShA, no. 1 (January 1976):3–10.

Vasil'yev, O. S., and Parkhitko, V. P. "Vozdeistvie na obshchestvennoe mnenie SShA" ["Influence on U.S. Public Opinion"]. In *SShA: Vneshnepoliticheskii mekhanizm* [*USA: The Foreign-Policy Mechanism*], edited by Yu. A. Shvedkov, pp. 231–53. Moscow: Izd. "Nauka," 1972.

Vladimirov, I. V. "Pered vyborami" ["Before the Elections"]. *SShA*, no. 10 (October 1974):40–45.

"Vstrechi v verkhakh" ["Summit Meetings"], editorial. *SShA*, no. 6 (June 1974):3–6.

Yakovin, Ye. Ye. "Okean i politika" ["The World Ocean and Politics"]. *SShA*, no. 5 (May 1976):76–82.

Yakovlev, N. N. *Prestupivshie gran'* [*They Exceeded the Bounds*]. Moscow: Izd. Mezhdunarodnye otnosheniya, 1970.

————. "SSSR-SShA: 40 let diplomaticheskikh otnosheniyakh" ["USSR-USA: 40 Years of Diplomatic Relations"]. *SShA*, no. 10 (October 1973):12–18.

Yanchuk, I. I. "Mekhanizm gosudarstvennogo regulirovaniya politiki v SShA" ["The Policy-Making Mechanism in the United States"]. *SShA*, no. 12 (December 1975):78–79.

Yermolenko, D. V. "O 'reideologizatsii' burzhuaznogo soznaniya" ["On the 'Re-ideologization' of Bourgeois Thought"]. *SShA*, no. 3 (March 1976):24–36.

Yur'yev, D. P. "Chto stoit za mifom o 'sovetskoi ugroze'?" ["What's Behind the Myth of the 'Soviet Menace'?" *SShA*, no. 9 (September 1976):62–68.

Zabliuk, N. G. "Lobbizm v politicheskom mekhanizme SShA" ["Lobbyism in the U.S. Political Mechanism"]. *SShA*, no. 12 (December 1974): 111–18.

Zhurkin, V. V. " 'Doktrina Niksona' i mezhdunarodno-politicheskie krizisy" ["The 'Nixon Doctrine' and International Political Crises"]. In *"Doktrina Niksona"* [*The "Nixon Doctrine"*], edited by Yu. P. Davydov, V. V. Zhurkin, and V. S. Rudnev, pp. 81–100. Moscow: Izd. "Nauka," 1972.

————. "Politika imperializma—osnovnoi istochnik mezhdunarodnykh konfliktov i krizisov" ["The Policy of Imperialism—The Main Source of International Conflicts and Crises"]. In *Mezhdunarodnye konflikty* [*International Conflicts*], edited by V. V. Zhurkin and E. M. Primakov, pp. 12–26. Moscow: Izd. Mezhdunarodnye otnosheniya, 1972.

————. "Rol'obshchestvennykh sil v razreshenii mezhdunarodnykh konfliktov" ["The Role of Social Forces in the Resolution of International Conflicts"]. In *Obshchestvennost' i problemy voiny i mira* [*Public Opinion and Problems of War and Peace*], edited by I. G. Morozov et al., pp. 88–102. Moscow: Izd. "Mezhdunarodnye otnosheniya," 1976.

————. *SShA i mezhdunarodno-politicheskie krizisy* [*The United States and International Political Crises*]. Moscow: Izd. Nauka, 1975.

—————. "SShA i mezhdunarodno-politicheskie krizisy" ["The United States and International Political Crises"]. *SShA*, no. 12 (December 1970): 14–26.

—————. "Vzglyad iznutri VPK" ["A View from Within the Military-Industrial Complex"]. Review of Elmo R. Zumwalt's *On Watch: A Memoir* (New York: Quadrangle/The New York Times Book Co. 1976). *SShA*, no. 1 (January 1977):79–81.

Zolotukhin, V. P. "Na puti v Belyi dom" ["On the Way to The White House"]. *SShA*, no. 6 (June 1976):15–29.

Zorin, V. S. "200-letie i 'konstitutsionnyi krizis'" ["The Bicentennial and the 'Constitutional Crisis'"]. *SShA*, no. 7 (July 1976):24–26.

—————. "Vnutrennie amerikanskie problemy 70-kh godov." ["Domestic American Problems of the 1970s"]. *SShA*, no. 8 (August 1971):3–13.

INDEX

AFL-CIO, 86

Acheson, Dean (Secretary of State): disagrees with Soviet experts in the State Department, 66; hostile to negotiations with USSR, 110

Adomeit, Hannes, 3

Albert, Carl, 55

All the President's Men, film part of campaign against détente, 91

Anderson, Jack, 90

Angola, 122

Anikin, A.V. 16

anti-communism in the U.S.: in the government, 62–64, 69–70, 72–73; in the trade unions, 86; in the media, 91; in leadership circles, 117–119, 143; begins to fade in late 60s, 119–123; increased distrust of USSR during 1976 elections, 129; deep-rooted "red menace" dogma persists, 131; liberals "chronic anti-communism," 143; nourished by Soviet dogmatism, 156; no longer a vital force, 157

Apollo-Soyuz mission, 168

Arbatov, G. A., director of the USA Institute

—political position of, 3, 149, 162; Soviet pragmatist, 162–163; on vulgar Marxism, 156; on the need for a "class approach," 149–150

—on the American economy, 17; U.S. technological pre-eminence, 12–13; the impact of military spending on, 19–20, 23

—on American politics: on the role of the state, 41; policy struggles within the leadership, 37–38, 65–66, 127–128; on liberals, 77, 108, 143; the enemies of détente, 131–132; the danger of fascism, 31; Richard Nixon, 96, 108, 143

—American public opinion: jingoism in, 86; the dread of nuclear war, 135

—American anti-communism: anti-Soviet attitudes of government officials, 62; the vices of Sovietology, 77; hostility toward the USSR, 117, 118, 120

—American foreign policy: loss of faith in, 25, 27; Cambodia crisis (1970), 99–100; Jordan civil war (1970), 102; Vietnam, 103–104; on U.S. as an "acceptable partner," 123

Arms race, impact on the U.S. economy: 19–23

Babbitt (Sinclair Lewis), 7

Barghoorn, Frederick, 2

Barnett, Richard, 78

Bay of Pigs, the, 43, 67

Berezhkov, V.M., 29, 91, 108n, 150–151, 170n8. See also SShA

Bernstein, Carl (*Washington Post*), 91

Bessmenykh, A.A., 65–66

"bipartisanship" in U.S. foreign policy, 54

"black liberation movement," weakness of, 29

Black Panther Party, chided for revolutionary romanticism, 17

Bobrakov, Yu. I.: reaction to 1974–76 economic recession, 10, 14–15; on "capitalist planning," 16

Boffa, Giuseppe (*L'Unita*), 31

Borah, Senator William, 126, 136–137

Bovin, Alexander, 6, 155–156

Brezhnev, Leonid Ilych: on Watergate,